The Faded Map

The Faded Map

LOST KINGDOMS OF SCOTLAND

Alistair Moffat

BIRLINN

This edition published in 2011 by
Birlinn Limited
West Newington House
10 Newington Road
Edinburgh
EH9 1QS

www.birlinn.co.uk

Reprinted 2012, 2014, 2018

ISBN: 978 1 84158 958 9
E-BOOK ISBN: 978 0 85790 057 9

British Library Cataloguing-in-Publication Data
A catalogue record for this book is available from the British Library

Designed and typeset by Iolaire Typesetting, Newtonmore
Printed and bound by MBM Print SCS Ltd, Glasgow

MIX
Paper from
responsible sources
FSC® C117931

For Hugh Andrew

Contents

�֍

List of Illustrations

✱

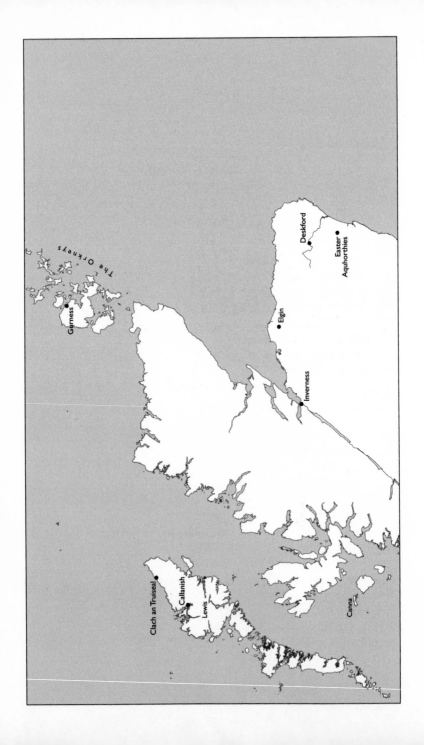

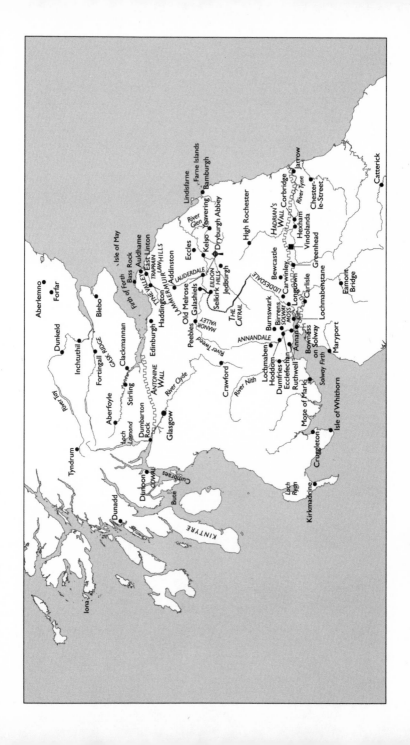

Introduction

✱

VERY LITTLE CERTAINTY, only occasional phases of continuity and hardly any clarity at all are the sorry string of characteristics to be found everywhere in this book. Scotland or, more precisely, north Britain in the Dark Ages seems a tangle of confusion, a story told in sometimes contradictory fragments and a few rare flickers of light. From late in the last millennium BC to AD 1000 and even beyond, it is a tale of shadows and half-lit edges.

Only the land, its rivers and lochs and the seas around it remain and, although the appearance of Scotland has changed over the course of a thousand winters and a thousand summers since, its fundamental shape and scale have endured. The sands and the tides, the hills and high valleys, the great rivers, the long-lost wildwood, the impenetrable marshlands and the ancient names of places have a rich story to tell. The land has its own certainty, continuity and clarity and, where it can, this book attempts to thread these into the weave of our early history.

Such as it is, much of what we might recognise as a history of Scotland in the first millennium AD has been supplied by outsiders. Greek travellers, Roman military historians and map makers, Irish annalists, Welsh bards and chroniclers now thought of as English have left us most of what passes for a narrative in what follows. Much has been lost and often it is the random discovery of an object, the recognition of a piece of dusty sculpture as great art or the realisation that some of the men of the north of Britain were very influential in their time that reminds us that a lack of a coherent history written by those who lived it is only an accident. Because records did not survive, we should not drift into the unthinking assumption that the society of Dark Ages Scotland was incapable of compiling them and was therefore somehow primitive and less sophisticated than others.

As a further discouragement, it should be made clear at the outset that the principal focus of this book is failure. The losers have, of course, been eclipsed by the winners in the history of Scotland. Excellent treatments of the rise of Dalriada, the Gaelic-speaking kings of the west and their eventual takeover of the whole country exist. And the story of the Pictish kingdoms, one of the great mysteries of our history, has been investigated and exhausted by talented historians. The Scots and the Picts appear in this narrative only when they shed light on the peoples they defeated or subjugated.

Instead a dim light is shed on the forgotten dynasties that died away and failed. Their lost kingdoms are the proper subject of this book. Where were Calchvynydd, Desnes Mor and Desnes Ioan, Manau and the land of the Kindred Hounds? Who were the Sons of Prophecy, the Well-Born, Macsen, Amdarch, the kings of Ebrauc and the treacherous Morcant Bwlc? What happened at Arderydd, Degsastan and Alt Clut? Where were the Grimsdyke, the land of the Haliwerfolc, the sanctuary of St Gordian, the Waste Land and the Raven Fell?

Most of these lost or half-remembered names are to be found in the landscape, overgrown by ignorance, pushed to the margins of our history by events elsewhere. The limitations of this book are all too obvious but its geographical limits require a little explanation. It is principally the 'faded map' of southern Scotland, the lands south of the Highland Line. Those lost kingdoms that spoke dialects of Old Welsh are much discussed and the final flourishes of the remarkably resilient Strathclyde Welsh close the narrative. The other significant language of Lowland Scotland was of course English and a concerted and extended effort is made to assert the Bernicians as one of Scotland's peoples. The arrival of their language and the glittering achievements of the dynasty of Aethelfrith are seen as a central part of Scotland's history. Bernicia is a kingdom lost to us in the pages of histories of England.

Finally, a note on the boxed notes in the text: these deal with snippets of detail and related information and are of incidental importance in a story which needs every bit of information it can find.

It is to be hoped that in these pages the 'faded map' of Scotland will acquire some colour once more. The story of our lost kingdoms is not merely a matter of footnotes for the curious. Failure has its own fascination. Losers in our history deserve our attention and perhaps our respect. Scotland was never inevitable.

Shadows

✺

I
N FEBRUARY AND MARCH, the hungry months of the late
winter, even the best fields are grazed hard, their grass pale
and nibbled to its roots. Good farmers use every inch of
pasture to nourish their pregnant ewes and, in the pillowy hills by
the River Tweed, it is surprising to see a copse occupy a long stretch
of good ground for no apparent reason. But it turns out that there is
one. Deep in the tangle of briars and hawthorns and surrounded by
a rusty barbed wire fence lies the shadow of an ancient kingdom.
Perched on a south-facing hillside between Galashiels and Selkirk in
the Scottish Border country, the long and prickly copse hides a
stone-filled ditch with a steep bank on its northern edge. The
farmer has fenced it to keep curious lambs from injury and mischief
and left the scrub and tumbled tree trunks as a welcome shelter
from the winter winds. Curious human beings who avoid becoming
hanked on the barbed wire and push their way through the briar
thorns will find themselves standing inside another time and
another place. In the still of a summer evening, the dense canopy
shades the lichen-covered stones of the ditch and in the quiet glade
there is a silence and the sense of a long past.

Nothing appears to be artificial – there are no obvious marks
of the work of men and women and no signs of occupation. The
deep ditch has been filled with stones picked up in the surrounding fields by generations of ploughmen and shepherds. None
seems to have been carved or worked in any way. And yet this

place was made by the back-breaking labour of many people, hacking soil and rock out of the earth with mattocks and picks, filling baskets, lifting them, carrying their loads to the bank above and piling the upcast ever higher. The ditch was deep – almost two metres in places – and, with the bank above it, the whole earthwork measured six metres across. This place was important. At least fourteen centuries ago, the ditch and its bank marked a frontier, the limits of two of the lost kingdoms of Scotland.

Known as the Catrail, the beginnings of the boundary have been traced a few miles to the north, near the banks of the Gala Water by Torwoodlee. As it climbs up the steep slopes above the flood plain, the ditch circles a broch, a stone tower probably built in the last centuries of the first millennium BC, perhaps occupying the site of an earlier hill fort. Formed with immensely thick drystane walls and circular in plan, the broch dominated the landscape, visible up and down the river valley, standing on a high and prominent spur. The frontier ditch skirted the great tower and it may be that, at some point in an overlapping history, the strength of one was associated with the integrity of the other.

After the line of the Catrail passes to the west of the modern town of Galashiels, it can be difficult to trace, often showing only as a shadow cast by early or late sun. When snow melts, the last of it sometimes lies where the old ditch has almost been ploughed out or filled in by farmers so that a slight depression is all that remains. As the Catrail reaches the tangled briar copse on the hillside between Galashiels and Selkirk, another tremendous fortification once reared up behind its line. On the summit of the ridge stands a plantation of spiky Norway spruces surrounded by a circular drystane dyke. Inside, screened by the evergreen trees, are the banks and ditches of an elaborate fort. Dug and palisaded some time in the first millennium BC, it is known as the Rink. An odd place-name, it is the stub of something longer and more revealing. Llangirick is, in part, an Old Welsh name coined by the communities who lived in the Borders before the arrival of English and the war bands who spoke its seventh- and eighth-century versions. Many Old Welsh place-names have survived. Peebles is from *pybyll*, which meant 'a tent' or 'a shelter' and probably referred to the shielings of shepherds or farmers. Kelso is from Calchvynydd, meaning 'a Chalky Hill'. In Wales there are many *llan* names and it usually refers to 'an enclosure'. There is a persistent local tradition that the second element of Llangirick is a memory of a Gaelic-speaking Scottish king. Giric reigned in the late ninth century and his war bands are said to have raided in the Tweed Valley. Perhaps they re-used the crumbling ramparts as a base for harrying the countryside around.

Below the Rink fortress, the frontier runs towards the banks of the Tweed and is picked up again immediately on the other side. What makes it almost certain that the Catrail was not a road but a boundary is the fact that it does not seek to ford rivers or pay much attention to natural features. In two places the ditch arrives at a sheer drop into a stream and carries on on the other side. Elsewhere its line goes from one side of a hill loch to the other and it often goes straight up ridges with no attempt to find an easier gradient.

Frontiers are the product of politics, of an agreement or bargain struck or at least a settlement of some kind, often a compromise. Another place-name suggests one. In the neck of land between the Tweed and the Ettrick before they meet below the Rink fort, lies Sunderland. An English name, it signifies territory separated or 'sundered' from a greater whole. The chronology may not fit (place-names are difficult to date) but in Sunderland there is a sense of an important boundary nearby, one which could not include it for some lost reason.

That reason may have been military. An alternative and equally plausible interpretation is that the construction of the Catrail was an act of war rather than an agreed peace. The ditch was almost always dug on the eastern or southern side of the earthwork and the bank raised to the north or west. That suggests that the Catrail was made to obstruct the advance of aggressors from the east, either mounted raiders or warriors on foot. And, if any did break through and had plundered cattle or other livestock, the ditch and bank would make it difficult for them to get away quickly with their stolen beasts.

The fact that several powerful fortresses lie close to the Catrail is also eloquent. They are always sited in the west or north and therefore behind the sheltering bank. And in turn that suggests strongly that this huge structure was thrown up by the peoples of the west and their kings.

Offa's Dyke supplies useful analogies. Built by the great Mercian king in the eighth century, it was intended to inhibit raiding parties riding out of the Welsh hills. Although on a much larger scale than the Catrail, its principles are the same; there is a wide and deep ditch to the west and a high bank on the east made from the upcast. At 150 miles in length, from the Severn estuary to the Dee, it was a vast project, the largest archaeological monument in Britain and the most impressive man-made frontier in Europe. Land was the most precious asset our ancestors had and kings did not hesitate to expend enormous energies to protect it.

To the west of Selkirk, the Catrail is much harder to detect as it climbs into the hills above the Yarrow Valley. It may be that this long stretch was dug at a different period and guided by different authority. After crossing the river near the Yarrow Feus, the frontier swings south through the high wastes of the old Ettrick Forest before becoming much more defined as it reaches the Borthwick Water. Now engulfed by commercial forestry, the last few miles are, nevertheless, again emphatic, the ditch cut in long straight sections before terminating in the western ranges of the Cheviot Hills, near Peel Fell.

Earthworks are notoriously difficult to date. The most persuasive evidence for Offa having caused his dyke to be built during his reign, from 757 to 796, is to be found in Asser's *Life of King Alfred*. Written 100 years after the event, the biography contains only one relevant sentence: 'Offa caused a great dyke to be built from sea to sea between Mercia and Britain.' The seas are assumed to be Severn Estuary and the Irish Sea while Mercia was

Offa's midland English kingdom and Britain was what is now Wales, seen by contemporaries as one of the last redoubts of the British. Written evidence like this is precious, much prized by historians of the so-called Dark Ages. And yet it is not entirely accurate. The northern section of Offa's Dyke was never built and to maintain its line to the Dee Estuary and the Irish Sea, another huge earthwork, which lay a few miles to the east, was used. Known as Wat's Dyke, it is forty miles long and was thought to be roughly contemporary with Offa's Dyke. But archaeologists have recently found a fire site under Wat's Dyke which was reliably carbon dated to around AD 446, much earlier than the reign of Offa.

No one has yet excavated the Catrail and parts of its fifty-eight-mile length may have been dug at different times or re-used older ditches and banks. Or the frontier may have been marked in different ways, and there were certainly substantial gaps where streams and sleep slopes seem to have sufficed. But the continuous 110 miles of Offa's great dyke was certainly built in the second half of the eighth century, and it was thrown up quickly because of military pressure from the Welsh kings of the west. It seems highly likely that the Catrail had similar beginnings and for similar reasons.

Solid, physically imposing frontiers were very familiar to the communities of southern Scotland. They lived between two mighty Roman walls, the Antonine across the Forth–Clyde isthmus and Hadrian's between the North Sea and the Irish Sea. But what was the military pressure in the western Tweed Basin that galvanised kings and lords to imitate the work of the legions?

In the seventh century, English-speaking war bands began raiding in the north. Riding out of the newly established kingdoms of Bernicia in Northumberland and Deira in Yorkshire, these warriors and their kings were ambitious, anxious to gain territory and prestige and successful in imposing overlordship in the Tweed Valley. In 603 a great general, Aethelfrith, led his war band to victory over the men of Aedan macGabrain, King of

Dalriada. They fought at a place called Degsastan by the chroniclers, probably Addinston in Lauderdale. By 637 the English were laying siege to the seat of the Old Welsh kingdom of the Gododdin at Din Eidyn, now Edinburgh. Not recorded are the forays they made to the west, to the fertile farms and fields of the Upper Tweed. But make them they did for the seventh century saw native kings shrink back into their upland fastnesses and try to stem the tide of English takeover.

It is likely that these defeated, retreating rulers determined to draw a line through the Border hills, the frontier which has become known as the Catrail.

Further down the Tweed, English-speaking warlords were renaming the landscape. The old fortress at the junction of the Teviot and the Tweed, the strategic pivot known for centuries as Marchidun, became Hroc's burh, the stronghold of the English warlord called the Rook. Roxburgh is the smoothed-out modern version. Much closer to the Catrail new settlements took a characteristic shape. At Midlem, originally Middleham, the village evolved as two rows of houses on either side of a central green and with long backlands behind. These were cultivated for many generations and show up well in aerial photographs. At Selkirk, on the flood plain of the Ettrick, a powerful magnate built a hall for himself and his warriors. It has left its name on the town. Selkirk is from Early English and it means the Hall Church. Only the faint traces of the wallstead, a large rectangle, can be seen from the air but the building was probably like its contemporaries. In the epic poem, *Beowulf*, King Hrothgar sat in a

> great mead-hall meant to be a wonder of the world for ever; it would be his throne-room and there he would dispense his God-given goods to young and old . . . The hall towered, its gables wide and high.

To the west of the Catrail few shadows remain. The kings of the west spoke Old Welsh to their warriors and their people, and the only recognisable legacy is the persistence of their ancient place-names. Indeed the frontier marks a striking division, even on a modern map. To the west, the landscape is speckled by many Old Welsh names. The poet and novelist James Hogg farmed at Altrieve in the Yarrow Valley. The older version is Eltref, which means 'Old Farmstead' in early Welsh. Some names, like Berrybush, sound very English but are not. Bar y Bwlch is the correct derivation and it means 'The Summit of the Pass'. *Pen* is Old Welsh for 'head' or 'a high hill' and place-names with pen abound in the western borders – Ettrick Pen, Penmanshiels, Pennygant Hill.

As the line of Catrail climbs west and up the Yarrow Valley, walkers come upon a much more substantial section. It bears an intriguing name, one which does more than hint at the purpose of the frontier. At first glance, Wallace's Trench sounds like a reference to the famous Scottish hero of the Wars of Independence. He campaigned in the Borders and, with his force of guerrilla fighters, hid in the wastes of the Ettrick Forest before being proclaimed Guardian of Scotland at the Forest Kirk in Selkirk. But why would a guerrilla fighter have his men dig a huge trench on the hillsides of the Yarrow Valley? Siege or attritional warfare was no part of Wallace's purpose. The historical reality is different – and fascinating.

Wallace's Trench long predates William and indeed has nothing to do with his exploits and everything to do with his name. In such records as survive, it is variously spelled as *Wallensis*, *Walays* and *Le Waleis*. All of these versions mean the same thing – 'William the Welshman'. To the great relief of many patriots, he did not come from Wales but Clydesdale in the old and half-forgotten kingdom of Strathclyde and his name probably recalls a native lineage which clung on to the old language – in other words, they continued to speak a dialect of Old Welsh into the early medieval period. Wallace's Trench is therefore the Welshmen's Trench, part of the long boundary between a developing English-speaking culture to the east and an ancient Celtic speech surviving in the hills to the west.

Place names support this interpretation and there is a striking clutch of them around Wallace's Trench. One in particular suggests a military tone. Tinnis occurs four times and it derives from the Welsh *dinas* meaning 'a fort'. And rising up west of the trench is Welshie's Law, probably a blunt, later echo of old differences.

Power names places and, when the English war bands penetrated far up the Tweed and Teviot valleys, their lords reordered the map. Many Welsh place-names gave way to new English names, especially when these were centres of wealth and prestige. At Sprouston, a small village on the southern bank of the Tweed near Kelso, there was a royal English township. Some time around 657, it was visited by a great man, probably King Oswiu of Northumberland, the Overlord of Britain or Bretwalda. Sprouston is a very early English name, after a man called something like Sprow, but the fact that it was a royal settlement with a great hall speaks of consolidation and firm ownership. If the Catrail was the frontier between Celtic and English kingship in the Borders, it lay far to the west and recognised that the fertile river lands of the plains had fallen to the invader and the hill country was all that was left to the defeated.

It is possible to hold up a map of Scotland and see the faint watermark of its lost kingdoms. Long earthworks pattern the landscape, running through fields, climbing hillsides, apparently leading nowhere, and enigmatic names remember the grass-covered undulations of ancient fortresses. Again, in the Borders, there is an elaborate structure known as the Military Road. It runs for about four miles and is not a road or track but an elaborate sequence of two banks and two ditches, the deposit of tremendous and well-organised labour. Historians have conjectured its construction to the first millennium BC and believe it to be related to the great hill fort on Eildon Hill North. The Military Road seems to guard the south-western approaches to the hills, and its function may have been to slow down an attack or prevent the rapid escape of raiders laden with plunder long enough for defenders to reach it.

In Perthshire, archaeologists have uncovered the Roman

frontier of the Gask Ridge, a series of watchtowers strung out in a line between Dunblane and Perth. Probably built by the legions commanded by the Governor of Britannia, Petilius Cerialis, some time around AD 73, it appears to have followed a pre-existing tribal boundary. To the west and north of the Gask Ridge ruled the kings of Caledonia while, to the east, occupying Fife and Kinross, lay the territory of the Venicones. Their Latinised name has been brilliantly parsed by an American scholar and it translates as 'the Kindred Hounds'.

Sometimes the memories of lost kingdoms are substantial, well documented and remnants survive. Strathclyde lasted until 1014 when one of its last kings, Owain, was killed in battle with the English at Carham on the banks of the Tweed and lingered almost certainly as late as 1070 when, according to one source, it was 'violently subjugated' by the kings of Scots. Others are little more than a few scattered fragments of a jigsaw. The kingdom of the Wildcats was undoubtedly powerful on both shores of the Moray Firth and its soldiers were willing to fight in its name as late as 1746. At Culloden, Clan Chattan fought with hopeless savagery. One of their captains, Gillies MacBean, killed fourteen government soldiers before his leg was shattered by grapeshot. When dragoons cornered the wounded man by a drystane dyke, Mac-Bean fought like a man possessed before being trampled by English horses. But who were the Wildcats? Caithness is named for them. Gaels call the Duke of Sutherland 'Morair Chat', his coastland 'Machair Chat' and the hill country 'Monadh Chat'.

Perhaps the most amazing survival is the kingdom of Manau. Its heartland lasted until 1974 in the shape of Clackmannanshire, Scotland's smallest county. Ignored by all but antiquaries, its talisman stands next to the old county buildings in Clackmannan. Clach na Manau is the Gaelic version of the origin name for the Stone of Manau, the core of the ancient kingdom and the derivation of Clackmannan.

These are not Ruritanian curiosities. The lost kingdoms of Scotland remember not only who we were before we thought of ourselves as Scots but, in so doing, they help unpack a much

The Kingdom of Moray

The ancient kingdom of Moray – or Moreb, an Old Welsh name meaning 'low-lying land by the sea' – was much larger than the modern county of Moray. Almost certainly the descendant of the Pictish kingdom of Fidach, it extended around both shores of the Moray Firth, running from Buchan in the east, taking in the lower Spey, Inverness and the north of the Great Glen and circling north up to Caithness. Even further back in history, it encompassed the old territories of the Cat People, what became the confederacy of Clan Chattan. A kingdom centred on the sea and the firth it bordered, its southern land frontier was the Grampian massif and the point near modern Stonehaven, known as the Mounth, where the massif almost reaches the shore of the North Sea. Two kings of Moray are noted in the Icelandic sagas in the tenth century – Mael Snechtai and Mael Coluim. These are Gaelic names and scions of a vigorous dynasty. The most famous king of Moray became king of Alba or Scotland and ruled between 1040 and 1057. This was Macbeth, a much more successful ruler than Shakespeare's drama allowed. Kings of Moray were seen as serious rivals to the line of Malcolm Canmore and, in 1130, his son, David I, mac Malcolm, finally annexed the old kingdom. He brought groups of settlers from the royal lands around the Tweed and these plantations were made on good land along the southern coasts of the Moray Firth. David I's policy created a linguistic frontier which can still be heard today. Between Inverness and Elgin, the local accent changes noticeably. This is because those from Inverness speak English learned by their Gaelic-speaking ancestors from the recent past while those to the east came from the south in the twelfth century and were already English speakers.

richer identity. They also remind us of political possibilities. If the Gaelic-speaking kings of Argyll had been less aggressive and less lucky, we might have lived under the rule of the Strathclyde dynasty. And we might have been worrying about the health of our native Welsh speech community or how fewer and fewer in the north were now speaking Pictish. What follows shows that Scotland was indeed never inevitable.

2

The Faded Map

✻

S OME TIME AROUND 320 BC, almost certainly in the benign months of the summer, a Greek explorer and scientist visited the land that would become Scotland. Pytheas had travelled an immense distance, beginning his remarkable and little-known journey at the prosperous trading colony of Massilia, modern Marseilles. He came north in search of knowledge, business opportunities and excitement. All three were recorded in *On the Ocean*, written on the traveller's safe return to the warmth of the Mediterranean. This fascinating book has been lost for almost two thousand years and all knowledge of it is derived from passages used in the surviving texts of later classical authors.

None of these scholars had visited Britain or Scotland and all of them depended on Pytheas' first-hand account. Some only included excerpts to mock him, calling him a liar and a fantasist. It was well known that human beings could not live in the hostile climate of the far north and the Greek explorer had simply made it all up. Others believed him intrepid and still more plagiarised his work without attribution. From an aggregate of all these references and some reasonable assumptions, it is possible to trace the voyage of Pytheas and even glimpse an occasional sense of what he saw.

As a serious scientist, Pytheas carried with him instruments capable of very accurate measurements and possessed enough geographical knowledge to translate his observations into data.

At midday, with a cloudless sky, he could calculate the height of the sun and this allowed him to work out how far north he had travelled from Marseilles. These measurements were later expressed as latitudes and, in turn, showed where Pytheas had been when he made them. One was almost certainly recorded on the Isle of Man. From there he sailed up through the North Channel, his shipmaster no doubt avoiding the boiling tide rips off the Mull of Galloway where the Atlantic surges in to meet the Irish Sea. Likely to have hugged the coast, both to take on regular supplies of fresh water and readily find safe night anchorages (early sailors were very reluctant to travel in darkness), captains preferred to voyage in short stages. And Pytheas slowly threaded his way up through the archipelagos of the Inner and Outer Hebrides. His ship made landfall at the Point Peninsula on the

Gnomon

Pytheas' ability as a mathematician was especially extraordinary when the rudimentary nature of his instruments is understood. On his epic journey to Britain, he calculated latitude on five occasions and each time he used nothing more sophisticated than a straight stick. Known as a gnomon, it was planted in the ground at an angle of precisely 90 degrees at noon, when Pytheas judged the sun to be at its zenith. If this could be done at the summer solstice, particularly when in unfamiliar territory, then so much the better. What mattered was the length of the shadow cast by the gnomon and its ratio to the height of the stick itself. Having presumably made a measurement at Marseilles or knowing what the standard ratio was, Pytheas moved north and made four more calculations. As the cast shadow lengthened slightly and the ratio to the height of the gnomon changed, Pytheas could work out degrees of latitude accurately. Working backwards from his calculations, it is possible to trace the extent of his journey. He planted his gnomon in Brittany (48 degrees north), the Isle of Man (54 degrees), the Isle of Lewis (58 degrees) and Shetland (61 degrees). The great scholar and admirer of Pytheas, Sir Barry Cunliffe, believes that the intrepid Greek probably made it as far north as Iceland (66 degrees). Gnomons are still used. The term now describes the triangular upright in the middle of a sundial.

eastern coast of the Isle of Lewis. That was where he made his last measurement of the sun's height, at the northern latitude of 54 degrees and 13 minutes, somewhere near the town of Stornoway.

What is even more startling was the Greek traveller's ability to work out distances very accurately. Reproduced in the work of another, later, Greek writer, Diodorus Siculus, here is Pytheas' general description of Britain:

> Britain is triangular in shape, much as is Sicily, but its sides are not equal. The island stretches obliquely along the coast of Europe, and the point where it is least distant from the continent, we are told, is the promontory which men call Kantion [Kent] and this is about one hundred stades [19 km] from the mainland, at the place where the sea has its outlet, whereas the second promontory, known as Belerion [Land's End], is said to be a voyage of four days from the mainland, and the last, writers tell us, extends out into the open sea and is named Orkas [Dunnet Head – opposite the Orkneys]. Of the sides of Britain the shortest, which extends along Europe, is 7,500 stades [1,400 km], the second, from the Strait to the tip [at the north] is 15,000 stades [2,800km] and the last is 20,000 stades [3,700 km] so that the entire circuit of the island amounts to 42,500 stades [7,900 km].

What astonishes all who read that passage is that Pytheas got it almost exactly right. The length of the British coastline, with all its indentations and deceptive distances is 7,580 kilometres. With only estimates of the speed of his ship, local knowledge of tides and currents to go on, he managed a level of accuracy unknown before modern times.

What is also striking is Pytheas' sense of enterprise in venturing into the unknown, far beyond the limits of Mediterranean knowledge of north-western Europe. With characteristic precision and reticence, Herodotus had mentioned the 'Tin Islands' that lay somewhere in the remote northern ocean but added immediately, 'I cannot speak with any certainty'. Tin was an essential ingredient in the alloy of bronze and, since deposits were rare along the shores of the Mediterranean, Greek merchants were always anxious to find new sources. Pytheas' epic journey was therefore not only motivated by curiosity and an evident sense of scientific enquiry but also by the needs of commerce. Tin was very valuable and, if the mists and monsters which guarded the chilly northern seas could be avoided, there was money to be made.

Contacts already existed. Tin was being regularly traded between southern Britain and the Mediterranean in the fourth century BC but almost certainly passing through several pairs of hands on its way south. If Pytheas could discover a feasible route from Marseilles to Britain, then perhaps a chain of expensive middlemen could be cut out.

He began his long journey overland, travelling first to the port of Narbonne and, from there, was probably rowed up the River Aude as far as the draught of a boat could reach and then onwards on foot or horseback up over the watershed and down to the headwaters of the River Garonne. From there a boat would have taken Pytheas quickly and comfortably to the great estuary of the Gironde and the Atlantic coast beyond.

This and several other overland and river routes to the north were well known to the Greek colonists of Marseilles and archaeology confirms a brisk trading network exchanging Mediterranean goods for the produce of the peoples of what is now France. On the shores of the Bay of Biscay, Pytheas will have found passage on local boats plying between shore markets further up the coast or possibly with merchants from his home port or with native traders who had done business with them. No doubt he avoided travelling alone and vulnerable – perhaps he had companions whose involvement is now lost to history. In any event, passage could be rapid and, if there were no significant breaks in his journey, the explorer could have found himself in Brittany, on the southern shores of the English Channel, less than 30 days after leaving Marseilles.

Pytheas was standing on the very edge of geography. As far as he knew, no Greek had come so far north and survived to record what he saw. Certainly Cornish tin was imported but none of his compatriots had come to the place called Belerion where it was panned from streams and hacked out of shallow pits. None had seen the charcoal-burners smelt the ore into astragal-shaped ingots weighing about 80 kilograms although many had passed through the markets of Marseilles. Several of these remarkable objects have been found at various stages of their journey to the Mediterranean. They were brought to the beach market between St Michael's Mount and Marazion on the Cornish coast, not far from Penzance. Once deals had been done and the tin loaded into boats, the rising tide refloated them and they trimmed their sails and swung away south out to sea. The sea captains navigated by pilotage, hugging the coastline, measuring progress by sea-marks and crossing the Channel when the French coast came in sight, often at Cap Gris Nez.

Cost, convenience and speed dictated that a sea journey, safely managed in the summer months, was always to be preferred to the slow and dangerous business of transporting goods overland. Quantities were necessarily smaller and robbers lay in wait. When the tin ships arrived at the mouth of the Seine, the Loire or the Gironde, they travelled as far up the rivers as they could. At the point when the keels began to scrape the river bed or become clogged in mud, the 80-kilo astragals were unloaded and transferred to packhorses. Their figure-of-eight shape allowed two to be carried by each animal, slung on either side of a wooden pack-saddle and lashed securely. The average packhorse could manage 160 kilos at a steady uphill walk without too much loss of condition. But these routes were only possible in summer when enough grass grew and could be grazed. Once a string of packhorses reached the banks of the River Rhône, the tin was untacked, set into boats and the current carried them quickly downstream to the sea and Marseilles.

Pytheas had travelled in the opposite direction and when he crossed the Channel, probably on a merchant ship bound for the well-known seamark of St Michael's Mount, he was about to enter unknown waters. Most likely in short hops, he made his way up through the Irish Sea to the Isle of Man where he took his second measurement of the height of the sun (the first having been carried out in Brittany). As he moved further north the climate would have cooled noticeably, the land grown more rugged and mountainous and the maritime culture changed radically. Pytheas almost certainly found himself travelling in a very different sort of craft from what he had been used to. Here is Rufus Festus Avienus' much later – and more poetic – version of the passage introducing Britain from *On the Ocean*:

> Lying far off and rich in metals,
> Of tin and lead. Great the strength of this nation,
> Proud their mind, powerful their skill,
> Trading the constant care of all.
>
> They know not to fit with pine
> Their keels, nor with fir, as use is,
> They shape their boats; but strange to say,
> They fit their vessels with united skins,
> And often traverse the deep in a hide.

These were seagoing curraghs, not unlike those still being built in the south-west of Ireland. In 320 BC, the waters of the Irish Sea and the Atlantic shores of Scotland and Ireland would have been crossed by many curraghs, some of them very large, all of them well suited to the swells and eddies of the ocean. Curraghs were quick, easy and cheap to construct. First a frame of greenwood rods (hazel was much favoured, and willow) was driven either into the ground or into holes made in a gunwale formed into an oval. Then the rods were lashed together with cord or pine roots into the shape of a hull, upside down. Once all was tight and secure – the natural whip and tension of greenwood helped this part of the process very much – the framework was then made rigid by the fitting of benches which acted as thwarts. Over the hull hides were stretched and sewn together (or 'united') before being lashed to the gunwales. When the hides shrank naturally, they tightened over the greenwood rods and the seams were then caulked with wool grease or resin. Large curraghs could take twenty men or carry two tons of cargo and, since they were so straightforward to make from materials widely available, they and their small, round cousins, the coracles, would have sailed the coasts of Scotland and Ireland in their many thousands.

In his magisterial *Life of St Columba*, Adomnan talked of how the Iona community used curraghs to bring materials from the mainland and also described how they could be rowed and sailed. To make passage easier, the saint intervened:

> [F]or on the day when our sailors had got everything ready and meant to take the boats and curraghs and tow the timbers to the island by sea, the wind, which had blown in the wrong direction for several days, changed and became favourable. Though the route was long and indirect, by God's favour the wind remained favourable all day and the whole convoy sailed with their sails full so that they reached Iona without delay.
>
> The second time was several years later. Again, oak trees were being towed by a group of twelve curraghs from the mouth of the River Shiel to be used here in repairs to the monastery. On a dead calm day when the sailors were having to use the oars, a wind suddenly sprang up from the west, blowing head on against them. We put in to the nearest island, called Eilean Shona, intending to stay in sheltered water.

But once again the power of the saint fixed the weather and the timbers were brought to Iona safely.

Pytheas claimed that his wanderings around Britain were not all seaborne. He travelled inland, but the hide boats will have helped him see much more than if he had gone on foot or even horseback. With a very shallow draught measured only in inches, coracles and curraghs could use rivers and lochs as their highways. Where rocky rapids or a watershed needed to be traversed, these hide boats were so light as to be easily carried. Turned upside down against the weather, they even made handy overnight shelters.

As he explored, Pytheas began to form strong but not always positive impressions of the peoples and especially the climate of the far north. Strabo, a Greek writer living in Rome after AD 14, considered *On the Ocean* to be little more than a catalogue of lies and exaggeration. But, in his vast, seventeen-volume *Geographica*, he used it nonetheless. Here is his, and Pytheas', version of the agriculture of the communities 'who lived near the chilly zone':

> Of the domesticated fruits and animals there is a complete lack of some and a scarcity of others, and that the people live on millet and on other herbs, fruits and roots; and where there is grain and even honey the people also make a drink from them. As for the grain, since they have no pure sunlight, they thresh it in large storehouses having first gathered the ears together there, because [outdoor] threshing floors are useless due to the lack of sun and the rain.

Some of this is little more than a Mediterranean view of long northern winters, cloudy days and the bewildering absence of several months of uninterrupted sunshine. The mention of millet is a fascinating misunderstanding. It does not grow in Britain but the reference, bracketed with 'other herbs, fruits and roots', is probably to Fat Hen, a nutritious plant now seen as a weed. Still known as *myles* or *mylies* in Scotland and cognate with the Latin word for millet, it was gathered, boiled and eaten as late as the eighteenth century by country people. Its seeds are rich in oil and carbohydrate and traces of Fat Hen have been found by archaeologists at sites dating back to the first millennium BC.

More generally, Pytheas was observing a society which still gathered in a harvest from wild places. In all likelihood, these were good locations for such as crab apples, hazelnuts or mushrooms and they will have been cared for and not overpicked. Our ancestors in Scotland ate – until recently – a wide range of plants now regarded as useless weeds.

Compared with Strabo's scorn, the tone of Diodorus Siculus' borrowings from *On the Ocean* is probably much closer to the original:

> Britain, we are told, is inhabited by tribes who are indigenous and preserve in their way of life the ancient customs. For example they use chariots in their wars . . . and their houses are simple, being built for the most part from reeds or timbers. Their way of harvesting their grain is to cut only the heads and store them in roofed buildings, and each day they select the ripened heads and grind them, in this manner getting their food. Their behaviour is simple, very different from the shrewdness and vice that characterise the men of today. Their lifestyle is modest since they are beyond the reach of luxury which comes from wealth. The island is thickly populated, and its climate is extremely cold . . . It is held by many kings and aristocrats who generally live at peace with each other.

Once again archaeology supports Pytheas' observations. Iron reaping hooks have been found at several sites in Scotland and the ancient method of cutting the grain near the top of the stalk is well attested into modern times. When cereals were grown in the old runrig system of long strips, the heads were cut so as to leave fodder for grazing animals. In the autumn, after the harvest, beasts came down from the summer shielings and were set on the reaped rigs to muck them, there being no other form of fertiliser. And cutting near the top also avoided the copious under-weeds of pre-industrial farming.

The last sentence of the extract from Diodorus is the first reference to British kingdoms and, although it is sketchy, even cursory, it has the virtue of simplicity. On his journeys around the coasts and inland, Pytheas clearly came across many kings and therefore many kingdoms. But Britain does not appear, at least not around the year 320 BC, to have been a squabbling anthill of competing autocrats. There were wars, the Greek explorer implied, but peace was the usual condition of life. As the nature of early Celtic kingship becomes clearer and the evidence supplied by outsiders more substantial, this observation will seem increasingly unlikely.

Pytheas noted few place-names in *On the Ocean* but one fascinating story was transmitted by Diodorus Siculus which hints at somewhere very specific in Scotland:

> In the region beyond the land of the Celts there lies in the ocean an island no smaller than Sicily. This island . . . is situated in the north and is inhabited by the Hyperboreans who are called by that name because their home is beyond the point where the north wind blows.

Mediterranean historians were in the habit of mediating exotic customs and beliefs to their readers and listeners through more familiar terms and, when Diodorus states that Apollo was worshipped on this distant northern island, he probably meant that there was a moon cult. Worship took place in 'a notable temple which is adorned with many votive offerings and is spherical in shape'. Diodorus goes on:

> They also say that the moon, as viewed from this island, appears to be but a little distance above the earth . . . The account is also given that the god visits the island every nineteen years, the period in which the return of the stars to the same place in the heavens is accomplished . . . At the time of this appearance of the god he both plays on the lyre and dances continuously the night through from the vernal equinox until the rising of the Pleiades.

Echoes of Pythean precision can be heard clearly in this passage and the movement of the moon does, in fact, run through an 18.61-year cycle at a particular northern latitude. When it is remembered that Pytheas' third measurement of the height of the sun was on the island of Lewis and that his calculation of 54 degrees and 13 minutes fits almost exactly with a lunar cycle of 18.61 years, the location of the spherical temple of the Hyperboreans slowly begins to come into focus.

Around 2800 BC the communities of prehistoric farmers on Lewis came together to build a spectacular temple – what is now known as the standing stones at Callanish. From the elliptical circle of outer stones, alignments run from the magnificent inner group to very particular seasonal configurations of the heavens. One aims directly at the southern moonset, another to the sunset at the equinox and a third to where the Pleiades first appear. But most telling is the fact that, every 18.61 years, the moon appears to those standing in the circle at Callanish to move along the rim of the horizon 'dancing continuously the night through'. This transit can be seen on clear nights between the spring equinox on 21st March and 1st of May. The latter date is the great Celtic feast of Beltane, now called May Day, a celebration of fertility and awakening after the long and dead months of winter.

By the time Pytheas visited the Isle of Lewis in 320 BC, the stones at Callanish had long been abandoned and a blanket of peat was forming around them. But tales will have been told of the Old Peoples who raised them, perhaps offerings laid at the feet of the great stones, Beltane celebrated, different gods honoured. Did Pytheas' curragh enter Loch Rog nan Ear where the stones can be seen from the sea? Did the oarsmen beach the boat at the head of the loch and did Pytheas talk to people who knew the old stories of Callanish and those who worshipped there?

Many of the ancient standing stones of the Atlantic shore were used as seamarks. North of Callanish, those sailing up the coast of Lewis could see clearly the huge Clach an Truiseal. Originally at the centre of another circle, this stone stands 5.8 metres tall and is immensely impressive. The beliefs which pulled it upright may have been long forgotten by the time Pytheas came to Lewis but it is not difficult to imagine a lingering reverence swirling around the Clach an Truiseal.

Stone circles were almost always placed carefully in the landscape, conspicuous but accessible, and, as the deposit of tremendous labour, they often retained their importance and traditions, even through periods of profound cultural change.

Stonehenge still inspires powerful devotion in the twenty-first century. In Aberdeenshire, not far from Inverurie, a small but striking circle has a very interesting name. The second element of Easter Aquhorthies is a Gaelic word which means 'Prayer Field', a clear recognition of what took place inside the ring of huge stones. But the important issue here is chronological. Gaelic arrived in Aberdeenshire much later than the date of Easter Aquhorthies' construction and probably millennia after the original religion of the prehistoric farmers of the Urie Valley who built it had begun to change. The gods were not the same but the traditions of reverence did not entirely fade and were understood. The stones of the Old Peoples were not fenced off and thought of as relics or monuments but were part of a changing landscape, of an aggregate of experience in one place.

Far to the south, a long way from Easter Aquhorthies and the Clach an Truiseal, another great stone circle retained all sort of significance. The Lochmaben Stane stands on the northern shore of the Solway Firth, near the outfall of the little River Sark and the modern border between England and Scotland. Pytheas probably saw it and its lost companions and, almost four centuries later, many more Mediterranean eyes looked at the huge round boulders. By AD 74, the invading Roman legions had reached Carlisle, the place called Luguvalium. Under the command of the governor of the new province of Britannia, Petilius Cerialis, soldiers built a fort on the eminence between the rivers Eden and Caldew, just to the south of their confluence. As the first professional army in European history, the Romans were methodical and, as Cerialis looked out over the grey waters of the Solway and to the flatlands beyond, his first thoughts will have been on the gathering of military intelligence. If the eagle standards were to be carried into the wilderness of the north and the legions were to march to glory behind them, then their general needed a map. As scouts rode out of the camp at Carlisle and began the long process of reconnaissance, what became Scotland began to emerge from the darkness of the past.

Markers in a largely treeless landscape will have proved

invaluable and the Lochmaben Stane is huge, a granite boulder standing more than two metres high and measuring more than six metres around. Very visible on the flat Solway plain, it would have been even more impressive when Cerialis' patrols saw it. The *New Statistical Account* of 1845 recorded a ring of nine large stones which enclosed a wide area of almost half an acre. Seven had been removed by the farmer at Old Graitney just before 1845 to allow him to plough more ground and an eighth had been dug out and rolled into a nearby hedge. Recent examination of the remaining megalith (almost certainly too big to shift) gave a date of around 2525 BC. And, when the Roman scouts rode north and west from Carlisle, the old circle was already ancient, still venerated and very useful.

Over the four centuries of Roman Britain, the first maps made for Petilius Cerialis and his fellow governors of the province of Britannia were added to and refined. Much later, in the seventh century AD, a clerk working at the Italian town of Ravenna used them to compile a composite map of Britain (and much of the known world) and he attached two place-names to the area. *Locus Maponi* supplies the initial elements of the name of the old stone circle but it was almost certainly more precisely applied to the town of Lochmaben ten miles to the north-west and, by extension, to the district between it and the Solway. *Locus Maponi* does not mean the 'Place of Mapon or Maben' but 'the Loch' or 'Pool' and, at Lochmaben, there are three. The Castle Loch is larger than the Kirk Loch and the Mill Loch is the smallest.

Mapon or Maponus was a god. His name derives from the Old Welsh root, *map*, which meant 'son of' and the predominant image is of a divine youth. Strong evidence of a local cult of Mapon has been found in a series of dedications at the slightly later Roman forts of the first century AD at Birrens, Brampton, Chesterholm (Vindolanda), Ribchester and the settlement at Corbridge. Most twin the Celtic god with Apollo and, as at Callanish, both may be further associated with memories of a moon cult at the stone circle on the Solway.

In the first millennium BC, Celtic beliefs were also associated with sacred water sites, especially small lochs. Having damaged it in some ritual manner, priests threw metalwork into watery places, probably as a means of propitiating potentially malevolent gods. And it may be that the lochs at Lochmaben were particularly sacred to Mapon and expensive swords, shields and other metal artefacts were deposited there. By contrast, the stone circle at the seashore may have directed worship to the sky and the transit of the heavens, perhaps to the moon. Although worship at each site probably did not occur even in the same millennium, there is a sense of a sacred landscape, the land of the people of Maben.

The clerk at Ravenna marked down another local name. Maporitum certainly denotes the stone circle for its meaning is clear. The ford of Mapon was still in regular use in the nineteenth century and, in fact, it gave its name to the Solway Firth. Ancient geography encouraged travellers, armies and any-one else on foot to cross the firth by one of three fords if they wanted to avoid a long detour to the east. Solway Moss and the boggy, shifting wetlands between the mouths of the rivers Esk and Sark could be treacherous and the more reliable bed of the firth was usually preferred. There were low-tide crossings be-tween Annan and Bowness, at the Sandy Wath between Torduff Point and the shore near Drumburgh and finally at what was known as the Sul Wath. The Vikings brought the word *wath* (cognate to 'wade') and it now exists in Scots and Cumbrian meaning 'a ford'. The *sul* was the pillar or the standing stone and it referred to the Lochmaben Stane. It marked the northern terminus of the shortest of the Solway (or *Sulvath*) fords and, in an otherwise featureless, flat land- and seascape, it was a vital aid to navigation. Travellers from the south anxious not to stray into deeper water kept their eyes fixed on the great stone.

Petilius Cerialis and his staff officers were not entirely ignorant about what lay north of Carlisle. From Pytheas, his imitators and detractors, they knew that Britain was a large island and that another, smaller island lay to the west. More information had been compiled by a Spanish geographer, Pomponius Mela. Writing just before the invasion of Britain in AD 43 by the armies of the Emperor Claudius, he also produced a map which shows Britain and Ireland in schematic outline, just as Pytheas had described it and in roughly the correct place in relation to mainland Europe. Significantly, Mela was the first to plot the location of the islands named as the Orcas in *On the Ocean*. Using the slightly different form of the Orcades, he places the archipelago off the northernmost point of Britain. There are thirty islands in the Orcades, according to Mela, and, not far to the west, he sets the Haemodes, the Shetlands. There are only seven of these. The arithmetic is not unreasonable and speaks of enquiries made, perhaps even at first hand, of people who had been there.

Ultima Thule

This was the phrase used by the Greeks, the Romans and Dark Ages' scholars to mean 'Farthest North', the frozen edge of the known world. Pytheas reckoned Thule to be six days' sail north of Britain and Pliny the Elder wrote that, in midsummer, there was no night and, in midwinter, no day. The word probably derives from the Greek tholos meaning 'murky' or 'indistinct'. It all added to the sense of mystery about the far north. When Ptolemy made his famous map of Britain, he turned Scotland north of the Tay through a 90-degree angle so that it bent abruptly to the east. The problem for Ptolemy was that, if he had plotted the north of Britain correctly, it would have extended to a latitude of 66 degrees north and, from the vantage point of the sun-drenched Mediterranean, the Greeks did not believe that human beings could survive north of 63 degrees. The inhabitants of Scotland's Atlantic coasts and islands were closer to the truth in every way. When they heard the call of the whooper swans and looked up at their V-shaped squadrons migrating north in the spring, they knew that there was land in the north. The great eighth-century historian, Bede, believed that Thule was Iceland and, a hundred years later, Dicuil, an Irish monk at the court of Charlemagne, described the long summers and winters of the north and the frozen seas beyond Iceland. Ultima Thule, 'Farthest North', turned out to be the vast subcontinent of Greenland and, when Viking longships sailed into its summer landing places, those classical writers who mocked Pytheas were once again proved wrong.

Pomponius Mela's map turned out to have historical as well as geographical consequences. When the legions had defeated the British kings of the south-east in AD 43 and advanced to the Thames, the Emperor Claudius hurried north from Rome. At the moment when his soldiers marched in triumph into the Trinovantian town of Colchester, it was vital that their Emperor and Commander-in Chief led them and was seen to be at their head. It was said that elephants were brought across the Channel to add to the impression of imperial might.

Political presentation had been at the heart of Rome's invasion of Britain – the entire exercise had been designed as a handy means of attaching glory to Claudius' name. Dragged on to the throne by the Praetorian Guard after the murder of Caligula, the new emperor's grip on power had been shaky and dissent was rumbling. But, if Claudius could outdo Julius Caesar and actually conquer the wild and misty island that lay across 'the Ocean' and all its dangers, then there was surely nothing that such an emperor could not achieve. And, when discussions about the proposed invasion began, someone from the staff of Narcissus, the freedman who was Claudius' Chief Minister, saw the map made by Pomponius Mela and the remote islands that lay far to the north in the sea beyond Britain, a propaganda coup appeared to present itself.

Diplomats were despatched to the court of the King of Orkney, and they almost certainly took with them or sent on containers of a very fancy liqueur made in the Mediterranean. At the elaborate broch at Gurness on Mainland, archaeologists have found shards of a type of small amphora which had become obsolete by AD 60 and which had been used to transport an exotic sweet drink, a gift from Rome – and perhaps a lubricant for delicate negotiations. Nothing less than a place in history for the Emperor was at stake.

When the fourth-century historian, Eutropius, listed as Claudius' greatest achievement that he had accepted the submission of eleven British kings at Colchester in AD 43, he took particular care to emphasise that 'he added to the empire some islands lying in the Ocean beyond Britain, which are called the Orkneys'. What transforms this detail from the incidental to something revelatory about the early kingdoms of Scotland was the logistics of the occasion.

Claudius was in Britain for only sixteen days. There was simply not enough time for a diplomatic mission to travel to Gurness, negotiate a treaty and then return to Colchester with the King of Orkney so that he could formally bow to the Emperor. The deal had to have been done well in advance – perhaps three months in advance when the general, Aulus Plautius, landed the expeditionary force of legionaries and auxiliaries at Richborough in Kent. And more, it shows a previously unsuspected intensity of contact, a clear knowledge of European politics in Orkney and a degree of political sophistication on the part of the royal council at Gurness. The reality was that the king and his advisors had no immediate need to submit to Rome, the legions had only just landed and the outcome was, at least, in some doubt. And the fighting was 600 miles away, far to the south and across the sea.

The journey of the Orkney king to Colchester was probably an eloquent comment on the relationship between the Orcadians and their neighbours on the Scottish mainland, in the northern Highlands. It is not stretching the significance of this submission too far to suggest that it was an attempt at making an alliance with the greatest military power in the world against the hostile kings of northern Scotland. For its part, Rome had played off many so-called barbarians against each other in the past and any such arrangement would have been well understood by both parties.

But, for Claudius, the coup of counting the King of Orkney as a subject of the Empire was a tremendous fillip which would silence opposition and garner support. Claudius the Conqueror had extended the power of Rome to the ends of the earth.

It became a famous achievement. When Britain's first really great scholar, Bede of Jarrow, sat down to write his *Ecclesiastical History of the English People*, the 'annexation' of the Orkneys into the empire was still seen as a signal moment. The islands 'which lie in the ocean beyond Britain' were witness to an imperial reach which knew no bounds.

Historians disagree on the identity of the first Roman governor to lead troops into Scotland. Julius Agricola had been appointed commander of one of Cerialis' legions, the XX Valeria Victrix, and, when he himself became governor of the province in AD 79 (or AD 78), it may be that he was indeed the first to enter what became Scotland at the head of a Roman army. Either way, intelligence about what lay in the north had greatly increased by the 70s AD.

Pliny the Elder was a remarkable man. A soldier, politician and scientist, he was killed at Pompeii in AD 79 when a fatal curiosity drew him too close to the eruption of Mount Vesuvius. Pliny was a prolific author but only his encyclopaedic *Natural History* has survived. In an age when men thought it possible to know everything and that all knowledge could be written down, he crammed an immense density of material into thirty-seven volumes. Here is part of Pliny's description of Britain, Ireland and the smaller islands off their coasts:

Hibernia lies beyond Britannia, the shortest crossing being from the lands of the Silures, a distance of 30 miles. Of those remaining [islands] none has a circumference exceeding 125 miles, so it has been said. Indeed, there are 40 Orcades [Orkneys] separated narrowly from one another, 7 Acmodae [Shetlands], 30 Hebudes [Hebrides], and between Hibernia and Britannia [lie the islands of] Mona [Anglesey], Monapia [Man], Riginia [Rathlin], Vectis [Whithorn], Silumnus [Dalkey] and Ambros [Bardsey] . . .

This is the first historical notice of the Hebrides but what immediately catches the eye is that the list includes Whithorn or, more correctly, the Isle of Whithorn on the northern coast of the Solway. Vectis was also the Latin name for the Isle of Wight but, given Pliny's sequence of names and the general accuracy of the information, the reference is almost certainly to Whithorn – another very early historical notice for a place which was to be of great significance.

In Book XVI of the *Natural History*, Pliny shivered as he wrote of the far north, the land under the winter stars of the Great Bear:

> The most remote of all those [islands] recorded is Thule, in which as we have pointed out there are no nights at midsummer when the sun is passing through the sign of the Crab, and on the other hand no days at midwinter; indeed some writers think this is the case for periods of six months at a time without a break. The historian Timaeus says there is an island named Mictis [St Michael's Mount] lying inward six days' sail from Britain where tin is found, and to which the Britons cross in boats of willow covered with stitched hides. Some writers speak of other islands as well, the Scandiae [Denmark?], Dumna, Bergos and Berrice, the largest of them all, from which the crossing to Thule starts. One day's sail from Thule is the frozen ocean, called by some the Mare Cronium.

Thule was probably the name the Greeks and Romans gave to Iceland while Dumna, Bergos and Berrice may be alternative names for the Outer Hebrides, from Barra to Lewis.

More writers added more mystery and foreboding about the far north. There was a great and dark forest, they warned, the Silva Caledoniae, and it was peopled by fierce warriors, the Caledonii. The Romans worried about a long tradition of danger in the depths of the woods. North of Rome the Ciminian Forest was ruled out of bounds for Roman armies by the Senate in the early days of the republic, and all their worst, visceral fears came to pass in AD 9 when Varus lost three legions in the Teutoberg Forest in southern Germany. To a man, they were slaughtered by the feral German warriors of the woods.

The effect of these tales of the north on Cerialis' soldiers cannot have been encouraging as rumours about what lay across the Solway flickered around their campfires. Others will have been more sanguine. What, wondered the more hardened veterans, did the Emperor want with such a cold, wet, difficult and useless place? What could it possibly be worth? Historians talked of the *pretium victoriae*, 'the wages of victory' earned by Rome's conquering armies – slaves, booty, sometimes precious and highly portable objects and even land. But what lay in the north except a dark forest full of screaming savages, six months of darkness and a frozen sea?

Glory – that was the answer to all the undoubted speculation in the ranks. Glory was what the Emperor sought – a stunning victory from his armies which had marched fearlessly to the ends of the earth that would translate into everlasting prestige in Rome and throughout the Empire. Legionaries would splash into the chilly waters of the Solway fords to keep the Emperor safe on his throne and to show that they and their comrades were the masters of the world.

What the northern part of that world looked like was made clearer by necessity. As reports came in from scouts and diplomats, knowledge of geography and politics expanded. Names became known, native alliances and hostilities better understood and attitudes to Rome made plainer. Perhaps Petilius Cerialis or more probably Agricola and his officers began to plan their advance. It seems likely that the Emperor Vespasian wanted to see and celebrate a conquest of the whole island and, since he himself had been a legionary legate in Britain during the Claudian invasion, he did not merely wave a hand in the air and command that his will be done. He knew what was involved.

The dates of events during his governorship are unclear but, some time between AD 71 and 74, Cerialis had successfully subdued one of the most powerful native kingdoms, the Brigantes. Almost certainly a federation of smaller kindreds, their territory straddled the Pennines and may have reached into the Cheviots and possibly Cumbria and the Eden Valley. Using the classical strategy of divide and conquer, Cerialis had his men build fortified roads through the hill, between the Parisii in eastern Yorkshire, the main Brigantian concentration in the Pennines, and the people known as the Carvetii in the Eden Valley and they created an important north–south split when they drove the Stanegate ('the Stone Road') through the Hexham

Gap. He had large forts built at Carlisle and Corbridge to control
the hill country around them. Similar tactics would work well in
the north.

Slightly later Roman sources talked of a kindred known as the
Anavionenses who lived in Annandale, broadly, the area between
the valley of the Nith in the west and the Moffatdale and Eskdale
Hills in the east. The name is clearly cognate with the town of
Annan, the northern terminus of the longest and westernmost of
the Solway fords and the name of the river which flows into the
firth. As seems fitting for the lands of the people of Maben,
Annan is another sacred name. In an Old Welsh form recorded
in 1124, the area was known as Estrahanent. The first element is
from *ystrad*, Old Welsh for 'strath or valley', and the second is a
rendering of Annan, an ancient Celtic goddess, sometimes seen
as a mother figure. In the Ravenna Cosmography, the name
of *Anava* is attached to the river valley and it seems close to
Anavionenses.

The name was unearthed at the site of Vindolanda, a fort near
Hadrian's Wall, in a long sequence of brilliant excavations by
Robin Birley. He and his team have found many hundreds of
letters and lists preserved in the anaerobic peat and they reveal
not only facts but attitudes. To the Roman colonists, the natives
were known as Brittunculi or 'wretched little Brits' and, in the
same report, the officer noted: 'the Britons are unprotected by
armour. There are very many cavalry. The cavalry do not use
swords nor do the wretched little Brits mount in order to throw
javelins.'

When Roman soldiers finally entered the territory of the
Anavionenses, they came into a cleared landscape. There was
no deep, dark Caledonian Forest. Analysis of ancient pollen
samples shows that southern Scotland was largely deforested by
the first century AD. For millennia, timber had been the source of
firewood for heat and cooking, of most building materials, most
tools and implements and, later, any form of wheeled transport.
By the first millennium BC, there is widespread evidence of a
marked increase in the use of stone for building work. And, by

the time Roman commanders rode north, there were few trees to be seen, far less any sort of forest, and timber had become a resource to be carefully husbanded and protected.

Apart from the lack of trees, either as the modern patchwork of densely planted evergreen forests, or shelter belts, or even small areas of wildwood, there were other ways in which the landscape looked different two thousand years ago. People had yet to raise pylons, criss-cross the countryside with overhead lines or the wide swathes of motorways and roads and the incessant hum of engine noise. From wherever the contours rose high enough, mounted Roman scouts looked out over a quiet scene, a hundred shades of green, brown, blue and grey, an entirely rural landscape of small farms, unbridged streams and rivers, lochs and distant hills. On still days many wispy columns of smoke rose into the air, seeping through the thatch of native roundhouses, themselves almost invisible, built from natural materials lying close to hand.

Roads were tracks, no wider than a narrow footpath and used by walkers, riders and very occasionally by carts in places where the ground was better and flatter. Wide areas of the landscape were covered with willow scrub and tall stands of marsh grass, undrained bogs which could be very dangerous to those ignorant of the safe paths. Someone who took a wrong step could disappear, suddenly be completely submerged, sucked into a boggy oblivion if helping hands were not quick.

In the first century AD, there was little or no traffic, at least in the modern sense. People moved much less, never for pleasure and only when they had to, and usually on foot. The land was quiet and only the lowing of beasts, cows at milking time, the bleat of ewes and the shriek of wildfowl were heard. Over many centuries, people had moulded where they lived, to be sure – clearing fields, husbanding and gathering a wild harvest of fruits, roots and fungi, and hunting and snaring wild animals – but they had not yet overpowered their environment. Moonless nights were black dark and common sense as well as fearfulness will always have kept everyone inside, snug in their warm and dry roundhouses. Even on the brightest day, from a distance, a modern eye would have seen what seemed an almost empty landscape.

The arrival of a Roman army in Annandale was a startling event. In the 70s AD, at least one legion, probably two, marched north and their appearance was unlike anything the native people had seen before. The sheer mass, such a huge number of men, 5,000 to 10,000, would have been dazzling – and terrifying. Roman soldiers did not wear uniforms, but rather a standard set of clothing and armour, and they carried similar equipment and a pack. Such uniformity would in itself have been disconcerting and the sight of a huge number of men marching in military order will have seemed like a giant, articulated animal snaking through the landscape.

Contingents of cavalry generally rode on ahead, sweeping the planned line of march for hostile activity and ambush. The column was led by a vanguard of auxiliary troops, men who were not legionaries but had been recruited from Rome's conquered provinces and sometimes those peoples whose territory lay beyond the boundaries of the Empire. They were expendable and would take the brunt of any frontal assault, preserving the more valuable, highly trained legionaries behind them. Batavians and Tungrians from what became modern Belgium and southern Holland were probably first across the Solway and into the Annandale Plain and they were led by their own aristocracy. Behind them came the command group with its bodyguard, the standard bearers and trumpeters. Following them were the legionaries who usually marched six abreast. Many armies sing or chant as they march but apparently the Romans moved in silence, accompanied only by the dull, rumbling thunder of their hobnailed boots thudding into the ground. Behind trundled the baggage train, carts, animals and slaves. And finally came the rearguard. Cavalry also rode out wide, protecting the flanks of the column. Even for a single legion on the move, its auxiliaries and baggage, the column could be more than two miles long – what must have seemed to those watching like an endless stream of men. And commanders expected a day's march to achieve at least fifteen miles. The vanguard of a large army of four or five legions would reach the site of its next overnight camp before the rearguard had left the last one. It was an impressive display, designed to discourage opposition and instil fear. And it must have.

Since they had crossed the Solway and made their way north, the long column of legions would never have lost sight of a striking landmark. Singular and with a flat summit, Burnswark Hill rose up out of the Annandale Plain. Almost seven centuries before the Romans saw it, the kings of the Anavionenses had commanded the building of a rampart, creating what archaeologists used to call a hill fort. Many ramparts were dug on prominent hills in the first millennium BC by the peoples of Lowland Scotland but they were probably not forts. It seems that their symbolism outweighed any military rationale. Difficult to defend against assault with such long perimeters and usually a lack of a reliable water supply, hill forts were meant simply to look impressive – a statement of power – but they are much more likely to have been temples. Rather than defending against what might attack them from the outside, their ramparts marked off a sacred enclosure where priests and kings (perhaps the roles were often combined) performed rituals.

Scotland's native society was Celtic in its nature when the legions marched north and hill forts may well have been the focus of the four main festivals of the year – Imbolc in late February, Beltane in early May, Lughnasa in August and, in late October, Samhuinn. These were the nodal points of the farming and stock-rearing year and the communities of Annandale, the Anavionenses, the people of Maben, almost certainly climbed Burnswark Hill to worship, celebrate and listen to the words of their priests and kings. When fires were lit inside the ramparts and music was played and sung, the gods drew near and the veil between the worlds lifted.

As was their prudent habit, Roman armies on the march dug overnight camps wherever they halted. Rudimentary affairs with a single ditch and a bank made from the upcast inside it, a camp could be created in a matter of an hour or two, such was the excellent training and coordinated command of Roman soldiers. It must have seemed extraordinary, even magical to anyone watching. The invading army dug a camp at Birrens, only three miles south-east of Burnswark Hill fort, probably their first since leaving Carlisle. Birrens was to have a long history, remaining occupied as a forward outpost even after Hadrian's Wall was built fifty years later, and then after the frontier settled there at the end of the second century.

Birrens Fort became known as Blatobulgium. An informative name, it meant 'the Meal-sack Place', a central depot where the cereal harvest bought by Roman quartermasters was ingathered. The garrisons of the Wall needed to be fed and the use of Birrens as a depot more than suggests Annandale as a fertile area for corn-growing native farmers. It lay conveniently near the western end of the Wall and its large and hungry garrison. In order to ensure a regular supply, the Romans must have paid reasonable rates and the local economy sufficiently efficient to produce a surplus. More than that, the commercial relationship is unlikely to have been with a series of small suppliers rather with a native government of some kind – kings or an aristocracy – able to organise and enforce collection, probably as an element in local taxation.

The line of the modern A74 was no doubt a well-trodden track two thousand years ago but it was also the Romans' chosen route north for another reason. From Corbridge in the east, another column also struck north, this time following what became Dere Street and finally the A68. The strategy was clear – a pincer movement to isolate the hostile territory which lay between.

The board had been set and the pieces now began to move into play. Between AD 79 and AD 83, imperial policy directed a huge and highly coordinated invasion and, when war burst over the native peoples of North Britain, it was to shine a vivid, even harsh, light on the land that was to become Scotland. For this was not to be a war fought in the half-light of ancient history but one which was recorded by a remarkable man. Tacitus wrote the *Agricola* only twenty years after the legions had waded across the Solway fords and, in its elegant and precise pages, Scotland's history first comes alive.

3

As If Into a Different Island

✖

FOR FIFTEEN YEARS, Publius Cornelius Tacitus had concealed his hatred for the Emperor Domitian, and concealed it very well. In AD 77 or 78, Tacitus married Julia Agricola, the daughter of a distinguished soldier and senator, and, soon after, began to climb the career ladder of Roman politics. When Domitian succeeded his brother Titus in 81, in suspicious circumstances, Tacitus continued to flourish, taking office as a quaestor, a magistrate with responsibility for public finances. Rising steadily in what the Romans called the *cursus honorum* ('course of honours'), he became commander of a legion and then, almost certainly, governor of a province. Ironically, with his cognomen of Tacitus meaning 'silent', he acquired an unmatched reputation as an orator in the law courts and as a writer. As the plotters in the imperial palace whispered behind their hands and the spies listened for murmurs of treachery, silence may have served Tacitus well.

By 93, Domitian had retreated into increasingly vicious bouts of paranoia and Tacitus became involved in a series of purges of suspect fellow senators. There is more than a hint of self-disgust when, at last, he felt able to write of his own complicity:

[T]he senate-house [was] under siege, the senate hedged in by armed men, the killing of so many consulars in that same act of butchery, so many noble women forced into exile or flight . . .

But soon we ourselves led Helvidius to prison, the faces of Mauricius and Rusticus put us to shame, we were stained by Senecio's innocent blood. Nero at least averted his gaze: he ordered crimes to be committed but did not look on. A special torment under Domitian was to see him watching us, our very sighs being noted down against us, and all the while that savage gaze was able to mark down so many who had turned pale with shock, that flushed face that saved him blushing with shame.

Having been installed in the Senate by Domitian and probably designated as Consul by him, Tacitus must have stood in some danger when the Emperor was at last murdered in Rome in 96. But despite his involvement in the purges, so frankly admitted, he took up office and a year later wrote a remarkable biography of his father-in-law, Julius Agricola. Brief and concise, it is the first coherent written record of early Britain and, in particular, of North Britain.

The publication of books in Rome was usually marked by a public reading in front of an audience, probably invited by the author. One of Tacitus' listeners is very likely to have been an interested party. Sextus Julius Frontinus had succeeded Petilius Cerialis as governor of Britain and been the immediate predecessor of Agricola. And he was living in Rome in 98. By that time Frontinus had become a grand old man and himself an author. Not only had he written a report on the state of the city's aqueducts as Water Commissioner, a very prestigious office, he had also published a treatise on military science, the *Strategemata*. Frontinus' own experiences in Britain are therefore likely to have been well known amongst the literate political elites and, while Tacitus may have been reporting events from the farthest ends of the empire, he will have known that an expert was listening and that rigour and accuracy were required.

After the reading of a new work, copyists then turned out several versions for sale or as gifts. Numbers must have been small for there is at least one example of an author recalling all the copies of one of his works in circulation so that he could make changes and corrections.

When Tacitus unrolled the first scroll of his *De vita et moribus Agricolae* and stood up to read from it, some time in 98, he must have relished the moment. Here, in a book, in a formal piece of history, was his opportunity to break his silence and speak his mind on recent events. The meat of the narrative is Agricola's successful campaigns in North Britain, his defeat of the Caledonians at the famous battle at Mons Graupius and a triumphant expansion of the boundaries of the empire. But the political background to all these achievements is often touched on. Here is an early passage:

> We have indeed provided a grand specimen of submissiveness. Just as the former age witnessed an extreme in freedom, so we have experienced the depths of servitude, deprived by espionage even of the intercourse of speaking and listening to one another. We should have lost our memories as well as our voices, were it as easy to forget as to be silent.

A few paragraphs later, Tacitus rounds off his extraordinary introduction:

> Nonetheless, it will not be an unpleasant task to put together, even in a rough and uncouth style, a record of our former servitude and a testimony to our present blessings. For the time being, this book, intended to honour Agricola, my father-in-law, will be commended, or at least excused, as a tribute of dutiful affection.

All history is partial and the *Agricola* was certainly written by a winner, a distinguished member of the Roman imperial aristocracy. But Tacitus' motives, the sense of setting down a proper history, of clearing the air after the cruelties and corruptions of the evil reign of Domitian, have bequeathed at least a degree of objectivity. Agricola is never criticised but the Roman Empire certainly is and the narrative feels uniquely balanced. The barbarians of North Britain are not portrayed as witless savages and Rome is not seen as the fount of all good.

Two more possibilities lend weight to this view of Tacitus' work. Agricola's cognomen means what it sounds like, 'the Farmer'. And it hints at an old jibe at provincialism. At the outset, Tacitus states that the great general came from Forum Julii, modern Frejus in Provence. The town lay in the province of Gallia Narbonensis and several very learned scholars believe that Tacitus' family also originated there. And, in the letters of the Younger Pliny, there is a probable reference to Tacitus speaking with a Celtic accent.

What should also inform a reading of the Agricola is the likelihood that the young man accompanied his father-in-law when he was appointed governor of Britain in 77 or 78. It was usual for powerful men to help in the advancement of the careers of their close relatives and Tacitus may have been appointed as a military tribune.

What all of this adds up to is an unusual sympathy for the subject matter of this short history. Accuracy may have been enhanced by some first-hand reporting and description of North Britain and its culture made more vivid by an understanding of a more distant Celtic milieu, that of Gallia Narbonensis. Gaulish was beginning to wither by Tacitus' time, as Latin slowly became the popular language, but he may have heard enough and observed enough to make better sense of what North British society was like.

The North British were very likely to have known a good deal about Roman society or, at least, the Roman army. Although no written records of their views have survived, it is impossible to believe that those who ruled the peoples of the north were ignorant of the greatest empire the world had yet seen. Perhaps some of these kings accompanied the Orcadians when they arrived at Colchester to submit to the Emperor Claudius in AD 43. The triumphal arch raised in Rome in AD 51 carries an inscription which counted eleven British kings bowing in subjection. One was almost certainly absent – a king who had sent warriors south down the hill trails to fight against the legions as they moved the imperial frontier up to the Cheviots.

As Roman provincial administration established itself in southern Britain in the decades after the Claudian conquest, an alliance was made with the Brigantes, the peoples of the Pennines, parts of west Yorkshire, Lancashire and possibly Cumbria. Tacitus called them 'the most populous state in the whole province'. Their queen, Cartimandua, was amenable to Roman diplomacy but her consort, Venutius, led a rebellion in the 70s AD. At Stanwick Fort, near Scotch Corner, Petilius Cerialis' legions overran the breakaway Brigantians. Tacitus reported that they had 'help from outside' and that can only be a reference to allies in the north.

These were almost certainly the Selgovae. Tacitus did not attach a name to the kindred which sent a contingent of warriors to man the ramparts at Stanwick (in fact, he supplied maddeningly few names) and they first appear on a map drawn by Claudius Ptolemy, a Greek geographer of the mid second century AD. He drew on information gathered before and during the invasion of the north. Agricola had sent ships to circumnavigate Britain, make contact with native kings and gather as much intelligence as possible. When Ptolemy came to compile his map, it is striking that the inland territories of kindreds and the general level of detail is much more precise and dense south of the line of the Forth–Clyde isthmus. To the north, names are plotted in coastal regions and there is a look of sparseness in the inland areas. Which implies a reliance on the information collected by the Agricolan ships.

The Selgovae appear to have inhabited the hill country of the upper Tweed Valley and stretched west to Annandale and south to the Cheviot ranges. Like several others noted by Ptolemy, their name means something. Derived form the Celtic root *seilg*, it meant 'the Hunters' and may have been a reference to an ancient way of life in a wilder part of the north. As hill peoples, they were probably stockmen who ran herds of sheep and cattle and continued the traditions of the hunt. It is more than coincidence that one of the greatest medieval hunting grounds, the Ettrick Forest, lay in the lands of the Selgovae.

In the heart of this ancient kingdom, at the foot of the steep slopes of Horsehope Craig in the Manor Valley near the modern town of Peebles, a shepherd was working his dogs in the spring of 1859. They were ingathering ewes, bringing them down off the hillsides at lambing time. It was a sunny morning and amongst the scatter of the scree at the bottom of the craig, the dull glint of metal caught the shepherd's eye. Lifting some smaller stones away from the base of a large boulder, he pulled out a beautifully made, socketed axe head and some small metal rings. Having marked the spot, the shepherd put the strange objects in his pocket and walked down the Manor Water to Glenrath to find the farmer, Mr Linton.

When both men returned that afternoon to the scree, they moved aside more stones to discover a large hoard of bronze objects. Another axe head came to light, many more metal rings,

---

The Yarrow Stone

High in the hills of the Ettrick Forest is a fascinating place. Near the farm of Whitehope is a surviving string of standing stones and one of them has a Christian inscription on it. It reads:

Here an everlasting memorial.
In this place lie the most famous princes, Nudus and Dumnogenus,
Two sons of Liberalis.

Whitehope is deep in the ancient territory of the Selgovae but this sixth-century gravestone hints at political annexation. 'Liberalis' is almost certainly a reference to the first powerful Strathclyde king, Rhydderch Hael. Hael means 'generous' and in Latin that translates as liberalis. *Perhaps the lands of the Selgovae had come under Rhydderch's sway. Nudus and Dumnogenus, with their Romanised names, may not have been his sons but his underkings.*

---

various metal bands and some small mountings with designs of concentric circles inscribed on them. Mr Linton and his sharp-eyed shepherd found twenty-nine objects in all and, apart from the axe heads, they were recognised as the components of a miniature wagon or cart, something made as a gift or for display, too small to be practical. A provisional date of 750 BC was attached.

The Horsehope Craig finds appear to have been a ritual deposit, an offering made to the old gods by a society which valued well-crafted metalwork and whose elites premiated horses, harness and horse-drawn transport. The early kings of the Selgovae and their men rode to war either on horseback or in chariots pulled by ponies. Other finds dating after 500 BC and later confirm the intimate link between the war bands of the Cheviots and Southern Uplands and their ponies and, even later, a generation after the Agricolan invasion of their territory, written sources from the Roman fort of Vindolanda agree that 'there are very many cavalry' amongst the kindreds to the north of the Stanegate frontier, the line which later became Hadrian's Wall.

The charioteers and the warriors they drove into battle spoke a Celtic language. It was an ancestor of modern Welsh, what language historians call P-Celtic or Continental Celtic. Tacitus would have heard its cousin dialects in Gallia Narbonensis, in Gaul itself and as far east as Dalmatia, even to the banks of the Danube. Place names, kindred names, like *Selgovae*, and the few personal names recorded by Ptolemy and other ancient geographers and historians support the notion of a wide distribution of Continental Celtic.

The language appears to have spread through trade and technology. In central Europe, north of the Alps, metalworking developed to a highly sophisticated degree and the first hard and very sharp iron spears and swords were hammered out by smiths who spoke Continental Celtic. As their much sought-after output moved along trade routes so did their language. And how they moved those goods was also important. Latin generally borrowed little from Celtic languages and the cultural traffic seems to have flowed in the opposite direction. But in the first millennium BC it seems that a clutch of vocabulary around the technology of wheeled vehicles was transferred. The words *carrus* for 'a hand-cart', *raeda* for 'a coach', *carpentum* for 'a carriage' and many other related Latin terms are derived from Continental Celtic. In this at least, it seems that the Romans had something to learn from the Celts.

Faded, almost unrecognisable and certainly forgotten, the relics of Continental Celtic can still be seen on modern maps. Just as they do to the west of Catrail, its ancient place-names tend to survive in groups, suggesting that Celtic speech communities in remote districts clung on for longer as the sea of English lapped around them. A good example is to be found in a high valley of the upper Tweed, not far from Manor and Horsehope Craig. Around an impressive, tottering ruin called Tinnis Castle (Tinnis is from *dinas*, 'a fort'), other Celtic names echo a lost history. Dreva Craig is from *tref* for 'settlement' and it lies below Trahenna Hill and Penvalla, both Celtic names. And around the flanks of this beautiful valley swirls the shade of a legend, a name forever linked to the retreat and defeat of an older Britain. Merlin or Myrddin is remembered at modern places like Merlindale and in much older names like Drumelzier (originally in the form of Dunmedler, 'The Fort of Merlin') and commemorated in an extraordinary stained glass window in the old church at nearby Stobo.

Merlin may in reality have been a druid, a last, lingering figure from the pagan past, but the associations with Tinnis and Drumelzier are tenacious. They survived in early Welsh poetry known as the Triads and in one fascinating notice in a sixth-century chronicle. But that is to anticipate events.

While the ancestor of modern Welsh, Continental Celtic, was establishing itself in mainland Britain, a distinct variant began to be heard in Ireland, the western coastlands and islands. Known to scholars as Q-Celtic or Atlantic Celtic, it grew into the modern languages of Irish Gaelic, Scots Gaelic and Manx Gaelic from the

Isle of Man. Notoriously difficult to date, the process of language spread and transfer can probably be approximately tracked by the archaeology of trade goods and the tracing of trade routes. It is probably safe to assert that the Selgovan kings and their contemporaries on the western seaboard were speaking these two different variants of Continental and Atlantic Celtic by the beginning of the first millennium BC. And they probably had difficulty in understanding each other.

As always languages change when they move and in Ireland and in the west, Atlantic Celtic developed in revealing and fascinating ways. These are historically very important and can be well illustrated by modern examples and comparisons. Scots Gaelic is not like English, German or any of the Latin-based languages of southern Europe. There is no word for yes or for no. If a Gaelic speaker asks *A bheil an t'acras ort?* ('Are you hungry?'), the answers use the verb forms *Tha* ('I am') or *Chaneil* ('I am not'). This makes for greater precision and clearer understanding on either side of a question.

Equally fundamental is word order. English and many of the Latin-based languages generally arrange a sentence in a subject-verb–object format while Gaelic usually prefers the verb first, followed by a subject and then an object. Conjugating prepositions are also widely used and they change the spelling and pronunciation of the word to which they are applied. This makes life difficult for learners. Often this mutation affects only the initial syllable of a word – 'in the paper', for example, is *anns a phaiper*, pronounced 'faiper' instead of 'paiper', as it would be if no preposition had been applied.

There are also strange and very intriguing forms to describe conditions or status or both. The earlier example, *A bheil an t'acras ort?* literally means 'Is there hunger on you?'. Or, in order to describe themselves as coming from the island of Lewis, a male Gaelic speaker would say, *Se Leodhasch a tha annam* – literally, 'It is a Lewisman that is in me'. This active means of expression appears in all sorts of forms. 'I am sleeping' is rendered as *Tha mi na mo chadal* or 'I am in my sleeping'.

These forms are very rare and do not appear at all in other European languages, and only about 10 per cent of the world's languages contain anything like them. Intriguing similarities can, however, be heard in the Near East and along the North African coast. Some Semitic, Berber and Egyptian languages and dialects use many of the same forms found in Atlantic Celtic. Vocabulary differs widely but sentence word order, conjugating prepositions and the use of active verb forms to describe status and condition as well as a dozen other similarities are widely found on the southern shores of the Mediterranean.

Until the reach and mechanisms of trade are taken fully into account, these seem unlikely connections. Amongst the most dynamic early traders in the Mediterranean were the Phoenicians. Originating from the coastal cities of Tyre, Sidon and what is now Lebanon and Israel, these intrepid merchants sailed immense distances into unknown waters in pursuit of profit and intelligence. Having found the great city of Carthage, near modern Tunis, they reached along the coast to the Straits of Gibraltar, the Pillars of Hercules, where they turned their steering oars either north or south. From their port of Gades, or Cadiz, explorer-merchants plied down the Atlantic coasts of Africa or up to Biscay and probably on to Britain beyond.

As these remarkable men traded, they needed to make themselves clearly understood. Vagueness has no place in commerce and incomprehension costs money. As trade intensified, language mixing or creolisation grew, much as it did in the great modern mercantile empires in Africa and the east. Forms, if not vocabulary, were shared and as Atlantic Celtic reached northwards, spreading like a coastal lingua franca, it absorbed much of original native language but imposed on it a structure which had developed out of the Mediterranean. In this way Scots Gaelic shares seventeen fundamental structural characteristics with the Berber languages of the Sahel.

Medieval Irish and Scots historians understood something of this ancient process. In the eleventh century monastic copyists produced versions of Ireland's foundation myth in what they called *An Lebor Gabala Erenn* (*The Book of Invasions*). Shrouded in the mists of ancient time, the fathers of the Irish nation were said to have sailed from a homeland in the Iberian Peninsula, part of a tradition known as the *immrama*, a series of myth-historical voyages made by holy men and heroes.

Kings, or at least men who would be kings, often reached for a foundation myth when politics demanded that a shaky position be shored up. And when Robert de Brus needed legitimacy to sustain his seizure of the Scottish throne, he asked the clever and resourceful cleric, Bernard de Linton, to cobble together a tale of how the Scots came to Scotland. Leaning heavily on *An Lebor Gabala Erenn*, he produced this – much less famous – passage from the Declaration of Arbroath:

> The which Scottish nation, journeying from Greater Scythia by the Tyrrhene Sea and the Pillars of Hercules, could not in any place or time or manner be overcome by the barbarians, though long dwelling in Spain amongst the fiercest of them. Coming thence, 1,200 years after the transit of Israel, with many victories and many toils they won that habitation in the west, which though the Britons have been driven out, the Picts effaced, and the Norwegians, Danes and English have often assailed it, they hold now, in freedom from all vassalage; and as the old historians bear witness, have ever so held it. In this kingdoms have reigned 113 kings of their own blood royal, and no man foreign has been among them.

In the early fourteenth century, when Bernard was writing, Scythia was generally understood to be the Bulgarian and Romanian shores of the Black Sea, and while the Tyrrhene Sea may be seen as a slight diversion, the general direction of travel agrees with the findings of language scholars. Although it should be made clear that de Linton was writing not of Pictish history or kings, or of that large part of the north which spoke Continental Celtic, but of the west, of the speakers of Atlantic Celtic and their traditions. Great migrations of peoples have certainly taken place throughout history but both the Irish *Lebor* and the Declaration of Arbroath are much more likely to be describing the journey of a language and those stories and fragments of a culture carried inside it.

If Agricola and his legions were not the first Mediterranean influence to reach the north of Britain, what can be said about the historical importance of language creolisation over such long distances? Only that contact and knowledge exchanged between cultures was likely to have been much more widespread and active than is currently believed. For good reasons historians place much greater reliance on written records and archaeology than on collective memory and tradition – but it is important to be wary of painting the world of 2,000 ago in stark colours. Simply because no written record of the north, its peoples and their kings survives and that, by contrast, Tacitus' account of his farther-in-law's campaigns does, we should not make the lazy comparison between illiterate, primitive and savage Selgovan kings and sophisticated Roman invaders. To twenty-first-century sensibilities, both probably shared shockingly brutal views of human life and suffering but it would be wrong to assume that one was more or less cultured than the other.

The Romans and the Greeks would not agree. They certainly saw themselves as superior. Barbarians were not simply the speakers of 'bar-bar' crude languages – they were also lesser beings. Just at the moment when the empire encountered the peoples of the north of Britain, Tacitus catches the complexities of this group of attitudes brilliantly:

> Thus [among the British] even our style of dress came into favour and the toga was everywhere to be seen. Gradually too, they went astray into the allurements of evil ways, colonnades and warm baths and elegant banquets. The Britons, who had no experience of this, called it 'civilisation', although it was part of their enslavement.

Tacitus' references were to southern Britain and they suggest how advanced – and subtle – the process of Romanisation had become. But the provincial government was not its only agent. In the first century BC, communities of Belgic Gauls had crossed the Channel to settle in what is now Hampshire, West Sussex and Berkshire. With them they brought a new economics, stimulated by the trade of the empire, and they introduced coinage to Britain and established markets at Silchester, St Albans and Colchester. Native British coins have been found in places below the Severn–Humber line but no further north. It seems that the kings of the Brigantes and those kindreds beyond them would continue to have more in common with those in Wales and Ireland. And throughout the long four centuries of the province of Britannia, the sort of Romanisation seen by Tacitus' withering eye would be confined to the south.

Once Petilius Cerialis had established secure fortresses at Carlisle and Corbridge and either he or Agricola had begun to advance beyond the Cheviots, logistics demanded at least some good relationships with native kings. Having executed an isolating pincer movement around the hill country of the Selgovae, Roman commanders could lead their long columns further north – but not without first securing sufficient supplies for their troops. The routes of march around Selgovan territory lay far from the sea and the fleet and foraging for such a large force was bound to be chancy. The solution was to find allies and in the kindreds known to Ptolemy as the Votadini and the Venicones, and it appears that Roman diplomacy succeeded. The territory of the Votadini included the lower Tweed Valley and the Lothians and seems to have been governed from a series of centres – Edinburgh's Castle Rock, the impressive acropolis of Traprain Law in East Lothian, Eildon Hill North near Melrose and Yeavering in north Northumberland. The power bases of the kings of the Venicones are much less well understood but in their kingdom of Fife there is no lack of impressive potential sites. It looks as though they were close allies of the Votadini, no doubt communicating by sea across the Firth of Forth, for Venicones means 'the Kindred Hounds'.

Both kingdoms have scant Roman remains, probably because

diplomacy had avoided the need for forts and roads. Roman military planners did not waste resources and a peace treaty was seen as almost as glorious as victory in war. At Newstead, at the foot of Eildon Hill North, a large depot fort was built by Agricola's legions. It acted not only as a centre for ingathering supplies (it lay on an ancient route-network and was next to the Tweed and a reliable ford) but also as a sentinel guarding the mouths of the Selgovan valleys of the Ettrick, the upper Tweed and the Gala Water. Around the walls of Newstead (which was rebuilt many times), archaeologists have found the remains of extensive corrals and ancillary fortifications and these appear to have been used to overnight animals – sheep, cattle and horses.

In Fife, the Roman invaders built no equivalent depot fort but sharp-eyed toponymists have detected the shadow of where one might have been. Near two small and temporary camps in the valley of the River Eden lies the village of Blebo. In an earlier version, it was Bladeboig. An unusual place-name, it is thought to relate to what the Romans called Birrens fort in corn-producing Annandale. Blatobulgium means 'the Meal-sack Place' and, in Fife, it seems to have been rubbed smooth by time into a contracted version. Supplying corroboration, Ptolemy places Horrea in approximately the same place and in English it means 'granary'.

Once the legions had reached the Firth of Forth and re-established contact with the captains of their supply ships, Agricola and his commanders will have pondered their next move. Reconnaissance will have given them two determinant pieces of intelligence. Beyond the Venicones lay trouble. Like the Selgovae, the Highland kings were likely to be hostile and if they made a secure alliance, they could muster a large army. However much the Romans longed to confront a native army in a set-piece battle where their superior discipline and equipment had delivered victory after victory, there was a difficulty – a lack of room to manoeuvre. Geography stood in Agricola's way – an enormously important feature of Scotland's geography which has now completely disappeared.

Stretching east from the foothills of the Lomond mountains, south of the Lake of Menteith and almost up to the cliffs of

Stirling Castle rock, Flanders Moss was a huge – and dangerous –
barrier. The residue of a prehistoric sea which reached as far
inland as the rising ground at Aberfoyle, it followed the meandering course of the River Forth and was almost five miles in
breadth in places. The name derives from two Scots words and
means 'a quivering or quaking bog'. Studded with stagnant pools,
some of them very broad and deep, the flat landscape was
punctuated by stands of birch and willow. Place names remember the old marsh – Birkenwood for the birches, East Poldar for
a bog beside a pool and Powblack for a peat-dark creek. In
winter, Flanders Moss was a bleak, sodden place, often flooded
as rain and snow swelled the Forth, and, in summer, the midgies
and mosquitoes will have been murderous.

It was not impassable or impenetrable. Under the thick blanket
of peat archaeologists have found the remains of prehistoric
wooden trackways made from cut logs and, around the fringes
of the Moss, there were settlements. Dangerous though it was, the
wetland was a reliable source of food for fowlers with their nets
and traps. Nests produced eggs in the spring and early summer,
and those with patience and a thick skin fished in the pools near
the course of the Forth where the murky water moved a little.

Crossing places were recalled in place-names such as Fordhead
and Causewayhead but, while native hunters and travellers knew
the safe paths, Flanders Moss was no place for armies. It was the
forgotten barrier which made Stirling and its dramatic castle rock
the gateway to the north and the Highlands and the strategic
hinge of Scotland. When Lord Kames began drainage operations
in the 1750s and the peat was removed to make flat and fertile
farmland, it was as though a door had opened.

Tacitus was struck by the importance of Flanders Moss and
could see clearly, probably at first hand, the effect it would have
on Agricola's campaign.

For the Firths of Clota [Clyde] and Bodotria [Forth], carried far
inland by the tides of opposite seas, are separated by a narrow
neck of land. This was now being securely held by garrisons and

the whole sweep of the country on the nearer side was secured: the enemy had been pushed back, as if into a different island.

Therefore in AD 82 Agricola had no choice but to march north under the shadow of Stirling Castle rock. It was just as well that the garrison was probably friendly. Later sources suggest that the kingdom of Manau was, like the Venicones of Fife, allied to the Votadini. In post-Roman records, the territories became twinned as Manau-Gododdin. Once again, place-names hint at its extent. For centuries Clackmannanshire was Scotland's smallest county (with the longest name) and its continued existence may have owed something to its having been the kernel of an ancient kingdom. As already noted (p.9), the name is from Clach na Manau, 'the Stone of Manau', and in the centre of the little town it can still be seen. Nearby Slamannan is 'the Moor of Manau'. And, around the fringes of the tiny county, more Celtic names, such as Powis Burn, imply the boundaries of a distinct territory.

None of the uncertainties of place-name evidence can cloud Roman actions after the breakthrough past Stirling. Along the high ground known as the Gask Ridge, the legions constructed one of the first fixed frontiers in the empire. It was a series of fortlets and signal towers linked by a road and at either end of the ridge lay a string of larger forts which were strategically sited at the foot of glens leading into the heart of the Highland massif. This was the territory of the Calidones, a kindred whose name came to be applied to all of the early peoples of the Highlands and the north of Scotland, eventually being adopted in modern times as Caledonia.

The whole Gask Ridge system ran from Loch Lomond in the west, skirting the Highland fault-line and reaching the North Sea coast at Montrose. As with other Roman frontiers it was porous, not aiming to stop armed incursion in its tracks – the individual forts and fortlets were not built to house garrisons large enough to achieve that. Instead the system was set up to police movement, gather intelligence and delineate an area outside of the empire, that of the Calidones, from an area inside, that of the Venicones. The Gask Ridge almost certainly ran along an older frontier between these peoples, between communities of hillmen and plainsmen. If substantial hostile movement was seen by mounted patrols at the mouths of the glens or indeed further into the interior, then messages could be despatched and retaliatory forces mustered. What is clear in AD 82 is the sense of a pause in Agricola's campaign. Having moved through the Stirling gap, he appears to be setting a limit to conquest, perhaps awaiting further instructions from Rome, and meanwhile building a defensive screen to cover his Lowland allies.

The impression made by the Gask Ridge frontier on the native peoples must have been startling. No doubt built quickly in the manner of most Roman military work, striking boldly across the landscape and regular in appearance, the line signalled the arrival of a phenomenon, an army and a culture able to tame the very landscape and make a mark still clearly visible 2,000 years later. Great and unprecedented power had marched north – that was the unmistakable message.

The new frontier was also the first recorded recognition of Scotland's most profound internal boundary, the Highland Line. And almost immediately it divided the land into Highland and Lowland, savage and subdued, what was to become Celtic in the north and English-speaking in the south.

But all of that lay in the future. Once the Gask Ridge frontier was established, Agricola turned his army westwards:

In the 5th year of the campaigns, he crossed in the leading ship and defeated peoples up to that time unknown in a series of successful actions. He lined up his forces in that part of Britain that faces Ireland . . .

It is possible that the reference to a leading ship indicates an expedition across the Solway Firth to Galloway but the difficulty with that interpretation is the mention of unknown peoples. Since Cerialis' men built the fort at Carlisle ten years before, it is inconceivable that the Romans would have had no knowledge of the kindreds on the opposite shores of the firth.

These were the Novantae and Ptolemy's map plots some intriguing detail. Their name may have meant 'the Vigorous People' and it compares with the Trinovantes, 'the Thrice Vigorous People', who lived in the south-east, mainly north of the Thames. The kindred name also seems to be related to Novios, the ancient version of the River Nith which runs through modern Dumfries. According to one medieval chronicler, it was seen as the eastern boundary of 'the wild realm of Galloway' and, more recently, it was where the counties of Kirkcudbright and Dumfries met, even though the river runs through the county town of the latter. The Novantae might simply have been the name of the first people that Roman reconnaissance patrols encountered, the kindred of the Nith, and their name was used for all those to the west of them. There are many analogies. The vast sub-continent of Siberia got its name from the Sabir, a tribe who lived immediately east of the Ural Mountains.

Ptolemy locates two settlements in the lands of the Novantae. The first element in Lucopibia means 'white' and seems to be another name for Whithorn. Rerigonion is on Loch Ryan, a

---

Desnes Cro, Mor and Ioan

On early medieval maps of Galloway, what approximates to Kirkcudbright-shire is described as Desnes Cro and sometimes Desnes Mor and Desnes Ioan. What do these names mean and where did they appear from? The great Welsh dictionary, Y Geiriadur Mawr, *offers no clues and Edward Dwelly's classic,* Faclair Gaidhlig Gu Beurla *(*The Illustrated Gaelic–English Dictionary*), notes a root word* des *which means, not very helpfully, 'land'. A* desreith *seems to have been an old term for 'a judge'.* Cro *can mean an enclosed area but one that is more like the size of a sheepfold than a large tract of land.* Mor *is simple – it means 'big' – but* ioan *and any variants seem impossible to work out. Enquiries made to more learned historians have produced nothing. Perhaps an enlightened Gallovidian reader might make some sense of what seems an impenetrable mystery.*

---

boiled-down rendering of the original. In Old Welsh, it was Rhionydd and it first came to notice in the cycles of poems known as the Triads. There it is joined with Gelliwig in Cornwall and Caerleon in Wales as one of the three national thrones of Britain, meaning Old Welsh-speaking western Britain. Rerigonion is 'Very Royal Place' and was one of the seats of the kings of the Novantae. That they were seen as a vigorous people there can be little doubt. When Hadrian's Wall was planned and built forty years later, a line of long sea defences, a sea wall, was laid out down the Solway coast of Cumbria. Attacks from Irish raiders and the Novantae were what the Roman military architects were anticipating and one of the largest forts in the north was built at Maryport. Situated on the Sea Brows, one of the few high points on that coastline, its towers looked for trouble sailing out of Galloway or the Irish shore.

Tacitus related what sounds like one of many conversations with Agricola, probably in Rome after his retirement:

> I have often heard him say that Ireland could be conquered and held with a single legion and modest numbers of auxilia. That would, he thought, be advantageous against Britain as well, if Roman arms were everywhere and freedom were, so to speak, removed from sight.

Even though his military judgement may have been overly optimistic, the invasion was considered a serious possibility: 'Agricola had given refuge to one of the minor kings from these people [the Irish], who had been expelled in a family quarrel. He treated him like a friend, keeping him in case an opportunity arose.' The phrase used by Tacitus, 'one of the minor kings', is instructive in that it shows some understanding of the shape of Irish politics in the first century AD. And it accords with later models. Law tracts of the seventh and eighth centuries describe three classes of Irish king. A *rí* was the lowest and most common sort, one who ruled over a kindred descended from the same ancestor, often a name-father. In this, they resembled the much later Highland clans of Scotland who usually adopted the form of, for example, MacLeod to show descent from Leod, the same name-father. The Irish kindreds may also have held ancestral lands as the clans did.

A *ruiri* was an overking of a group of several kindreds who were almost always neighbours and he, in turn, might bow to the power of a provincial overking, a *ri ruirech*. To top off the royal pyramid, Ireland had, from time to time, a High King who ruled over all, having been inaugurated at the sacred Hill of Tara. In reality, these relationships must have been much less tidy and they probably fluctuated as reputations waxed and waned and different traditions imposed themselves in different places. But it may be that the man who sat at Rerigonion on Loch Ryan, the Very Royal Place, was a provincial overking, the highest rank, who could control lesser rulers, perhaps all the way east to the banks of the Nith and the limit of the territories of the Novantae.

There exists no direct evidence for the structures of northern kingship in the first century AD but Ireland's cultural influence may have sailed across the narrows of the North Channel. A modern land-based society which thinks in terms of road transport often forgets the historical important of the sea as a highway and how people and ideas crossed it readily – much more easily than on land. And the kingdom of the Novantae was a sea-based polity, without doubt. Galloway's indented coastline supplied shelter for ships and good beaching was available in many places. A journey from the royal centre at the top of well-defended Loch Ryan to the mouth of the Nith could be made in the fraction of the time it took a traveller to make the same trip overland. And the watchers in the fort at Maryport and the sea wall on the Cumbrian coast inhibited a response to a naval capability of some strength.

If Atlantic Celtic spread through trade and maritime contact, it is possible that it was spoken on both shores of the North Channel and perhaps in the southern Hebrides. The names on Ptolemy's map of the north are not all incontrovertibly Continental Celtic in character. Early links between Ireland and the western coasts of Scotland became increasingly important as time went on.

British Gaulish

The Celtic dialects of France, collectively known as Gaulish and spoken on both sides of the Alps, began to die out only generations after the conquest by Julius Caesar. It lingered until the second century AD *when the Bishop of Lyons, St Irenaeus from Asia Minor, reported that he could not always manage in Latin and had 'to learn a barbarous tongue'. But a dialect of Gaulish, perhaps introduced by the Belgae in the first century* BC, *did survive and thrive in Britain. Personal names show the influence clearly, especially amongst kings and queens. In Gaulish, Cassivellaunos means 'Oak-dominator', Tasciovanos is 'Badger-slayer', Cunobelinos is 'the Hound of the God, Belenos' and Boudicca means 'Victory'.*

If a provincial overking ruled at Rerigonion, some measure of his power might be drawn from later sources and comparisons with the Celtic peoples of Gaul a century before. In *Commentarii de Bello Gallico*, Julius Caesar recorded a society of some diversity. Kindreds were sometimes governed by kings, occasionally by elected magistrates (who had to come from different families so that the grip of oligarchy was slacker), but all were dominated by a military aristocracy. The members of these leading families were themselves warriors and often maintained small war bands at their own expense. It is important to stress that numbers were not large. Few had the resources to maintain more than dozens of warriors.

In order to justify themselves, feed their prestige and hone their fighting skills, these warriors needed to fight. Caesar wrote that the kindreds of Gaul went to war, 'well-nigh every year', in the sense that they would either make wanton attacks themselves or repelling such, and other commentators saw these Celtic people as 'war-mad'.

Poems known as the Ulster Cycle were first transcribed in the eleventh century but scholars believe them to be very much older. The most famous, *An Tain Bo Cuailgne*, 'The Great Cattle Raid of Cooley', describes a pre-Christian Ireland and it may first have been recited in the courts of kings in the first century AD.

The language used has been dated to the seventh and eighth centuries but even though much of the narrative is clearly mythic, the detail of weaponry, chariots and the traditions of the war band locate the stories even earlier, in the first and second centuries AD. Their great value is to supply atmosphere – to say something colourful and memorable about how Celtic warriors societies behaved and how they saw themselves.

The *Tain Bo* is a tale of heroes and superhuman deeds. Queen Medb of Connaught has mustered a great army from all her underkings and is marching to invade Ulster to steal a considerable prize, the Brown Bull of Cooley. All that stands in their path is the boy-hero, the seventeen-year-old Cuchulainn. The following description of the ritual before battle, of how warriors worked themselves into a frenzy and intimidated the enemy in front of them, is clearly fantastical but its brilliant images light up the ferocious culture of combat in Celtic Ireland:

> The rage-fit was upon him. He shook like a bullrush in the stream. His sinews stretched and bunched, and every huge, immeasurable, vast ball of them was as big as the head of a month-old child. His face was a red bowl, fearsomely distorted, one eye sucked in so far that the beak of a wild crane could scarcely reach it, the other eye bulged out of his cheek. Teeth and jawbone strained through peeled-back lips. Lungs and liver pulsed in his throat. Flecks of fire streamed from his mouth. The booming of his heart was like the deep baying of bloodhounds, or the growl of lions attacking bears.
>
> In virulent clouds sparks blazed, lit by the torches of the war-goddess Badb. The sky was slashed as the mark of his fury. His hair stood about his head like the twisted branches of red hawthorn. A stream of dark blood, as tall as the mast of a ship, rose out of the top of his head, then dispersed into dark mist, like the smoke of winter fires.

Cattle were seen as a measure of wealth in early Celtic societies and cattle-raiding was an important means of venting an overheated warrior society. Raids and counter-raids were honourable, added status, were a cause for celebration and feasting and they involved the use of martial skills. Most of all they were much less wasteful of men than all-out battle.

The kings of the Selgovae, the Votadini, Manau and the other kindreds of the north almost certainly sanctioned cattle-raiding, probably originating persistent traditions in the Border hills and the Highland glens. In Continental Celtic, the warriors of these royal war bands were known as the *teulu*, literally meaning 'the family'. In modern Welsh the adjective *teuluaidd* means 'aristocratic' but members of the Selgovan king's *teulu* need not have been related to him or even high-born. What mattered was military prowess and the numbers of these household warriors will only have been large in the halls of overkings but, even then, only exceptionally more than a hundred. In a later reference, *The Anglo-Saxon Chronicle* defined an army as more than thirty men.

The royal war band depended absolutely on the king and he on them. Their leader, the *penteulu*, was constantly in the king's company as a bodyguard and a counsellor, and both men knew that the loyalty of the war band was the whole basis of royal authority and stability. Consequently warriors received a flow of gifts and favour, usually from a division of the spoils of raiding or war. And there was a regular cycle of feasting and drinking to reinforce these bonds of dependence. When the *bardd teulu* sang in their hall, he celebrated the valour and virtue of the war band collectively and by name. Healthy competition was encouraged and the traditions of feasting, such as the award of the hero's portion, the best cut of meat from the cauldron, came to be famous.

Soldiers have always spent most of their time not fighting and so the war band took on other responsibilities in the royal household from an early date. *Gwestfa* or 'food rents' were owed to the king by his kindred and, in order to collect and consume these efficiently, the household was peripatetic, moving on from each place as the rents ran down. In the territory of the Novantae, this annual journey was probably undertaken by sea since at least three ancient royal sites, at Loch Ryan,

Cruggleton and the Mote of Mark, are on the Galloway coast. Known as the *cylch* in later Welsh sources, it was organised and its collections enforced by the *penteulu* and his men.

At each royal centre it is likely that the king took care to show himself and restate his authority. While the *teulu* was the core, he needed a larger force to augment it if war became imminent. When Agricola's legions appeared in the north after AD 79, there can be little doubt that farmers and shepherds were pressed into service, even if only for show. Such a host was called the *gosgordd*. But, by itself, it is unlikely that the host of any northern king could hope to be a match for the armies of Rome.

When Agricola crossed in the leading ship to defeat unknown peoples before, in a curious gesture of intent or perhaps defiance, lining up his forces to face Ireland, he was probably campaigning in the Kintyre peninsula. From the Mull of Kintyre, it is possible to make out Fair Head and the Antrim coast even on a cloudy day. And the unknown peoples his men defeated could credibly have been the Epidii, 'the Horsemen'. When Ptolemy marked their name on Kintyre, he added a little more when he identified the Mull as Epidion Akron, 'the Promontory of the Horse People'. In a fascinating survival, Kintyre was seen in the eighteenth century as the homelands of the Clan MacEachern. The extended version of the name is Mac Each Thighearna and it means 'the Son of the Horse Master'.

Horses were central to Celtic warfare in the first century AD and for long after. But not in the same way as the great destriers which carried armoured medieval knights or those brave juggernauts which galloped with the Light Brigade into the valley of death. These were big, heavy and sometimes aggressive beasts trained to trample over opponents in the ruck of battle or to knock them down with the irresistible impetus of a determined charge. The horses bred and broken by the horsemen of the Epidii or Kintyre were not at all like that. They were small ponies, their withers often reaching no higher than a man's chest. Archaeology confirms (both with skeletal remains and tack) that these were most likely bred from wild native stock. Tough,

nimble, intelligent and with tremendous stamina, these fell
ponies (to use a much later definition) were also very adaptable.
Warriors could use their ponies for riding in cattle raids, they
were able to travel long distances over difficult country and then
be used as herders on the way home with the spoils. Or they
could become cavalry ponies and fight at close quarter, respond-
ing to a rider's shift in seat or to guidance with the legs as he used
both hands for a weapon and shield. The impetus of a horse
could add immense weight to the delivery of a blow or its fast
reactions avoid the full force of one.

Celtic warriors adored their horses, even venerated them, and,
when they harnessed the smaller ones to the yoke of a chariot,
their bards became lyrical. Here is another passage from the *Tain
Bo Cuailgne*:

> Cuchulainn's war chariot was both broad and fine, shining like
> white crystal, with a yoke of gold, great panels of copper, shafts
> of bronze, wheel-rims of white metal, light-framed. It could
> reach the speed of a swallow or a wild deer racing over the plains
> of Mag Slebe. The chariot was drawn by two well-yoked horses,
> swift, strong, roan-breasted and long-striding. One was supple,
> hard-pulling and great-hoofed. The other was curly-maned,
> slender-hoofed and sleek.

The habit of plaiting the manes and tails was not something
dreamed up by modern Pony Club competitors for the County
Show. It was done by the grooms of the war band to avoid
tangles with harness and bridles, a matter not of decoration but
potentially of life and death if the manoeuvrability of horses was
not to be fatally impaired. While a groom drove a chariot (no
mean feat to keep it steady on rough ground), probably crouch-
ing low on his haunches as a warrior stood behind with his
weapons, bracing on the bouncing floor to keep his balance.
Often charioteers drove warriors into the midst of a battle where
they dismounted to fight. And as they moved about a battlefield,
flicking and checking with the long reins, drivers could display

tremendous skill. Julius Caesar watched amazed as charioteers ran back and forth along the pole between their galloping ponies and stood like acrobats on the curved double yokes.

After the expedition to Kintyre, Agricola's attention turned northwards once more. No doubt with imperial approval from Domitian, the Roman war machine rumbled again through the Stirling gap. Here is Tacitus:

> To resume the story, in the summer in which he began his sixth year in post, he enveloped the states situated beyond the Bodotria [the Firth of Forth]. Because there were fears that all the peoples on the further side might rise and the land routes be threatened by an enemy army, Agricola reconnoitred the harbours with the fleet.

The campaign almost immediately met with near disaster. For the first time, according to Tacitus, '[T]he peoples who inhabit Caledonia turned to armed struggle'. Agricola had brigaded his legions and auxiliaries into an invasion force of at least 17,000 men, probably more. It seems likely that Agricola's own legion with whom he had served on an earlier tour of duty in Britain, the XX Valeria Victrix, had marched north with him in some strength. The II Adiutrix were with them and part of the IX Hispana had been summoned from their garrison at York. In addition there were regiments of auxiliaries, the Batavians and Tungrians from the lands near the mouth of the Rhine. It was a substantial, battle-hardened and experienced army.

To meet this challenge, the kindreds of the Highlands and the coastal straths of the north-east had formed an alliance. In what must have been a series of rapid negotiations conducted as the Romans advanced, the northern kings had combined their household war bands and almost certainly mustered the host, the *gosgordd*. If the Celtic society beyond the Forth was indeed as combative as that of Gaul (there may be an instructive but long-range comparison with relations between the Highland clans of the historic period and how each chose sides in the

Jacobite rebellions of the eighteenth century) and had regularly raided cattle from each other, then these differences were quickly patched up. It seems likely that there were some pre-existing interlocking loyalties which could be brought into play for the size of the army needed to confront the Romans must have involved not scores but hundreds of different war bands. Perhaps there was indeed a network of overkings between whom an alliance could be forged.

In any event, the size of the Caledonian confederate army turned out to be enough to give Agricola pause and persuade him into a tactical mistake. Tacitus of course nowhere concedes this, merely stating, 'To avoid encirclement by superior forces familiar with the country, he himself divided his army into three divisions and advanced'.

The leaders of the confederate army were aware, had good intelligence and showed themselves sufficiently flexible to take advantage. There follows one of the most vivid pieces of reporting in Tacitus' *Agricola*. Perhaps he saw events unfold with his own eyes or perhaps the old general told a good tale of a close-run thing:

> When the enemy discovered this, with a rapid change of plan they massed for a night attack on the Ninth Legion, as being by far the weakest in numbers. They cut down the sentries and burst into the sleeping camp, creating panic. Fighting was already going on inside the camp itself when Agricola, who had learned of the enemy's route from his scouts and was following close on their tracks, ordered the most mobile of his cavalry and infantry to charge the combatants from the rear and the whole army was to raise the battle-cry. At first light the standards gleamed.

Agricola's army was shadowed by the Classis Britannica, the Roman fleet, and, as the advance continued northwards, they probably supplied the troops. The Caledonian generals had different problems of supply. As in the night attack on the IX Legion, the confederate army had favoured guerrilla tactics, always avoiding the set-piece battle in open country. With their tight shield-walls, short, sharp, stabbing swords and iron discipline, the legions had defeated Celtic armies again and again. They were professionals and their drills and skills had been honed by centuries of experience. But problems of supply were pressing hard on the confederate generals and at last they were forced to take the decision to stand and fight in pitched battle.

The problem was timing. Tacitus wrote of Agricola's campaign beginning in the summer of either AD 83 or 84, what commanders had traditionally seen as the fighting season. By the time of the attack on the IX Legion and the advance up through Angus and the Mearns, harvest-time had passed. This allowed the *gosgordd*, the Caledonian army of farmers finally to muster. And it also forced them into a set-piece battle. A huge Roman army of more than 17,000 hungry mouths consumed everything in its path and the native granaries of the north had just been filled. If the Caledonian generals wished to defend their food stores and avoid a starving winter for their people, then a battle was inevitable.

'So he came to the Graupian Mountain. It had already been occupied by the enemy,' wrote Tacitus. What Agricola saw was a massed host of perhaps 30,000 men arrayed on the slopes of the mountain, probably Bennachie in Aberdeenshire. At its foot stood the Caledonian vanguard, most of them warriors from many royal *teulus*. Leading the host was Calgacus, not a king but a man 'outstanding among their many leaders for his valour and nobility'. His name means 'The Swordsman' and he was almost certainly a warrior of tremendous reputation, a real Cuchulainn and not a myth-hero.

Faced with such numbers stationed in a superior position, looking down on the battlefield, Agricola immediately saw that his men might quickly be outflanked, surrounded and annihilated. He extended his lines to counter even though it thinned the ranks. The disposition of Roman forces was otherwise standard. In the centre of the line stood 8,000 auxiliary infantry, their shields locked, their short swords bristling. On the flanks 3,000 cavalry guarded against encirclement and behind the centre 'the legions were stationed in front of the rampart: victory in a battle where no Roman blood was shed would be a tremendous honour; if the auxilia were driven back, the legions were a reserve'.

In the awful moments before battle was joined, the confederates behaved like a Celtic army. Warriors sallied out to issue challenges, charioteers made 'a din as they rode back and forth'. Individual bravery in the Caledonian ranks was not doubted but it would be collective discipline that would triumph. After each side had exchanged volleys of javelins, the auxiliaries attacked in formation. Despite a period when the Caledonian cavalry looked as though they might indeed outflank Agricola's army, the Roman front line ground forward. Pushing, stabbing and always staying together, they forced their way up the hillside and cut their way into the heart of the confederate army.

It was a defeat but, while Tacitus tried hard to portray it as a rout, the battle was not absolutely decisive. His tally of 10,000 Caledonian dead is a suspiciously round number but only a figure of 360 Roman casualties is probably accurate. Mons Graupius saw the end of native resistance for the time being but the Highlands were never penetrated by Roman roads or forts and never would be.

4

Kingdoms Come

Y RHUFEINIWR, 'THE ROMANS', had lost their emperor. Their High-King, Hadrian, had at last succumbed to a wasting disease. When his sick heart ceased to beat, the elders of Rome had hailed a new emperor. Antoninus Pius was his name, and he had been anointed by the dying Hadrian as he groaned through his last months of agony and misery. But the passage of power from one High-King was always uncertain – even more so when there was not just a kingdom at stake but the mightiest empire the world had ever seen. Y Rhufeiniwr knew it and, as they sat with their warriors and discussed the vicissitudes of Roman politics, the kings of the northern kindreds knew it too.

After Hadrian's death in 138, there was war. Across the waist of Britain, from the eastern sea to the western shore, the Romans had built a mighty stone wall. Painted white with lime-wash, it sliced like an obscenity through the lands of the plainsmen of the lower Tyne Valley, the Textoverdi and the Corionototae and it divided the hill country of the Brigantes and the Selgovae and the Carvetii in the west. It was an affront and a challenge. Here is the Greek writer, Pausanias: 'Also he [Antoninus Pius] deprived the Brigantes of most of their territory because they had taken up arms and invaded the Genounian district of which the people are subject to the Romans.'

Leaving aside the mysteries of Genounia, probably a scribal error or a simple mistake of geography, the thrust of the passage is clear enough. The British kings and their war bands had ridden out of their upland strongholds and probably ambushed columns of soldiers or attacked forts. It seems that, by 'Brigantes', Pausanias meant the hill peoples of the north in general. After the slaughter of Mons Graupius, no native general would risk a set-piece battle and none is reported or celebrated. Skirmish and guerrilla tactics were preferred. The hit-and-run stings of fast-moving cavalry and possibly squadrons of chariots were certainly disruptive but occasionally Roman retaliation was effective and gruesome.

Native warriors were decapitated, either in action or by execution, and their heads spitted on poles and planted as a dire warning at the gates of at least two Roman forts in the north. On Trajan's Column, soldiers are depicted doing exactly this in the Dacian wars of thirty years before. In the early 1900s, Trimontium, the large fort near Melrose, was excavated by James Curle, a local solicitor. In rubbish pits dug close to the walls of the fort, he found several skulls but no skeletons associated with them. Unlikely to be burials, these were almost certainly the heads of Selgovan warriors either captured or killed in battle by the garrison. In the shadow of Hadrian's Wall, at Vindolanda, another skull was discovered much more recently. This time, DNA testing was used to determine that this was the head of a native warrior, probably a member of the *teulu* of the king of the Anavionenses. Forensic analysis confirmed the excavators' suspicions. The head had certainly been spitted on a pole and no doubt displayed as a grisly trophy in a prominent place.

War in Britain was quickly seen by the incoming regime on the Palatine Hill as an opportunity. Like every new emperor, Antoninus Pius needed to establish military credentials and amongst his first acts was the appointment of a governor of Britannia. He found a remarkable man to take over the troubled province.

Quintus Lollius Urbicus was born in the Roman province of Numidia, modern Algeria. His father was a modest landowner, himself the son of a Berber tribesman. It was a dazzling transformation – a triumph of merit over the class rigidities of imperial Rome. Lollius Urbicus was clearly an excellent soldier and, as Antoninus Pius well knew, he depended absolutely on the emperor's favour for advancement.

The new governor began his mission to Britannia by repairing and refurbishing the fort at Corbridge, just south of Hadrian's Wall. With the II Augusta legion in the van, the empire drove northwards once more. Here is the relevant notice in a biography of Antoninus Pius: 'Through his legates he carried on many wars; for he conquered the Britons through Lollius Urbicus, the governor, and, after driving back the barbarians, built another wall, of turf.'

Before he could set his soldiers to the task of building yet another frontier wall, Urbicus had to subdue the kings of southern Scotland. The campaign cannot have been easy for it lasted at least two and possibly three years. Since this was a war of conquest, aimed at bringing more territory into the empire and thereby enhancing the emperor's early prestige, it required a systematic occupation. Striking north along the well-established line of Dere Street, Urbicus garrisoned forts at Risingham and High Rochester in north Northumberland before climbing up and across the Cheviot watershed and rebuilding Trimontium on the Tweed.

The large fort was the hub of the Roman occupation of the south of Scotland. It commanded the head of the gently undulating and fertile river valley just at the point where the Tweed emerges from the western hill country. Probably deliberately placed on the frontier between the Selgovae and Votadini, Trimontium could both protect and police. Well-placed to act as an ingathering depot for the agricultural produce needed to feed the occupying forces, it also overlooked a crossing of the Tweed, at first a ford just above Leaderfoot and then almost certainly a bridge.

Communications were good. With their usual briskness, Roman surveyors climbed the sacred mountain of Eildon Hill North and planted a signal station smack on the summit. Ringed by a three-mile-long symbolic rampart, Eildon Hill had been a sacred precinct for the peoples of the middle Tweed Valley for a thousand years. Now it suffered detachments of soldiers signalling to their comrades to the south and north, using either a white flag system or polished, reflective metal sheets. Modern experiments have shown that signals sent from Eildon Hill could be picked up on Ruberslaw where there was another Roman station, fifteen miles to the south. This abuse of holy ground was another affront – part of the cost of subjection.

The mechanics of subjugation depended heavily on the Roman main road clearly visible from the top of the hill as it runs arrow-straight up to Ancrum Moor. Dere Street began in York, the headquarters of the VI Adiutrix Legion (and much later part of the Anglian kingdom of Deira, hence the name of the road) and it made its way over the Cheviots, down past Trimontium, up the Leader Valley, over Soutra and down to Edinburgh. No longer clearly traceable under the modern city after it reaches the junction at Nether Liberton, the great road is thought to have turned west and run on through the Stirling Gap and as far north as Perth.

The precise terminus for Dere Street was probably intended to be a huge legionary fortress at Inchtuthil on the River Tay. It was begun in AD 83 on the orders of Agricola and intended to house his favoured legion, the XX Valeria Victrix. Vast, the largest fortress north of York, Inchtuthil was planned and its building organised on a grand scale. At fifty-three acres, it could accommodate 6,000 soldiers inside the stone-walled perimeter. There was a hospital, extensive workshops, many barracks blocks and an elaborate headquarters building. All of this suggests that Agricolan Scotland was about to be fully integrated into the provincial administration of Britannia. But events at the other end of Europe derailed those intentions – and thereby changed the course of the history of the north. The Dacians, of modern Romania, had rebelled and plunged the area of the lower Danube into chaos. From Chester, the II Adiutrix was withdrawn to shore up the eastern European frontier and in turn the XX Valeria Victrix was forced to abandon the great building project at Inchtuthil and march south to replace them.

The huge fort was being constructed in the territory of the Caledonians and, when the news came from Dacia, the native kings will have understood why the XX Legion had to depart immediately. With so much activity and the intensive contact with native communities that this implies, information will have flowed and the military intelligence amongst the Caledonians improved. The notion that Rome operated a separate, much more sophisticated world unintelligible to native elites is often too readily and thoughtlessly assumed. Southern Britain had been occupied for forty years, some northern kings had become subjects of Rome and knowledge of and contact with the Empire is likely to have been much more intense and regular than surviving records allow.

Rome was suddenly distracted by the flaring of invasion from Dacia but, after the slaughter at Mons Graupius, the kings of the north are unlikely to have entertained any notion of taking a military advantage. Nevertheless the abrupt abandonment of so much work is still striking. In order to bring stone from nearby quarries inconveniently sited at the top of rising ground, the Romans built a sophisticated road system. At a fork at the foot of the incline empty ox-drawn wagons were led up a steeper gradient while moving down the other, more gently sloping road were fully laden wagons. There was always a danger that beasts could be pushed by a great weight of building stone and crushed. It was an elegant solution. But one day the wagons stopped rolling, the roads were left empty and the stone stayed in the quarries. Once equipment had been loaded instead and the legion and its auxiliaries formed up in marching order and anything useful to an enemy which could not be carried away south had been set ablaze, the Empire moved south of the Tay. Then as now, soldiers were used to sudden changes of plan and, as the smoke plumed over the building site by the riverbank, few will have given all that useless work a backward glance

When archaeologists dug the site of Inchtuthil in 1950, they came across a remarkable find. In a deep pit, 750,000 iron nails had been carefully concealed. The commanders of the XX

Valeria Victrix knew the value of so much smelted iron to Caledonian blacksmiths and were unwilling to leave such handy war materials behind. Too heavy to carry away, all of those nails were needed for the new fortress, probably marked on Ptolemy's map as 'Victoria'. Perhaps the soldiers also thought that, one day, they might return but it would need to be soon if the location of the pit was not to be forgotten.

When the legion and their auxiliaries marched out of Inchtuthil in AD 87, they probably did not really believe that they were leaving behind a serviceable military installation which would be of use to their enemies. While there is later evidence of native use of Roman forts along Hadrian's Wall after its abandonment in the early fifth century, it was usually partial. These huge facilities were designed on a different scale, intended for use by an incoming occupying force and not suitable for people who already lived around them. When native kings or warlords occupied the sites at Birdoswald, Housesteads or South Shields, they used only the parts of the fortifications which had remained intact – gatehouses, corner towers and the like. It is very unlikely that the empty acres of Inchtuthil attracted new occupants after AD 87 except perhaps in those places where sheep and cattle could be handily corralled.

Rome's roads were more durable and useful. They were also very new and different. Before Agricola and other generals came north, native travellers who used long-range routes preferred good ground, avoided the marshlands by rivers and in valley bottoms or steep climbs and preferred a long way round if it was safer and they could remain dry-shod. In the south, native trackways followed the tops of gentle ridges where the drainage was good. Military imperatives and the availability of thousands of soldiers to work on them drove Roman roads through the landscape with what might have seemed like brutal directness. Cutting straight across farmland, dividing holdings and bringing traffic where there had been none before, their impact must initially have been startling.

Dere Street was no narrow artery. So that two, wheeled vehicles travelling in opposite directions could pass, it was 7.7

metres wide on average and the metalling or bottoming was usually more than 30 centimetres deep. The principles of road building had been refined by centuries of experience. The surface was not flat but had a pronounced crest in the middle; this road mound was known as the *agger*. Drains ran on either side collecting water running down from the road mound. Bad weather was the greatest enemy and once a puddle was established, wheels splashed the gravel out of it and, if not repaired, it grew ever larger. Archaeologists have discovered that where one puddle was not repaired quickly, cart wheels bounced out of it and created a series of potholes of decreasing but destructive size in a straight line after it. Roads were routinely repaired after the winter rains, otherwise they would soon have disintegrated beyond effective use. While Roman roads were well maintained, they were not universally excellent. At the fort of Vindolanda a letter dated around AD 100 was found with a comment that travel was not advisable '*dum viae malae sunt*', 'while the roads are bad'.

The visual impact was also striking. Not only were the straight roads a new and unnatural colour in the landscape, they took up a great deal of space. On either side lay open pits where road stone had been quarried (and where road menders could find more if needed) and, beyond them, the scrub and woodland had been cut back where possible. Roman commanders worried about ambush. In the upper Clyde Valley, near the small fort at Crawford, not far from the modern A74, the old road avoids the flat ground by the banks of the river and instead climbs up a hill to the north. The reason for all the additional labour – and making the soldiers sweat – was fear of ambush. The route by the Clyde was flat but it passed through a narrow valley and native warriors could easily have surprised a Roman column from the higher ground.

There are more than 400 miles of Roman roads in Scotland and they helped shape history long after the fall of the Western Empire. Armies continued to march on them in both directions. When Edward II of England came north before his fateful encounter with Robert the Bruce at Bannockburn, he led his soldiers along Dere Street. As the road climbed up through the

Cheviot Hills and the English army slowed, it was said that it was strung out for more than twenty miles.

The old road had more peaceful uses and the section from Melrose to Edinburgh was known as 'the Malcolmisrode' after the medieval Scottish kings of that name. Also recorded as 'the Via Regis', it carried a good deal of mercantile traffic and was kept in decent condition. Up on the windblown wastes of Soutra Hill, about a mile west of the modern A68, a long run of Dere Street is still clearly visible. What brings it out of the heather and bracken are the dead straight lines of the ditching on either side.

There are also hints that Dere Street acted as a political boundary for one of the more shadowy kingdoms of the Dark Ages. Calchvynydd was said to be based at Roxburgh Castle near Kelso in the sixth century and its territory extended westwards between the Tweed and the Teviot as far as the line of the road.

Once Lollius Urbicus had refortified Trimontium, he led his army north to the Firth of Forth. Antoninus Pius needed a blaze of glory, something triumphant to give the city of Rome and all of its factions and interests the sense that not only was he capable as a commander-in-chief but he could also expand the empire. Hadrian had made himself deeply unpopular with his policy of retrenchment. 'What could not be held would be given up' made good military sense but was bad politics. Rome's ruling class of senatorial families and those who aspired to it had grown wealthy on the expansion of the empire and, in the defeat and subjuga- tion of barbarians, there had been prestige as well as profit. When, at the beginning of his reign, Hadrian had ordered the murder of four alleged plotters – senators and men of consular rank – he had alienated the Roman elite and never been forgiven for it. It was one compelling reason for him to spend eleven years of his long reign out of the city, touring the provinces and the imperial frontier. Antoninus Pius was determined on a different course and so Lollius Urbicus was ordered north to resume conquest, what had been seen as Rome's divine mission.

Hadrian's Wall was abandoned and replaced with what has become known as the Antonine Wall. Much shorter, it ran for thirty-nine miles from Old Kilpatrick on the Clyde to Bo'ness on the Firth of Forth. Work appears to have begun in the east, probably in the spring of 142. Less elaborate than the wall a hundred miles to the south, it took only two years to complete.

Once surveyors had pegged out the line, making sure the wall took the commanding ground at every opportunity, soldiers dug out shallow foundations. Having laid a stone footing with kerbs on either side to prevent spreading, they then built it up to height with turfs. These were large and Trajan's Column shows men carrying them on wooden backpacks. After it had been topped with a wooden palisade and the turf had dried and settled, the wall stood at thirteen feet high. A ditch was dug on the northern side to make it seem more massive and, to the south, a military road ran behind. Beyond the ditch *lilia* were hidden. Small pits filled with sharpened stakes and covered over with brush, these vicious traps show that the wall was certainly seen as a defensive rampart expecting trouble from the north. With seventeen forts and about forty fortlets built along its length, the wall amounted to a densely packed and formidable garrison. The Romans did not often waste resources and some of their more peaceful frontiers could be very thinly manned. Lollius Urbicus packed the Antonine Wall with soldiers because beyond it, and also perhaps behind it, lay substantial threats.

Either before or after completion of the huge building project, the peoples of the Clyde Valley were subdued. Coins commemorating a Roman victory were minted in 142 or 143. On Ptolemy's map the Damnonii, sometimes Dumnonii, are marked as the kindred controlling the Clyde Valley and the lands around the shores of the Firth. One of their principal strongholds was on the summit of the remarkable Alt Clut (Dumbarton Rock) which rises almost sheer on the north-western coast of the estuary.

The Damnonii share their name with Dumnonia, a Celtic kingdom of the south-west of England. Its likely derivation might have arisen out of the geology of both areas. Damnonii probably means 'the Deepeners' – those who deepen the earth, miners. Coal could be dug from heughs or outcrops in several places along the Clyde and in Devon and Cornwall tin was mined and a lucrative trade created around its production.

No record of a campaign against the Damnonii survives, only the conquest of their territory. Their dramatic acropolis at Dumbarton Rock is immensely old and it has the longest documented history of any stronghold in Britain. Its modern name derives from Dun Breatainn, Atlantic Celtic for 'the Fort of the Britons', while the older name of Altcluit is a Continental Celtic form for 'the Rock of the Clyde'. By 144 and the completion of the great wall which reached the Clyde only three miles to the east, the ancient fortress was one of the northernmost bastions of the Empire.

The effect of the Antonine Wall must have been dramatic, jaw-dropping. Warfare between the kindreds had certainly had political effects and no doubt been destructive and bloody but the defeat of one war band by another had not altered the landscape in the way the legions had. Landward movement between north and south was severely restricted and tightly controlled, as was any unauthorised activity in the military zone along its length. Since its location depended on strategic imperatives and these ignored everything else, many farms were either destroyed or made very difficult to manage. Pastoral societies must have the ability to move flocks and herds around and relieve grazing from too much pressure.

But it was not destined to last. After only twenty years, the Antonine Wall was abandoned as the imperial frontier retreated south to Hadrian's Wall. Under the Emperor Marcus Aurelius, retrenchment once again became Roman policy. It is likely that the more vulnerable turf wall was cast down by those who were affronted by it and resented its presence and who wished to move freely again. But what remained, and is still the most obvious relic of the Antonine Wall, was the defensive ditch in front of the rampart. At Rough Castle and at Watling Lodge and Callendar Park in Falkirk, there are stretches where it is very impressive. Apart from historians, few knew it as the Antonine Wall until present times. The ditch appears to have conferred its earlier name. *Greim* is Atlantic Celtic for 'a bite' and the wall became known as 'the Grimsdyke' as though men with mattocks and shovels had taken a bite out of the ground. Sometimes written as Graham's Dyke, this version probably came from Greumaich, the Gaelic equivalent of 'Graham'.

Although Scotland south of the Forth–Clyde line was part of the Empire for only twenty years, this brief period of Romanisation may have had more than a passing effect. With so much left behind, so much military architecture obvious in the landscape – two walls as boundaries, thirty forts and other substantial installations and long stretches of roads – there is a growing sense that the kings of this part of the north saw themselves differently.

No record of the diplomacy undertaken by Lollius Urbicus and his officers survives but, if Antoninus Pius intended southern Scotland to become part of the empire, discussions and negotiations with native kings and their counsellors must have taken place. Rome was always anxious to avoid the waste of men and materials if accommodations could be found. Peace was cheaper and examples from all over the empire illustrate Roman willingness to absorb new peoples by treaty and agreement. On Traprain Law in East Lothian, one of the power centres of Votadinian kings, significant finds of second-century Roman artefacts have turned up. These may well have been gifts, encouragements to the kindreds of the south-east to remain friendly.

Tacitus described how Agricola took care to make the benefits of Romanisation attractive in the south where 'the toga was everywhere to be seen' amongst native elites, and there is no reason to think that policy had changed under the governorship of Lollius Urbicus and his successors. For twenty years – a generation – the kindreds of the south of Scotland were part of the empire and many of those who ruled over them probably found the notion attractive, even exotic. Like Syrians, Egyptians and Numidians, they were now with Rome and, like Lollius Urbicus' family, they may have seen the empire as an opportunity, a career. And even in 163, when the frontier was pulled back to Hadrian's Wall, those glamorous aspirations may only have dimmed a little – the Empire might return, the infrastructure was waiting.

Successful ambush obviously depended on surprise but what could convert surprise into disabling shock was speed and earth-shattering sudden noise. At Deskford in Banffshire, the source of the latter was accidentally discovered in 1816. According to a later report:

> There was found, about twenty years ago, on the confines of a farm called Leichestown, the resemblance of a swine's head in brass, of the ordinary size, with a wooden tongue moveable by springs. It also had eyes, and the resemblance in every respect was wonderfully exact. It was found at a depth of about six feet, in a mossy and knolly piece of ground on a bed of clay. The ground abounded with hazel-nuts, which looked entire, but upon being opened, were found empty.

It was a carnyx, a famous type of Celtic trumpet. Diodorus Siculus wrote that 'their trumpets again are of a peculiar barbarian kind; they blow into them and produce a harsh sound which suits the tumult of war'. The beautiful boar's head with the wooden clapper was mounted on a long vertical tube which terminated in a mouthpiece turned towards the player in an elongated s-shape or j-shape. On a well-known cauldron found at Gundestrup in Denmark, three carnyx players are shown holding up their tall instruments to their mouths.

Like the Highland clans with their bagpipes, the northern kindreds charged into battle at the sound of the carnyx. And just as pipers could act as buglers, sounding different orders over the din of war cries and screams, so the carnyx was used by native commanders to control their warriors.

When presented with a replica of the Deskford carnyx, the musician, John Kerry, discovered a surprising range. Most interesting was the ability of the instrument to imitate animal noises and, in particular, those made by a charging wild boar.

Like the Australian didgeridoo, it was also possible to reproduce sounds like proto-speech very loudly. Several carnyxes blasting into life at the same time must have been terrifying.

Animals were long seen by the northern kindreds as tremendously powerful symbols. And, since carnyx heads could be cast to represent a great range of creatures, it may be that the men who raised their weapons and charged when the Deskford trumpet sounded felt themselves both protected and empowered by the aggressive virtues of the wild boar. When Ptolemy plotted the names of the kindreds of the furthest north, he marked down the Orkoi, the Boar People of the Orkneys, the Caereni, the Sheep Folk of the north west, the Lugi, the Ravens of Sutherland as well as the Epidii, the Horse Masters of Kintyre and the Venicones, the Kindred Hounds of Fife.

The second requirement for a successful ambush was such speed as to allow little or no time for the enemy to react, organise themselves and form into anything other than a ragged defensive alignment. Chariots and cavalry racing from cover out across the open ground on either side of a Roman road could achieve devastating speed. Tacitus mentioned chariots at Mons Graupius and thought them ineffective. Caesar disagreed and here is what he saw in southern Britain in 55 BC:

> In chariot fighting the Britons begin by driving all over the field hurling javelins. Generally, the terror inspired by the horses and the noise of the wheels are sufficient to throw their opponent's ranks into disorder. Then, after making their way between the squadrons of their own cavalry, they jump down from the chariots and engage on foot. In the meantime, the charioteers retire a short distance from the battle and place their vehicles in such a position that their masters, if hard pressed by numbers, have an easy means of retreat to their own lines. Thus, they combine the mobility of cavalry with the staying power of infantry.

Celtic metalwork was much prized and the long slashing sword described by Tacitus, the *spatha*, could be fearsomely sharp. It was more effective as a cavalry sabre and usually only members of a *teulu* could hope to own a battle sword. Spears were much more common and warriors generally carried two – a heavier for thrusting in close-quarter combat and a lighter for throwing. In Europe, Celtic armies were known as *Gaesatae*, 'the Spearmen'. Shields carried by cavalry troopers were necessarily small and used for parrying rather than protection. Infantry carried longer and larger shields and both sorts had a metal boss in the centre, in front of the handgrip, so that it could be used as an offensive weapon.

Roman commentators often remarked on the Celtic habit of fighting naked. Wearing only a helmet, a torc around the neck and a sword belt, warriors were seen charging into battle wearing no protection whatever – at least none that a Roman would recognise. But it was there in the minds of the naked warriors. Most men wore tattoos that they probably saw as powerful talismans. Animals appear to have been especially revered – the horse, the wild boar, the hound, the raven and the bull all had characteristics, either real or imagined, which warriors believed would help them. There are obvious links between kindred names, the sounds of the carnyx which sent them into battle and what had been impregnated on their bodies. No doubt the Romans thought nudity made Celtic warriors easier to kill.

No written records exist to support these likely suppositions – or indeed the heroics or ignominies of native soldiers and their *teulus*. Roman reaction is almost always the only guide and the appearance of particular sorts of coins suggests that, in the 150s, there was war in the north once again. It seems that the kings of the Anavionenses attacked and destroyed Blatobulgium, the fort at Birrens in Annandale. A coin issued in 155 celebrates an important Roman victory in Britain, almost certainly successful retaliation for the attack. The usual way of illustrating the defeat of native forces was to show the figure of Britannia (very much like the image on old pennies) with her head bowed. Remarkable archae-ology has uncovered evidence of Roman campaigning against the Anavionenses – although its dates are by no means certain.

On the summit of Burnswark Hill stood the principal hill fort of the kindred and, at some point after the war with Rome in the 150s or possibly later, it may have become a military refuge as well as a sacred place. At its foot lie two temporary Roman camps, one on the north side and another on the south, probably the remains of a siege. Outside the walls of the latter stand the clearly defined outlines of three mounds. They were ballista emplacements, where the Romans set up artillery to fire missiles at the ramparts on Burnswark Hill. When archaeologists dug around the three gateways of the hill fort, they found large numbers of stone ballista balls. The Roman bombardiers were apparently skilled – able to gauge the range of their powerful trebuchets very precisely. There is also evidence for the use of large mechanical crossbows which could fire deadly iron-tipped bolts over long distances. In the campaigns in southern Britain after the Claudian invasion of 43, it was said that the garrisons of native hill forts were persuaded to surrender by the mere sight of ballistas being emplaced. The Burnswark fort was used later as a training ground for the much feared artillery of the Roman army.

During the second half of the second century, conflict broke out regularly in the north. Because it was the only notable military success of his reign, the conquest of southern Scotland had to be maintained while Antoninus Pius was emperor. When the frontier was pulled back to Hadrian's Wall after his death, aggression from the north did not abate. During the reign of the deranged Commodus, serious trouble threatened the whole of Britannia. The northern kindreds burst through the wall defences and into the province where 'they killed a general at the head of his forces'. This may have been the governor, probably the victim of ambush or surprise attack. Archaeology at the forts of Rudchester, Halton Chesters and Corbridge suggests that the northern army invaded down Dere Street and broke through in the east.

Commodus sent Ulpius Marcellus to restore order and it may be that the siege-works at Burnswark were undertaken on his orders and date to the 180s, in an attempt to crush the Anavionenses. Even if it succeeded, the native kings could claim overall victory. The forts north of Hadrian's Wall were never again occupied and despite the issue of coins in 184 with Britannia bowed and the assumption of the title of Britannicus by Commodus, Rome had been forced to retreat – and not by events elsewhere in the empire but as a result of native military pressure. It was a century after Mons Graupius and the kings of the north were once again resurgent.

Commodus' chaotic reign marked the abrupt close of a long period of stability, the era of the so-called adoptive emperors. These were men appointed by their predecessors (often by a process of elimination – Hadrian had preferred several alternatives to Antoninus Pius) and not the result of the lottery of primogeniture, as it was with the succession of the crazy Commodus, the son of Marcus Aurelius. After his inevitable assassination on the last day of 192, Septimius Severus emerged as the new emperor, having disposed of most of his rivals. The only survivor, Clodius Albinus, governor of Britannia, was more tenacious and his claim to the throne lasted until his defeat and suicide at Lyons in 197.

The British-based legions had marched behind Albinus and the weakened provincial garrison quickly came under pressure from the northern kings. War bands raided in the south, according to the historian, Herodian, 'laying waste the countryside . . . carrying off plunder and wrecking almost everything'. In 197 Septimius Severus sent Virius Lupus to Britain to calm the situation and secure the Hadrianic frontier. The two kindreds in the van of all that trouble were named as the Maeatae and the Caledonians. The former were new and place-names hint at their territories. Dumyat, the Dun of the Maeatae, is an impressive hill standing out from the southern range of the Ochils, and not far away is Myot Hill. These obvious geographical features with the name of a kindred attached are likely to have stood on a southern frontier. The lands of the Maeatae therefore lay to the north of the kingdom of Manau. They may have held the beautiful valley of Strathearn, the upper reaches of the Teith and the high ground to the north-east. And north of the Maeatae are two more place-names which might signify the southern marches of the Caledonians in a similar way. Dunkeld was known in the ninth century as Dun Chaillden, 'the Dun of the Caledonians', and the second element of the striking, singular peak of Schiehallion also contains a version of the kindred name. Both may have been so called because they lie on the edge of their lands.

Virius Lupus brought cash to Britain rather than soldiers. Dio Cassius reported: 'Because the Caledonians did not keep their promises but had prepared to assist the Maeatae . . . Lupus was compelled to buy peace from the Maeatae for a large sum, and he received a few prisoners of war in exchange.'

These last may have been Romans or prominent native allies of Rome. And Dio's report says something about diplomacy. It was the Maeatae who were raiding in the province and taking prisoners while the Caledonians had either supported them or were about to. In any event the deal stuck. For ten years there appears to have been peace in the north. Perhaps regular subsidies were handed over. No doubt the kings of the Maeatae were content with their gold, but Septimius Severus was a tough soldier with a long memory and an utterly ruthless nature.

Aerial photography has revealed evidence of his ruthlessness, a series of four extraordinary structures in southern Scotland – a string of temporary marching camps on the line of Dere Street, from Trimontium to Pathhead and the high ground south of the Firth of Forth. What is extraordinary is their size. Each extends to more than 165 acres and they are located only eight miles apart. They show the trail of a vast Roman army on the march in 208. Forty thousand men were being led by the Emperor himself on a spectacular mission to invade and pacify the north. Septimius Severus' patience with the Maeatae and the Caledonians was at an end. Dio Cassius again:

> The Britons having broken their agreements and taken up arms, Severus ordered his soldiers to invade their territory and to put to the sword all that they met, adding the Homeric quotation that 'they should let nobody escape, not even the children hidden in their mothers' wombs'.

Genocide was what the Emperor planned – a ruthless campaign of extermination. As the Grand Army marched down from Soutra Hill and saw the Firth of Forth in the distance, another measure of the might and reach of Rome came into view. Bobbing at anchor in the firth were no fewer than four imperial fleets brigaded together to join the invasion. Under the flagship of the Classis Britannica, the British Fleet, was the Rhine Fleet and two fleets from the Danube. Such was the scale and the sweep of Roman military planning that these last had sailed out of the Black Sea many weeks previously, travelled the length of the Mediterranean, up the Atlantic coast of France, through the Channel and up the North Sea coast. Perhaps 200 ships, triremes, biremes and liburnae waited in the Forth Roads. Signallers from the Grand Army may have made contact while they were on the high ground at Soutra.

Marching six men abreast, their eagle standards glinting in the sunshine and the low thud of their hobnailed boots thundering on the road, the British legions and their auxiliaries made up the bulk of Severus' force. Because he led them in person, the Praetorian Guard had come from Rome, 9,000 strong, and there were also detachments from European legions. With their baggage train, the infantry column stretched for six miles. Out wide on the flanks, squadrons of cavalry, perhaps 10,000 troopers in all, swept the countryside for any hostile activity. As the rearguard left the camp they had dug the night before, the surveyors were pegging out the site for the next one. It was probably the largest army ever to invade Scotland and, as the foraging legions moved slowly across the landscape, they devoured all in their path, like a plague of locusts.

When Severus and his officers reached the Forth, likely near Cramond, they divided the Grand Army into three groups. A legion was left at the base to guard the rear. Another, larger group marched north through the Stirling Gap and up to Strathmore before arcing round to the North Sea coast at the Montrose Basin where they could ultimately embark on the imperial fleet and be taken south. But, before that could happen, Severus sent the remainder of his army on by sea. Their landing point was at Carpow on the Tay Estuary where the banks and ditches of a large camp have been excavated. It was a classic pincer movement and it choked the Maeatae and the Caledonians into negotiation.

Possibly to the fortress at Carpow in 209, the kindreds sent a delegation. It was led by Argentocoxus. His name means 'Silver-Leg', perhaps a reference to a habit of wearing greaves in battle. The discussion prompted this surprising anecdote from Dio Cassius:

> A very witty remark is reported to have been made by the wife of Argentocoxus, a Caledonian, to Julia Augusta. When the Empress was jesting with her, after the treaty, about the free intercourse of her sex with men in Britain, she replied: 'We fulfil the demands of nature in a much better way than do you Roman women; for we consort openly with the best men whereas you let yourselves be debauched in secret by the vilest.' Such was the retort of the British woman.

It is difficult to know what to make of this. Julia Augusta, better known as Julia Domna, was certainly in Britain with her husband. A powerful influence at the imperial court, perhaps too powerful to be left behind amongst the plots and conspiracies of Rome, she also had a reputation for licentiousness. Perhaps the most surprising aspect is the presence of wives at the peace negotiations – and, making sour remarks to each other, a Caledonian princess successfully besting a former Syrian aristocrat, the Empress of Rome. Contemporary commentators were always taken aback by the active roles of elite Celtic women. Queens Boudicca and Cartimandua had occupied centre stage at pivotal moments in the early years of the province of Britannia and here was another influential women – this time one very well informed about the shady rumours slithering around the imperial entourage. If not a fabrication of Dio Cassius (he was not an enthusiastic supporter of Severus), the anecdote is a good example of how much the leadership of the northern kindreds knew about their enemies.

Free Love in the Flat Highlands

Such is the sparseness of source materials for the early history of Scotland that historians are sometimes tempted into hypotheses that totter like inverted pyramids. The remains of Roman goods have been found mainly in high-status sites in southern Scotland, and around the North Sea coasts such goods are found in brochs, the extraordinary drystane towers built for the powerful between 220 BC and AD 100. On the Atlantic coasts and in the landward areas of the Highlands, fragments of Roman goods appear to be more evenly distributed with significantly less emphasis on high-status sites. The beginnings of a hypothesis but still a little blurry. C. Julius Solinus, the third-century Roman author of On the Wonders of the World, *a title which might just include fables, reported that men in the Northern Isles shared their women in common and that the King of the Hebrides was an impoverished mendicant hoping 'to learn justice through poverty' and a man who shared the wives of his subjects. Add these scraps together and the vision of a less hierarchical, 'flatter' society in the north finally comes drifting into view.*

At all events, the treaty negotiated by Argentocoxus did not hold and fighting once more broke out. While planning another campaign in Scotland, to be launched from the legionary fortress at York, Septimius Severus became ill. He suffered badly from gout. His son, known as Caracalla, led the Grand Army up the north road once more and this time appears to have carried out a merciless programme of destruction and killing, perhaps reaching the Moray Firth coastlands. But fate intervened to cut short the bloodshed when, in 211, Septimius Severus died and Caracalla hurried south to protect and further his own dynastic interests. His expedition was the last time the eagle standards were seen in the north.

5

After Rome

✹

THE HISTORIAN Ammianus Marcellinus described dramatic events in Britain in 367:

After setting out from Amiens on a rapid march to Trier, [the Emperor] Valentinian was shocked to receive the serious news that a concerted attack by the barbarians had reduced the provinces of Britain to the verge of ruin. Nectaridus, the count of the coastal region, had been killed and the general, Fullofaudes, surprised and cut off . . . Finally, in response to the alarming reports which constantly arrived, Theodosius was selected for the task and ordered to proceed to Britain without delay. He had a great reputation as a soldier, and, getting together a tough force of horse and foot, he set out on his mission with every prospect of success . . . [A]t that time the Picts, of whom there were two tribes, the Dicalydones and the Verturiones, together with the warlike people of the Attacotti and the Scots, were roving at large and causing great devastation. In addition the Franks and Saxons were losing no opportunity of raiding the part of Gaul nearest to them by land and sea, plundering and burning and putting to death all their prisoners.

This pivotal episode in the history of Britannia is known as the Barbarian Conspiracy, 'a concerted attack' on the province by two Pictish kindreds, the Scots from Ireland, the Attacotti, perhaps from the Hebrides and war bands of Franks and Saxons in Gaul. These incursions were all the more devastating for having been planned and coordinated and their success seriously undermines the popular image of screaming hordes hurling themselves at the stones of Hadrian's Wall. Clear leadership and precise military planning and timing appear to have achieved unprecedented success. It was a culmination of sixty years of intermittent aggression.

In 305 and 306 the Emperor Constantius Chlorus was in Britain campaigning against the Caledonians and 'other Picts'. What sounds like a soldiers' nickname for warriors wearing tattoos, it is the first use of this term for the northern kindreds by Roman historians. In many societies military body decoration, which in this case probably resembled early versions of the designs on Pictish symbol stones and jewellery, was used by bands of warriors not only to identify themselves as a brotherhood but also to invoke the power and protection of the symbols themselves. Roman soldiers also wore more modest legionary tattoos.

Trouble flared along the frontier again in 315 and, this time, Rome claimed victory. Nevertheless, coin hoards dating to the second and third centuries found in the north suggest that occasional successful military action was also mixed with regular subsidy. Britannia was seen as an important province and, in a period of relative peace, the Emperor Constans 'clove the ocean' and made what sounds like an impromptu imperial tour:

> He sent no advance warning to the cities there, nor did he make any prior announcement of his sailing, or wish to create a stir with his plans before he had completed the venture ... As it was affairs in Britain were stable.

By 360 the situation had deteriorated. Ammianus again:

> [T]he wild tribes of the Scots and Picts broke their understanding to keep peace, laid waste the country near the frontier, and

caused alarm amongst the provincials, who were exhausted by the repeated disasters they had suffered.

And four years later a momentum was building – 'the Picts, Saxons, Scots and Attacotti were bringing continual misery on Britain' which would lead to the disaster of the Barbarian Conspiracy.

When they crossed the Wall or landed in their ships in 367, the Picts, the Scots and the Attacotti had no intention of invading, occupying or settling. Raiding was what mattered to them – acquiring as much plunder as they could carry off. And, as their war bands looted, raped, burned and killed, the province began to bleed to death. Within fifty years, Britannia would cease to be part of the empire, becoming increasingly weak and vulnerable, and the damage done by the northern kindreds was an important contributory cause.

When Count Theodosius restored order in 369, he will have done his best to shore up the Wall defences. It seems that what remained of the garrison had been implicated in the Barbarian Conspiracy and the *areani*, the scouts who operated forward of Hadrian's Wall, had been bribed. The Pictish kings will have wanted no reports of a build-up of forces to reach commanders in the south and so silence was bought. And it worked: 'Fullofaudes was surprised and cut off', probably ambushed.

Notable absentees in the reports of 367 were the kindreds who lived between the Roman walls. The Damnonii, the Votadini, even the Selgovae and the Novantae appear not to have been involved. Understandings of some sort with the Pictish leadership (unless they sailed around the walls) about neutrality may have been reached or threats issued. In any event, it seems that Theodosius himself reached a different understanding with those kindreds once Britannia and the wall had been secured.

For kings and royal families, genealogy has always been important. It conferred legitimacy and, in the sixth and seventh centuries, the rulers of the Celtic kingdoms of Britain seem to have valued glittering ancestors more than most. King lists compiled in early medieval Wales contain flights of historical fancy but four names appear around the period between 370 and 380 which speak of imperial policy rather than pretension. Quintilius Clemens ruled on the Clyde, over the Damnonii, Antonius Donatus over the Novantae in the south west, Catellius Decianus over the northern Votadini and probably Manau and, governing in the Tweed Valley, Paternus, son of Tacitus. Paternus had a nickname which has survived. Pesrut means 'the man in the red cloak'. Who were these men?

Scholars have argued that the king lists are so late and corrupt as to be of little or no value – or that the assumption of Roman names was an affectation, probably signifying nothing more than a conversion to Christianity. If so, then these are very early Christians indeed. And four kings of the four principal kindreds all converting and all adopting the correct Roman form of nomen and cognomen at the same time? This stretches coincidence and a particular piety to breaking point.

Two years after he had pacified Britannia, Count Theodosius was in North Africa on a similar mission. Ammianus reported that he had calmed the situation 'by a mixture of intimidation and bribery and put reliable *praefecti* in charge of the peoples he encountered'. Corroboration came from someone who lived in the region at exactly that time – St Augustine of Hippo: 'A few years ago a small number of barbarian peoples were pacified and attached to the Roman frontier, so that they no longer had their own kings, but were ruled by prefects appointed by the Roman Empire.'

An intriguing and recent archaeological find offers support for very late Roman involvement with the four kingdoms between the walls of the north. At Springwood Park near Kelso, more than a hundred low denomination Roman coins have been found. They date to after the Barbarian Conspiracy and were turned up in a field just across the Teviot from the mighty, old castle of Roxburgh. Although no archaeology has ever been permitted, the shape of the castle mount and the ditching at its west and east ends strongly suggest a long history. Before it acquired an Anglian name in the early seventh century (Hroc's Burh, meaning 'the Stronghold of a Man Called the Rook', probably the leader of a war band), Roxburgh Castle was known as Marchidun in Old Welsh. It means 'the Cavalry Fort'. Were Theodosius' prefects sent north to the kindreds with a squadron of cavalry to back their authority? And was Paternus Pesrut's red cloak seen on the ramparts at Roxburgh as he ruled over the Votadini of the Tweed Valley? And were his soldiers used to being paid in coin?

Serving in Britannia with Count Theodosius was a young Spanish officer who would also lend his name to native dynasties and gain a remarkable enduring fame in Wales. Magnus Maximus led the British field army to victories over the Picts in 381 and, as the empire in the west began to fragment, he was proclaimed emperor by his soldiers in 383.

The Welsh called him Macsen Wledig, 'the General', and believed that he was the first to fly the dragon standard. It is certain that he transferred most of the British garrison to support him in Gaul where he established himself as western emperor based at Trier. From there he controlled Britain, Gaul, Spain and Africa. At Aquileia in 388, Macsen was defeated by the forces of his rival, Emperor Theodosius I, the son of Count Theodosius. Although he was summarily executed, his fame amongst the Celtic kindreds of Britain was undying.

Persistent tradition insists that Macsen married a Welsh princess, Elen Lwyddog, and the emerging dynasties of the kingdoms of Powys, Dyfed and Gwent all claimed him as a founding ancestor. Only twenty years after Maximus' death, Britannia slipped out of the control of the dying empire. In 409 the southern cities and the ruling provincial elite had refused to accept Constantine III as emperor and, a year later, his rival, Honorius, advised the cities of Britannia to look to their own defences.

Conventionally seen as a turning point, the moment when the light of civilisation went out in Britain, 410 is perhaps better understood as an important date in a process. After the withdrawals of troops by Macsen and subsequent usurper-emperors, there were probably few soldiers left to leave. The Roman garrison in Britain may only have consisted of remnant detachments on Hadrian's Wall and at the legionary fortresses at York, Chester and Caerleon. In any case the Roman army had not been Roman for a very long time. By 410 many of its soldiers were likely to have been natives and there is evidence of families living at Housesteads, a major fort on the Wall, in the third and fourth centuries. In addition, a long tradition of hiring bands of barbarian mercenaries was well established in Britain. Most were Germans, warriors from the kindreds north of the Rhine, and the Roman commanders named in the reports of the Barbarian Conspiracy had German names, Nectaridus and Fullofaudes.

However, the year 410 did see a truly world-shaking event, something which reverberated not only in Britain but all over the empire. King Alaric and his Gothic army besieged Rome and sacked the great city. Occasional enemies and occasional allies of various factions in the struggle for control of the western empire, the Goths became exasperated at the deceits and treacheries of the Emperor Honorius and his refusal to pay subsidies. Even though the imperial capital had been removed to Ravenna, a city protected not by mighty walls but a ring of impenetrable marshes, Alaric decided to attack Rome. Here is the final paragraph of Edward Gibbon's magisterial *The Decline and Fall of the Roman Empire*:

The crime and folly of the court of Ravenna was expiated a third time by the calamities of Rome. The king of the Goths, who no longer dissembled his appetite for plunder and revenge, appeared in arms under the walls of the capital; and the trembling senate, without any hopes of relief, prepared by a desperate resistance to delay the ruin of their country. But they were unable to guard against the secret conspiracy of their slaves and domestics, who either from birth or interest were attached to the cause of the enemy. At the hour of midnight the Salarian Gate was silently opened, and the inhabitants were awakened by the tremendous sound of the Gothic trumpet. Eleven hundred and sixty three years after the foundation of Rome, the Imperial city, which had subdued and civilised so considerable a part of mankind, was delivered to the licentious fury of the tribes of Germany and Scythia.

To contemporaries the world appeared to shift suddenly on its axis. In Bethlehem, St Jerome wailed, 'When the brightest light on the whole earth was extinguished . . . then I was dumb with silence'. A shining symbol had been shattered and a sense of shock rippled around the empire. Even so, Alaric's 'licentious fury' was somewhat muted. By 410, the Goths were Christians and no religious buildings in Rome were to be touched and only a modest three days of plunder were permitted. This half-heartedness is echoed in a remarkable declaration by Athaulf, the son and heir of Alaric, at Narbonne a year after Rome had fallen:

> To begin with, I ardently desired to efface the very name of the Romans and to transform the Roman Empire into the Gothic Empire. Romania, as it is commonly called, would have become Gothia; Athaulf would have replaced Caesar Augustus. But long experience taught me that the unruly barbarism of the Goths was incompatible with the laws.
>
> Now, without laws there is no state. I therefore decided rather to aspire to the glory of restoring the fame of Rome in all its integrity, and increasing it by the means of the Gothic strength. I hope to go down to posterity as the restorer of Rome, since it is not possible that I should be its supplanter.

These surprising sentiments were by no means unique, and in Britain those called barbarians by Rome actively attempted to preserve much of what had been Roman. And closely allied to that cluster of ideas and traditions, such as the rule of law, so admired by Athaulf, was the spread and prestige of Christianity. After the Emperor Constantine's endorsement in 312, it had become the state religion, it thrived in that most Roman of institutions, the city, it was mediated in Latin and the leader of the church was the Bishop of Rome. Nevertheless, the earliest glimmers suggest Christianity was one of many faiths. When visitors to the hot springs at Aquae Sulis, at Bath, wanted to ask a favour of the goddess, Minerva, they had messages scratched on small sheets of lead which were then cast into the bubbling waters. One man wanted to recover stolen money from a pickpocket 'whether they were pagan or Christian'.

Several British bishops attended an early church council at Arles in France in 314 and they probably represented York, London, Lincoln and Cirencester. As the fourth century wore on, each British city almost certainly acquired a bishop and a church. To be a Christian in fifth-century Britain was to maintain more than a spiritual link with the immediate imperial past. Christendom was to be the eventual successor of the empire in the west.

Near the western terminal of Hadrian's Wall and the location of an important fortress, Carlisle would have seen the ordination of its bishop and the consecration of its first church, almost certainly little more than a room, a modest meeting place. It was certainly a substantial Roman city and, far from the wealthy and much preyed-upon south, continued as a viable community for a very long time, at least two centuries after the collapse of the western empire. And its survival was of great importance to the emerging kingdoms of southern Scotland.

When Count Theodosius had pacified the frontier in 369 he:

put in hand many necessary reforms. He restored cities and garrison towns, as I have said, and protected the borders with guard posts and defence works. The recovery of a province which had fallen into the hands of the enemy was so complete that, to use his own words, it now had a lawful governor, and the emperor, treating the matter as a triumph, decreed that henceforth it should be called Valentia.

Since Carlisle was already the principal town in the civitas of the Carvetii, the long established territory of the kindred at the west end of the Wall, it is likely that it also became the capital of the new province of Valentia. Its boundaries are far from clear but, if indeed Theodosius attempted the Romanisation of the four kingdoms between the two walls, then it made every sort of sense to bring them within the empire and confer on them the prestige of an enhanced status, perhaps even citizenship. Carlisle may have become the principal city of a remnant of the Roman province.

Two saints supply some concrete sense of its survival. In his *Ecclesiastical History of the English People*, Bede wrote of St Cuthbert's visit in 685. The Queen of the Northumbrians, whose war bands had taken control of the Eden Valley and Carlisle, was there:

> Cuthbert, leaning on his staff, was listening to Wagga the Reeve of Carlisle explaining to the Queen the Roman wall of the city, and the citizens conducted him around the city walls to see a remarkable Roman fountain that was built into them.

If what was remarkable about the fountain was the water pouring out of it, then the Roman aqueduct supplying Carlisle was clearly still working and had been maintained over the two centuries by 'the citizens' since the fall of Britannia.

When a church in the city was dedicated to Cuthbert some time after 698, its orientation was dictated by the position of the Roman streets and the angles at which the grid plan ran. And the building does not stand in the conventional east to west axis but square on to a road which has now disappeared. If the city had declined and was deserted then this sacred imperative might have been ignored but there were other occupied buildings around it and a community still living inside the walls Wagga thought so exceptional as to be worthy of both saintly and royal attention in 685.

In fact, civic buildings were still standing well into the Middle Ages and the twelfth-century historian William of Malmesbury noted a large vaulted stone building, perhaps the market place or 'basilica', which carried an inscription to Mars and Venus. Paved Roman streets were still in use at that time and the excellent repair of Carlisle's west walls and the stonework of the cathedral owe a great deal to Roman masons.

The second saintly informant on the early life of the city is more surprising. After a brilliant analysis by Professor Charles Thomas, it is now clear that the family of St Patrick originated in late Roman Carlisle. Unusually, Patrick, or Patricius, left two surviving texts by his own hand. His *Letter to Coroticus* described a singular but important incident but his *Confessio* is a memoir, and very revealing.

Broadly, the story opens with Patrick being abducted by Irish pirates and sold into slavery in Ulster at around the age of sixteen. After six years as a shepherd boy in the 420s, he escaped and probably made his way to Gaul. On his return to Britain, Patrick underwent religious training of some kind and was ordained as a deacon. Then, traditionally in 432 but probably later, he returned to Ireland as a bishop and began his famous mission of conversion.

But it is Patrick's often overlooked origins which shed a fascinating light on the history of northern Britain. In the *Confessio* he wrote that he had been captured at a place called Vicus Banna Venta Berniae, which lay near his father's estate. Since Patrick was certainly a Roman Briton, his home will have almost certainly been in the north-west. That part of the old province faces Ulster, where the pirates sold him into slavery and where he returned to preach the gospel. And there was also a place called 'Banna' – it was the name of the Roman fort on the Wall now known as Birdoswald. While *vicus* and *venta* denote a village and a market, *berniae* stood for a pass or ravine. All of these elements fit the location of the modern village of Greenhead where the Tipalt Burn tumbles down a rocky defile on its way to join the South Tyne.

Patrick's father, Calpurnius, and one of his grandfathers offer more insights. Calpurnius was not only an estate owner but also a *decurion*, a member of an *ordo* or town council. The only possible town was Roman Carlisle, where Patrick's father had also been a Christian deacon. Potitus, his grandfather, had been ordained a priest and his church almost certainly stood somewhere within the walls of the city. What is very striking in all this is the sense of a cultural atmosphere. If Patrick flourished in the mid fifth century, then his father's town council was still functioning after the end of Britannia and his grandfather was involved with a very early and flourishing church in the late fourth century. In the far north-west of the empire, far from the trouble engulfing the south-east and Gaul, apart from the raids of Irish slavers, life seems to have been conducted within a framework of law, order, Latin, urban life and the growing Christian church – and, after 369, perhaps conducted in the new province of Valentia.

When St Patrick wrote his letter to Coroticus, he was furious, raging at the king for capturing Irish converts and selling them into slavery. No doubt personal experience added extra vehemence. But two details are intriguing. Coroticus was almost certainly a king of the Damnonii, with his citadel on the Rock of the Clyde, and he was himself a Christian. The king lists also call him grandson of Quintilius Clemens. In excommunicating Coroticus and his war band, Patrick called them his 'fellow citizens' and 'fellow citizens of the Holy Romans'. Just as it began to die in the west, did the Roman Empire once again stretch as far north as the Clyde? Another fascinating but shadowy passage of post-Roman politics supports the sense of a lingering but powerful memory of Britannia in the north.

The context for events in the fifth century in Britain is notoriously difficult to set, so little evidence has survived. There are three principal literary sources and all are highly problematic. The one closest to contemporary events is also the least informative and most frustrating. 'On the Ruin of Britain' is a glorious rant written by Gildas, a sixth-century monk who lived either in the Old Welsh-speaking west or in the kingdom of the Damnonii on the Clyde. He supplies few names and only one certain date but the gist of Gildas' account has become widely adopted as authentic.

After the end of Roman Britannia, he writes, 'the councillors together with a proud usurper' made the catastrophic mistake of inviting 'the fierce and impious Saxons' to settle in Britain. When the money to pay them as mercenaries (against the marauding Picts) ran out, the Saxons rebelled and began to take control. More and more came across the North Sea and eventually most of Britain was lost to them or, in Gildas' view, 'ruined'.

The second literary source for the fifth century used 'On the Ruin of Britain' as its basic text. In Bede's *Ecclesiastical History of the English People*, the name of the 'proud usurper' was mentioned. Bede called him Vortigern and added a date, now widely accepted, for the beginning of the end of Britain and the birth of England. In 446, he reckoned, the ships of the Angles, the Saxons and the Jutes first made landfall.

As the title of the third text implies, the *History of the Britons* saw events from a native point of view and saw them somewhat differently. Compiled by Nennius, another monk, this fragmentary text mixes myth with what sounds like history and it was compiled later than both Gildas and Bede, probably dating to the early ninth century. Engagingly, the introduction freely confesses

---

Knife and Spear People

In contemporary sources there is a fleeting sense of the Saxons being thought of as more savage than the angelic Angles. Perhaps it is because they took their name from a weapon, the seax *knife. A long blade, sometimes half a metre, it seems to have been the Saxons' favoured weapon. Its unlikely fame endures in the arms of the modern counties of Essex, the East Saxons, and Middlesex, the Middle Saxons. Both carry the device of three* seax *knives, although they look more like scimitars. Franks also invaded the declining Roman Empire in the west and they took their name from the* franca, *a throwing spear or javelin. When the first crusaders reached the east in 1099, the horrified Greeks and Muslims called them all Franks, no matter where they originated. That name has also been persistent and the Egyptian word for any westerner is* firengi.

---

confusion, surprising eclecticism and the shortcomings of the chronicler:

> I have presumed to deliver these things in the Latin tongue, not trusting to my own learning, which is little or none at all, but partly from traditions of our ancestors, partly from writings and monuments of the ancient inhabitants of Britain, partly from the annals of the Romans, and the chronicles of the sacred fathers . . . and from the histories of the Scots and Saxons, although our enemies, not following my own inclinations, but, to the best of my ability, obeying the commands of my seniors; I have lispingly put together this history from various sources . . .

Disarming, possibly alarming, this history is nevertheless occasionally very enlightening. In common with ranting Gildas and sober Bede, it agrees upon a picture of Britannia at bay in the early fifth century. Without the support of the empire and its soldiers, however illusory or sketchy, the old province had become vulnerable to attack.

They came in their ships – the Irish, the Saxons and, most destructive and persistent, the Picts. Gildas wrote of the Saxons' *cyulis* or 'keels', 'as they call their ships of war', and these were almost certainly plank-built wooden boats. The Irish and probably the Picts sailed in seagoing curraghs, what Gildas called 'canoes', but, whatever craft were used, they must have come in small fleets. No ship sailing in northern waters in that period was large. There exists a fascinating document which offers some sense of what might have sailed out of nowhere to attack the vulnerable coasts of Britannia.

Some time in the seventh century, the kindreds of the Gaelic-speaking kingdom of Argyll were counted in a census known as the *Senchus Fer na h'Alban*, the 'History of the Men of Scotland'. It is an accidental survival illustrating a process of some antiquity. The numbers were compiled to assess military obligations and, given the geography of the Atlantic coastline, it is scarcely surprising to see these expressed in naval terms. Seven-benched seagoing curraghs seem to have been standard and these needed fourteen men to row them and a steersman in the stern and a lookout in the bow. Some will have been larger but sixteen marines to one ship is a reasonable approximation and it prompts the notion of a Pictish or Irish raiding party consisting of several boats and ones with a shallow draught able to penetrate far inland up the wider rivers.

. The sharpest weapon in the armoury of seaborne raiders was surprise. There was no warning until their ships came within sight of land and, even when a Pictish fleet was seen hugging the coastline, they could arrive at their target faster than news could reach it overland. But a pattern of landings must have emerged. Estuaries and riverbanks were preferred to coasts open to the sea and bad weather and gently shelving beaches allowed vessels to be dragged well above the high-tide line if a coastal landing was unavoidable.

By the late fourth century, Pictish raiding parties had been seen in the Thames and Gildas spoke of them as *'transmarini'*. Defences had been built along the North Sea coast by the Roman provincial administration – what was known as the Saxon Shore. Forts guarding landing areas in East Anglia, Kent and Sussex hoped to contain incursion from across the North Sea while a line of watchtowers down the North Yorkshire coastline waited for the threat of Pictish attack.

When government in Britain reverted to native control after 409–410, all of the sources give the impression of continuity. Cities had almost certainly been self-governing for some time and a council and a figure in overall authority are mentioned. Perhaps Bede's and Gildas' use of *'superbus tyrannus'* or 'proud usurper' speaks of imperial pretention. Like Magnus Maximus, there had been several ambitious men who had made their bid for the throne from Britain. In any case, 'Vortigern' is not itself a name but a title. In its various versions, it means something like 'High Lord' or perhaps 'Overlord'.

Whatever his precise status, the Vortigern appears to have taken decisive action. Archaeologists have excavated a series of early Germanic cemeteries near the estuaries of the Humber, the Wash and the Thames. The earliest burials date to well before the 440s and the Saxon rebellions described by Gildas and Bede and they suggest that bands of Germanic mercenaries were placed at these strategic locations to defend against Pictish – or incoming Saxon – attack. In Latin, such groups were known as *foederati* or 'federates' and they were used all over the empire to guard its frontiers. More early cemeteries have been found around south London and near Oxford, again suggesting a defensive deploy-ment of *foederati* by the Vortigern and his council.

The overall strategy appears to have worked for there are no more reports of Pictish raids in the south after 410. Another, more radical redeployment also had beneficial effects. The kingdoms of southern Scotland seem to have been sufficiently well organised to force Pictish raiders to sail around their territory. They were also able to produce two talented military leaders and enough well-trained soldiers to achieve something unique in the disintegrating western Roman Empire.

Some time around 430, probably on the orders of the Vortigern, an expeditionary force set out from the kingdom of Manau-Gododdin. In Old Welsh, Votadini had transmuted into 'Gododdin'. Probably a large cavalry troop, it was led down the Roman roads to the old legionary fortress at Chester. Almost 20 per cent larger than any other fort in Britain and with an amphitheatre with seating for more than 8,000, Roman Deva or Chester was a substantial base. At the head of the riders from Manau-Gododdin rode a remarkable figure, another man with a Celtic military title. This was the Cunedda, the Good Leader. It has come down to us as the popular Christian name of Kenneth and the Welsh genealogies name him tautologically as Cunedda Wledig, the General. In the fifth-century lists, the Cunedda is also described as the grandson of Paternus Pesrut and the son of Aeternus. It is a signal of a culture in transition when a Celtic epithet was preferred to a Roman name.

The Cunedda's mission was to remove the Irish settlers who had taken over the Lleyn Peninsula of North Wales. It seems likely that their war bands had been raiding as far west as Viroconium, modern Wroxeter, and the civitas of the Cornovii. The Irish raiders had originated in Leinster and Lleyn is a cognate name. The peninsula was left undefended when Magnus Maximus took the garrison at the Roman fort at Segontium, Caernarfon, with him to Gaul in his bid for the empire. No details of the Cunedda's campaign have survived, only notice of its success. Deserted farms and shielings in that part of North Wales were long known as *cytian yr Gwyddelod*, 'the huts of the Irish'. Tradition holds that the Vortigern was from the *civitas* of the Cornovii and his wish to see the Irish expelled might have had personal as well as political motives behind it.

The cavalry warriors from the northern kindreds did not ride home after their victories. Under the Cunedda's leadership, they established themselves in Wales. The old kingdom of Gwynedd is named after the Cunedda and, according to modern Welsh scholars, it retained an atmosphere of Romanitas for the following two centuries. Early Welsh literary sources seem almost obsessed with a need to explain the origin of place-names but the traditions that the Cunedda's sons, Meirion and Ceredig, founded the kingdoms of Meirionydd and Ceredigion are unlikely.

What is remarkable about the expedition to Wales from Manau-Gododdin was that it was the only occasion when invading barbarians were permanently expelled from inside the frontiers of the old empire. And, just as importantly, it showed the central authority of the Vortigern as far-reaching, extending to the northern and western edges of Britannia. Given that and the successful use of well-placed Saxon colonies of mercenaries against the Picts, it seems that the first thirty years of post-Roman Britain were a time of increased security and administrative continuity, and the old province was a safer place to live than it had been in the previous forty years.

Economically, however, there was decline. As part of the Roman imperial trade network, Britannia had exported both agricultural and manufactured products and imported a wide

---

Dark Ages Recession

For about 300 years, in the period immediately following the fall of Britannia around 410, the economy in Britain operated without coin. Currency production ceased and barter took its place. Core manufacturing also ceased abruptly with wheel-turned pottery absent from the archaeological record until the seventh century after having been abundantly available in the Roman period. Urban life shrank dramatically. The British economy took almost 600 years to return to the levels of production and activity in Britannia – a very long recession. In 2010, the Financial Times *ran an article on the post-Roman economic collapse because 'it put recent crises in the shade'. Possibly.*

---

variety of goods on some scale. But, after 410, the use of coinage began to fade when the remnants of the army and the administration ceased to be paid. If new coins were minted anywhere in Britain after 410, none have survived. The industrial manufacture of pottery declined sharply and quickly disappeared. This was not simply a matter of a lack of good tableware – pottery of every sort was used in the transport of food and drink. And, if agricultural surpluses could not easily be moved, they could no longer be traded over any distance. This, in turn, removed the motivation for farmers to produce surpluses and pushed communities towards subsistence. Roads on which goods might be carted were left unrepaired in many places and, by the close of the fifth century, towns were certainly in decline in the south. Once again, this inhibited trade tremendously as concentrations of population thinned and dispersed and markets ceased to be held.

Both Gildas and Bede ignore the containment efforts of Vortigern (who need not have been the same man between 410 and the early 440s) and they focus exclusively on his great epoch-changing blunder. Having brought the Saxons and, no doubt, other Germanic kindreds to Britain and having failed to meet their demands, he had invited the wolf into the fold. From their strategically placed strongholds, the rebel mercenaries rose up and were quickly able to establish themselves in the south and east. This view takes no account of the undoubted fact that there were already many Germanic groups in Britain. At all events, in the 440s, battles were fought and lost in Kent, the Vortigern was killed at the beginning of the war and, from their bases, it seems that the Saxons raided towns and villas in the west and probably along the Thames Valley. Gildas takes up the tale:

> [S]ome of the wretched survivors were caught in the hills and slaughtered in heaps; others surrendered themselves to perpetual slavery in enemy hands ... others emigrated overseas ... others entrusted their lives ... to the rugged hills, the thick forests and the cliffs of the sea, staying in their homeland afraid, until, after some time, the savage plunderers went home again.

Roman authority still held across the Channel in Gaul. In 433, Aetius, a nobleman originally from Moesia, modern Bulgaria, was appointed Consul and General-in-Chief on behalf of the young Emperor Valentinian III. Effectively emperor in all but name, Aetius maintained the rule of Rome in the west for thirty years. His greatest achievement was the defeat of Attila and his ferocious Hunnic army in Gaul in 451. When the Saxons rose up against the Vortigern in the 440s and killed him, Gildas wrote that a letter was sent across the Channel:

> 'To Aetius, thrice Consul, come the groans of the Britons ... the barbarians drive us into the sea, and the sea drives us back to the barbarians. Between these, two deadly alternatives confront us, drowning or slaughter.' The Romans however, could not assist them.

Plague had visited Britain in the 440s and there is also some evidence of catastrophic climate change with the rise of sea levels and widespread flooding. As people fled westwards from the Saxon raids, many decided to go further. Emigrations across the Channel to Gaul began and so many went to the district of

Armorica that it became known as Brittany, Little Britain. Gildas takes up the story:

> After a time, when the cruel raiders returned to their home, God strengthened the survivors . . . Their leader was a gentleman, Ambrosius Aurelianus, who perhaps alone of the Romans had survived the impact of such a tempest; truly his parents, who had worn the purple, were overcome in it. In our times his stock have degenerated greatly from their excellent grandfather. With him our people regained their strength, challenged the victors to battle and with the Lord acceding the victory fell to us. From then on now our citizens, and then the enemies conquered . . .

Ambrosius Aurelianus is one of the few names noted by Gildas and it sheds a flicker of light on the society of post-Roman Britain. With the formal nomen and cognomen (the praenomen was often written as an initial or even dropped), it signifies a family known as Ambrosius with the Aurelianus element saying something about their origins. The name may have been famous and powerful for it has survived in Welsh as Emrys, and in the earliest sources Ambrosius is hailed as Emrys Wledig, the General. Sometimes the cognomen refers to an emperor or a dynasty under which the family came to prominence and between 270 and 275 Aurelian ruled. Although his reign was short, it was very effective, pulling the empire together, building new walls around Rome, defeating rivals in the east (including the exotic Queen Zenobia of Palmyra) and restoring the discipline of the army. Aurelian's name conferred prestige and it may be that Ambrosius' family adopted it towards the end of the third century.

Gildas is untypically clear in this passage, stating that not only were the Ambrosians a noble family, Romano-British rather than native (in implied contrast with the Vortigern) but also that they 'had worn the purple'. This may mean a connection to Magnus Maximus or Constantine III, both usurper-emperors with British origins, or, more likely, that Gildas intended to convey that

Ambrosius Aurelianus was one of the old senatorial class or perhaps even someone with the inherited rank of military tribune. Formally both were entitled to wear the *toga praetexta*, a toga with a broad purple border.

'[W]ith the Lord acceding', Ambrosius defeated the Saxons, wrote Gildas, and this is unequivocal evidence that the general was a Christian. Moreover, it suggests that he came from the more urbanised south. In the fourth and fifth centuries, Christianity in Britain tended to flourish in the towns (the term *pagan* is from the Latin *paganus*, 'a country person', and is also the origin of 'peasant') and there is a persuasive argument for locating Ambrosius around Amesbury in Wiltshire. The place-name seems to be derived from the family name and it may have been close to the power base from which attacks were launched against the Saxons in the east.

Gildas concludes with a passing observation that, after the success of Ambrosius' campaigns, hostilities with the Saxons

---

Brittany and Amesbury

Place names often record no more than description or location – Newtown, Ford, Rockcliffe, Castletown and so on – but sometimes they remember people. Roman emperors were fond of naming cities after themselves, perhaps the most famous example being Constantinople, and it may be that more obscure figures in Dark Ages Britain are commemorated in this way. In his magisterial The Age of Arthur, *John Morris traced a pattern of place-names in the south-east of England which may relate to the native general of the fifth century, Ambrosius Aurelianus. So-called 'Ambros' names only occur there – Amesbury, Amberley and Ambrosden. More certain is a clutch of names across the Channel in Brittany. By the 540s and 550s, a series of migrations from Britain had led to the establishment of Little Britain or Brittany in the former Roman district of Armorica. The Breton language is related to Cornish (although some scholars now believe it preserves remnants of Gaulish as well) and Welsh and a scatter of place-names, such as Bretteville or Briteville, reaches as far east as Normandy.*

ebbed and flowed with neither side gaining a decisive advantage. '[O]ur citizens' won battles and sometimes 'the enemies conquered'. With the beginnings of a sense of there being a common front in the war for England, a new word came into currency. *Combrogi* meant 'fellow countrymen' or, more precisely, 'those who share a common border'. The Saxons began to recognise the term and talked of the *cumber*, 'the native British'. It survives in many place-names spread all over the map, from Camberwell in south London to Cumberbatch in Cheshire. The most obvious relic is Cumbria and its predecessor, Cumberland.

Gradually *combrogi* also mutated into the Welsh word for Wales, Cymru, and Cymry for the Welsh. Its first surviving appearance is in a praise poem to a seventh-century Welsh king, Cadwallon, and it is spelled as Kymry. Although the word slowly became dominant in common speech, the poets clung for centuries to the past when they sang of Brython for Wales and Brythoniaid for the Welsh. But in reality the greater part of Britain was to be conquered by the Saxons and England would become Lloegr, 'the Lost Lands'.

If, indeed, the wars of Ambrosius Aurelianus concluded with the sort of stalemate suggested by Gildas, then life in the west of Britain will have carried on relatively undisturbed. Archaeologists have found evidence of long-distance trade – Mediterranean pottery dating to the fifth and sixth centuries in North Wales, Ireland and the south-western and western coasts of Scotland. Many of these pots and their precious contents were probably delivered by ships operating out of the Biscay and Brittany ports and, in the *Life of St Columba*, describing the second half of the sixth century, the community of monks on Iona waited for 'Gaulish ships arriving from the provinces of the Gauls'. All sorts of goods were traded on what were almost certainly regular visits – wine for communion and colours for illuminated manuscripts from as far away as Syria and even India.

Ideas also travelled in the Gaulish ships and some seem to have found landfall in Galloway. With his community at Marmoutier, near Tours in Gaul, St Martin is often seen as the founder of western monasticism. He was revered and influential in the early church and the survival of a fascinating group of inscribed stones in south-western Scotland strongly suggests the long reach of his teachings. At Kirkmadrine (a metathesis for Kirkmartin), two bishops were remembered on one memorial. Viventius and Mavorius appear to have led a congregation of some substance in the Rhinns of Galloway, the most westerly peninsula. It is thought that the Kirkmadrine stones date to 500 but even earlier is the inscription to a man called Latinus found at Whithorn. It listed three generations of his family, presumably all Christians, and close by the remains of an early cemetery have been found.

The most famous name associated with early Christianity in Galloway belongs to Ninian. First mentioned by Bede, he is said to have converted the southern Picts and was a saintly bishop of the British. His church was built in stone, 'in the Roman manner, *Ad Candidam Casam*', at the White House. In the later seventh century, it became known as Whithorn when the Angles took power in Galloway. Scholars periodically dispute the existence of Ninian but there can be little doubt that Christianity first entered the north through Galloway and moved over the watershed hills to the Borders and the Forth and Clyde Valley. As it declined and shrivelled, the city of Carlisle and its church appear to have had less and less influence.

In his monastic life, St Martin's inspiration was a group of Near Eastern ascetics known as the Desert Fathers. To escape persecution in the towns and cities and to find a more solitary, undistracted and contemplative life, they sought out remote, even harsh, places in the deserts of the interior. Lacking seas of inhospitable sand to surround and isolate a community of monks in Western Europe, St Martin substituted the wildwood of central Gaul. Deep in the forests at Marmoutier he and his brothers could shut out the temporal world and seek communion with God. When Martin's ideas travelled north, the wastes of the sea replaced the tangle of the woods but the name the Gaels gave to these remote, windswept places remembered their eastern

---

Saints

It was not until the eleventh century that the papacy took control of the making of saints. Before Urban II insisted that only the pope could confer sainthood, it had been a matter for local prelates and local tradition. In the early church, martyrdom automatically made the victim a saint but, after the fourth century, the definition became more elastic. When the quality of 'heroic virtue' was observed in monks and priests and occasionally in the laity, that could, in itself, be a qualification. The notion behind this was best illustrated by ascetics – those who willingly suffered all manner of privation for their faith. Their holy suffering was seen as analogous to the torture and often appalling deaths of real martyrs and, after a suitable period of what was known as 'bloodless martyrdom', they could become saints. In the Middle Ages, the Congregation for the Causes of Saints was formalised and a centralised bureaucracy was set up in Rome. Cases were tried as in a court of law with the Postulator arguing the case for conferring sainthood and the Devil's Advocate taking up the case against.

---

origins. These remote communities were called *diseartan*, 'deserts', and the town of Dysart on the coast of Fife is derived from the memory of the ascetics of Syria and Palestine.

The island of Iona is perhaps the most famous *diseart* and sources talk of a community which did much together under the guidance of their abbots but whose members lived alone in cells built of stone and turf. The word monk, from the Greek *monos* meaning 'single', originally described a solitary person.

One of the most remote *diseartan* is on the island of Canna. Sgor nam Ban-Naomhan, 'the Skerry of the Holy Women', was home to a convent of nuns, probably founded in the seventh century. Their *diseart* is cut off from the main island by a steep escarpment and was only easily accessible by sea and then only in fine weather.

Behind a drystone walled enclosure was a group of small buildings, almost certainly monastic cells. Some huddled against the enclosure wall seeking shelter from the Atlantic winds.

Others, perhaps eight in all, were arranged around a well-house and a building where saddle querns (for grinding corn) have been found. These holy women must have suffered in the hard and unrelenting winters, the wind-driven rain finding its way into their bare cells, and they were genuine ascetics anxious to know their God through extraordinary privation. It is not clear how they survived or for how long or where the corn for their querns came from. Perhaps they depended on the kindness of the islanders or Canna or on an aristocratic patron or on the gifts of visitors.

The Sgor nam Ban-Naomha never lost its atmosphere of sanctity. Pilgrims seeking cures were brought into the ruins of the ancient enclosure as late as the nineteenth century. Companions laid the sick and the crippled on stone beds known as *leaba crabhach*, 'sacred couches'. It was an enduring belief which brought the pilgrims down the dangerously steep path through the scree. The prayers and exemplary lives of generations of the holy women had drawn God nearer to the drystone walls of the Sgor and imbued its very ground with a powerful sanctity. By simply being there, in contact with its stones and soil, the pilgrims could summon the help of the Almighty to ease or even cure the suffering of the infirm. More than that, the soil itself in such a place was thought to have the power to cleanse bodies of earthly sins. In the Middle Ages many wealthy noble-men gave generous gifts to Scottish abbeys and churches in exchange for the right to be buried inside the precincts and often as close to the high altar as possible.

In their remote and rainswept *diseartan* the early monks and nuns of the north of Britain brought a different Christianity into being. It stood in high contrast with the ministries of the bishops and priest of the cities and towns of the south who engaged with the world and all its sins and temptations. But it would be misleading to think of two versions of Christianity moving in different doctrinal directions. Their approaches to God and their sense of a Christian life were very different but not their fundamental beliefs.

St Gildas

The author of On the Ruin of Britain *has a more rounded historical personality than virtually any other figure of the fifth and sixth centuries. Ordained in the church, he composed a monastic rule and was also the subject of an early biography.* 'The Life of Gildas' *was written in the ninth century by a monk based in Brittany at a place called Rhuys. It tells of Gildas' birth in Alt Clut, Dumbarton Rock on the Clyde, the kingdom which later became Strathclyde. He was sent to the monastery of Llan Illtud Fawr in Wales and later to Ireland. After his studies were complete, Gildas came back to Strathclyde and the Old North where he preached and converted pagans. Towards the end of his life, he came to Brittany and settled on the island of Rhuys where he lived as a hermit. Later he founded the monastery which eventually produced his biography. Gildas' story shows a Celtic west where there was routine movement over considerable distances and, with the exception of his short stay in Ireland, movement between communities speaking dialects of Old Welsh. Breton was probably introduced into the north-western corner of France by migration from Cornwall after the Saxon invasions.*

Much of Gildas' holy rage arose from what he saw as a badly managed contest between Christian British kings and pagan Saxon invaders. If only the native dynasties would cease their squabbling and sinfulness, then the hosts of the Lord could unite and drive the heathens into the sea. The early gains made by the Saxons in the east appear to have been consolidated and a truce was holding at the time Gildas wrote. He spoke of 'our present security' but nowhere does he explain how the peace was won. The sole clue is a reference to a final battle:

After this, sometimes our countrymen, sometimes the enemy, won the field . . . until the year of the siege of Badon Hill, when took place the last almost, though not the least slaughter of our cruel foes, which was (I am sure) forty four years and one month after the landing of the Saxons, and also the time of my own nativity.

Scholarship conventionally dates the composition of *On the Ruin of Britain* to the 540s and sets the year of Gildas' birth as 516 – the year, therefore, of the siege of Badon Hill. Who fought this action, gained this mighty victory which stemmed the westward rush of the Saxon tide and created 'our present security'? As usual Gildas does not say but Nennius' *History of the Britons* offers an explanation, details of a victorious campaign and the name of perhaps the most famous warrior in British history:

Then it was, that the magnanimous Arthur, with all the kings and military forces of Britain, fought against the Saxons. And though there were many more noble than himself, yet he was twelve times chosen their commander, and was as often conqueror. The first battle in which he was engaged, was at the mouth of the River Gleni, the second, third, fourth and fifth, were on another river, by the Britons called Duglas, in the region of Linnuis. The sixth on the River Bassas. The seventh in the Wood of Celidon, which the Britons call Cat Coit Celidon. The eighth was near Guinnion Castle, where Arthur bore the image of the Holy Virgin, the mother of God, upon his shield, and through the power of our Lord Jesus Christ, and the Holy Mary, put the Saxons to flight, and pursued them the whole day with great slaughter. The ninth was at the City of the Legion, which is called Cair Lion. The tenth was on the banks of the River Tribruit. The eleventh was on the mountain Bregion, which we call Cat Bregion. The twelfth was a most severe contest, when Arthur penetrated to the Hill of Badon. In this engagement, nine hundred and forty fell by his hand alone, no one but the Lord affording him assistance. In all these engagements the Britons were successful. For no strength can avail against the will of the Almighty.

Scholarly reaction to this text varies enormously. Some dismiss it as late, corrupt and ultimately fanciful, while others are more vehement, seeing it as the poisonous seeds of pointless myth-history. To this way of thinking, Arthur, king or otherwise, never existed outside the imaginations of a few Celtic clerics and chroniclers. There are other references. In the tenth century *Annales Cambriae* and the death songs known as *The Gododdin*, composed around 600, Arthur is mentioned but those who take these doubtful historical notices seriously are characterised as no-smoke-without-fire-mongers not rigorous scholars.

Others take a different view. The primary sources for the period between 400 and 600 are so sparse, even those transcribed much later, that all evidence should be treated with respect. One eminent scholar wrote of the period as 'the lost centuries' of British history. But, if Arthur is not remembered in any texts, he certainly has his memorial in the British landscape. Hundreds of place-names remember the great hero and, even though the mythology swirling around him can be wildly romantic, the core of the story has always seemed credible. A successful native general, the successor of the Vortigern, the Cunedda and Ambrosius Aurelianus halted the tide of Anglo-Saxon invasion sufficiently to allow Gildas in the 540s to enjoy his 'present security'.

The Nennius text appears to be a version of an older praise poem, something composed by bards to honour the achievements of Arthur, the conqueror. Remnants of poetic conventions are detectable in the alliteration of Cat Coit Celidon, and a rhyme-scheme with Celidon, Guinnion, Bregion and Badon. All of which persuades the sceptical to redouble their doubts – the needs of poetry outweighing the demands of historical accuracy! But why should poetry and accuracy be mutually exclusive? Poems are still composed with real events as their subject matter and they often derive added power for that reason. But then there is the inherent unreliability of oral traditions, history becoming distorted and embellished as it passed down in memory from one generation to another. But why should word of mouth be more untrustworthy than a written source? Who would rely on the British tabloid newspapers of the last thirty years as an honest record of anything? The bards of the fifth, sixth and seventh centuries are to be trusted no less – and no more – than the scribes of the same period.

The central difficulty with Nennius is one of comparison. In his great history, Bede generally excluded fanciful elements (if saintly miracles are taken at face value) and concentrated on what he believed to be true. No dragons flew and only a little lightning rent the air. But, in his apparently forensic rigour, Bede was an unusual chronicler. Most, like Nennius, included an undifferentiated jumble of material uncritically set down, sometimes in a very eccentric order. And that is the problem. Not far from the passage about Arthur is the tale of a boy (the young Ambrosius Aurelianus) brought into the presence of the Vortigern to be put to death in some sort of blood sacrifice. He avoided his fate by the unlikely means of pointing out that two dragons dwelt under the foundations of the Vortigern's fortress. This sort of thing is seen as a fatal taint, invalidating everything around it. But, in fact, the tone of the Arthur text and other material is markedly different, almost certainly indicating a separate source.

The Nennius text is careful to point out that Arthur was no king but a man appointed by kings as a war leader like his predecessors. There is a sense of unity, of a common purpose and a common enemy, of native kings combining their forces, what Gildas despaired of them doing in the 540s, what he knew had been successful forty or fifty years before he was writing. Alliances of this sort were not uncommon and there would be two famous concerted native efforts against the enemy at the end of the sixth century in the north.

As well as politics, geography is important as Nennius lists twelve battles won under Arthur's leadership, the last of them corroborated by Gildas, what the sources call the siege of Badon Hill. Four out of the twelve are identifiable, clearly real places where the armies of Celtic Britain tasted victory. And they can be found on maps of north Britain.

'Gleni' is the River Glen which flows east out of the Cheviot Hills in what is now north Northumberland. Arthur was likely a *penteulu*, the professional warrior at the head of a royal war band and a man who had attracted a powerful reputation. But why did he form his men up for battle on the banks of an obscure and windswept river in the wilds of north Northumberland? Because a royal enclosure stood by the Glen, perhaps even a complex of buildings which could be described as a palace. Yeavering was brilliantly excavated in the 1950s by Brian Hope Taylor and, amongst later material, the rare remains of a fifth- and sixth-century native presence were recorded. Kings lived by the little river.

Like the battle at the Glen, others take place at sites by rivers, almost certainly at fords. Tactically they were good places to lay an ambush, perhaps with cavalry charging a surprised straggle of infantry. 'Bregion' is attested as another name for Bremenium, the old Roman fort at High Rochester in Redesdale. It stands astride Dere Street, near the head of a valley reaching into the heart of the Cheviots, on what became the traditional invasion road for armies marching north. And it too lies near a ford over the River Rede and is only ten miles south of the Glen. The 'Wood of Celidon' later became Ettrick Forest, north of the Cheviots, and it appears in more than one early source in that guise.

Three battles within less than a day of each other – this concentration suggests the faded reports of an ancient campaign fought in the north by Arthur and his squadrons of Celtic cavalry. The siege of Badon Hill is believed by many to have taken place in the south-west, near Bath. But across the valley from High Rochester stands Padon Hill. Perhaps four battles were fought in the north. And, if they were, who opposed Arthur and his allied army? And when did they fight?

Archaeologists have discovered Germanic cemeteries in the north (and therefore evidence of settlement) dating from as early as the late fourth and fifth centuries. The massive forts of the Saxon Shore were built at the end of the third century and there exist several notices of German warriors in Britannia. With the end of the Roman province and the ebb and flow of war, it is very likely that groups of Anglo Saxons were establishing themselves in Yorkshire and the north-east. The rebellion of Germanic mercenaries against the Vortigern in the early fifth century might well have been repeated elsewhere. Did Arthur go to war against the ancestors of warriors who would later establish the magnificent and powerful kingdom of Northumbria? It seems likely.

Gildas and other sources offer unexpected help and general agreement on the dating of Arthur's great campaign against the barbarians all Britain called the Saxons. Many were Angles from Angeln on the borders of modern Denmark and Germany, others were Jutes from Jutland, to the north of them, Frisians to the south and there were even Swedes and Franks amongst the settlers and land-grabbers. But, in all of Britain's Celtic languages, the word is the same – *Sais* in Welsh, *Sasunnaich* in Gaelic and variations in Manx, Irish and Cornish. Gildas called them *furciferes*, literally 'fork-bearers' or 'servants', and it is sometimes translated as 'rascals'. In any event, he and other chroniclers rejoiced at what they saw as an emphatic, momentum-halting defeat at the siege of Badon Hill and they reckoned that the battle was fought in 500.

Since that date attracts unprecedented consensus amongst the sparse sources, it ought to be taken gratefully as a fixed point. And, if it was such a final and decisive encounter, then it strongly suggests that Arthur's campaign against the Saxons was fought in the 490s. The latest mention of the great general is in a battle said to have been fought at a place called Camlann in 517. The entry

---

British Cuckoos

A Cornishman who spent much of his professional life in Scotland, Professor Charles Thomas, was more aware than most of the links between the ancient lands of the Old Welsh-speakers. He noticed a trio of place-names in Dumfries and Galloway and East Lothian – Terregles, Penpont and Tranent – and compared them with three in Cornwall – Treveglos, Penponds and Trenance. This sort of awareness is to be applauded but it is not recent. Sir John Clerk of Penicuik was the origin of Walter Scott's The Antiquary *and he called his home Mons Cuculi, a Latin version of the Old Welsh name and it means 'Cuckoo Hill'.*

in the annals reads: 'The battle at Camlann, in which Arthur and Medraut fell, and there was plague in Britain and Ireland.' Castlesteads Fort on Hadrian's Wall was known as Camboglanna and, like Camlann, it means 'Crooked Glen' or 'Valley'.

Medraut is a Celtic name, certainly not a Saxon one, and Camlann sounds like a battle between British kings, their generals and their war bands. Gildas complained that this sort of internecine bickering was a principal cause of the ruin of Britain. Tradition insists that Arthur and Medraut, or Mordred, were enemies and, in what Lord Tennyson called 'the last, dim, weird battle of the west', the great hero may have died.

Arthur's legacy has been enormously powerful and almost all of it has clung to the south-west of Britain, to Glastonbury, Tintagel, Cornwall and Wales. Many of these associations were confected in the Middle Ages, and such traces as can be found in the threadbare historical record of the fifth and sixth centuries suggest a northern figure, a general who rode out of the half-forgotten Celtic kingdoms of southern Scotland.

At the Battle of Guinnion Castle, which may have stood in the valley of the Gala Water, another route to the Forth and the north, Nennius recorded that 'Arthur bore the image of the Holy Virgin, the mother of God, upon his shield, and through the power of our Lord Jesus Christ, put the Saxons to flight, and pursued them the whole day with great slaughter'. By 500 and Badon Hill, all of the native kingdoms of Britain were Christian and those in the north talked of the war against Y Gynt, 'the Gentiles', 'the Heathens', by which they meant the Saxons. When they sang of the deeds of their own armies, the royal bards sang of Y Bedydd, the warriors they called 'the Baptised'.

6

The Baptised

✶

I N THE 530S, THE Roman Empire was resurgent. Under
Justinian's dynamic rule, generals led seaborne expeditions to
recapture Italy, North Africa and even parts of southern
Spain. Perhaps Rome might reach out as far as Britain once more
and come to the aid of the *combrogi*, the fellow citizens. The Vandals,
the Goths and the Visigoths had all been vanquished and surely the
Saxons could not resist the legions of the emperor as the Mediterranean again became a Roman lake. But it was not to last.

In order that the glorious progress of reconquest was properly
recorded for a grateful posterity and the needs of present politics,
Justinian's ministers had sent the historian, Procopius, with the
expeditionary forces. In 536 the dashing general, Belisarius, sailed
west to North Africa and defeated the Vandal kingdom but, as
Carthage and other cities were retaken, the skies began to darken
and the sun was dimmed. All eyes were raised to the Heavens and
men were terrified, wondering if the end of days was at hand.
Procopius wrote, 'During this year a most dread portent took
place. For the sun gave forth its light without brightness . . . and it
seemed exceedingly like the sun in eclipse, for the beams it shed
were not clear.'

A catastrophic event on the other side of the world was the
cause. What happened in 536 was recently confirmed by an
expedition led by the geologist, Harald Sigurdsson and recorded
by Ken Wohletz of the Los Alamos National Laboratory in the

USA. On the seabed between the Indonesian islands of Java and Sumatra, Sigurdsson's bathyspheres discovered a huge caldera with deposits which could be reliably radiocarbon-dated to the sixth century. This volcanic depression was vast, measuring an astonishing 40–60 kilometres across, and it lay near the point where the island of Krakatoa famously blew itself apart in 1883. What happened in 536 was of a different order of magnitude – so devastating that it might have severed Java from Sumatra and created the Sunda Straits.

Computer modelling has postulated worldwide effects on every continent which lasted for at least two years. When the eruption broke through and boiling magma was met by inrushing seawater, a huge volume of vapour rocketed into the sky. The plume may have been 50 kilometres high. Mixed with vaporised seawater were huge volumes of superfine volcanic dust and as it rose through the stratosphere, great ice clouds were formed. As much as 100 cubic kilometres of ash and ice crystals then began to dissipate as the stratospheric winds created by the eruption began to blow and a significant cloud layer quickly darkened over the northern and southern hemispheres. This reflected much of the sun's light and warmth back into space, allowing very little to penetrate.

Chroniclers in every part of the world had seen nothing like it and, where records survive, they speak of cataclysm, of incomprehension and of what the scientists at Los Alamos have reckoned to have been the most sudden and severe cooling of the climate in the last two millennia. Snow fell in August in China, there was a 'dense, dry fog' over the desert countries of the Middle East and a severe drought in Peru. As the vast volcanic clouds cast over the skies above Britain and Ireland, the Annals of Ulster recorded 'a failure of bread' in 536 and the monks at Innisfallen, near Killarney, wrote that the famine lasted from 536 to 539. The Dark Ages were beginning. And there was worse to come.

Imperial Constantinople was a vast city – the largest in the western world by far and home to more than half a million people. Like Old Rome, New Rome was also in a state of political ferment. Emperors could be made and unmade by the mob or, more correctly in Constantinople, by two rival mobs. Politics had polarised around the Hippodrome, the huge stadium which stood in the centre of the city, adjacent to the Imperial Palace. Opposing factions, known simply as the Blues and the Greens, gathered there to support their chariot-racing teams and also to give vent to their opinions. Wise emperors courted the Hippodrome crowds and hoped to bask in a form of politics by public acclamation. It was with this in mind that Justinian married the amazing Theodora, a dancer and daughter of one of the managers of the Green faction. She was streetwise and shameless and she understood the collective mind of the mob. According to Procopius, who clearly sniffed at such a scandalous marriage, Theodora once performed what amounted to an open-air striptease in front of the vast and delighted crowds at the Hippodrome. He also insisted that she once complained that 'God had not endowed her with more orifices to give more pleasure to more people at the same time'. Apparently Theodora was able and intelligent and one of the most successful empresses in history.

Apart from striptease and a supply of salacious gossip, what sustained the politics of the mob in Constantinople was Egyptian grain. The city imported many shiploads each year to dole out to the mob and to feed its more respectable citizens. But the corn loaded into the holds on the quays of Alexandria was often infested with rats and, in 541, the rats themselves were infested with deadly fleas.

That autumn bubonic plague sailed into the harbours of the Golden Horn and, in such a densely packed mass of people, it spread like wildfire. At its terrible peak, the pandemic killed around 5,000 people a day. The city authorities could not cope and corpses were piled high in the forums and the streets. Scholars conservatively estimate a population loss in Europe of between 50–60 per cent. After the bewildering drama of volcanic winter in 536 and 537, it was a second devastation and the ambitions of Justinian to reclaim the western empire were stopped dead in their tracks as his soldiers died and the tax revenues needed to pay them dried up all across the stricken empire.

Western Britain and Ireland were the northernmost tangent of the Mediterranean trading system but the plague took some time to reach their shores. In 549, the Ulster annalists wrote of a '*mortalitas magna*', literally a 'great death', that was stalking the land. Seven aristocrats, probably sub-kings, died and across the Irish Sea in Wales more devastation was reported. The *Annales Cambriae* noted that the Great Death had carried off Maelgwn, King of Gwynedd.

Ireland, Wales and the south-west were almost certainly ravaged by bubonic plague. The trading enclaves at Tintagel and Cadbury-Congresbury by the Severn Estuary appear to have been deserted in the second half of the sixth century and the surviving Roman town at Wroxeter shrank and ceased to hold markets. Records of the terrible aftermath have perished – except in one unexpected quarter. The powerful image of the Wasteland finds its way into early medieval stories such as the *Mabinogion* and the Arthurian romances. They tell of an empty landscape, of farmers lying dead in the fields where they fell and of how 'no animal, no smoke, no fire, no man, no dwelling' could be seen for miles.

It is likely that the scourges of famine and plague weakened the native kingdoms of the west of Britain but impossible to know how relatively badly the Saxons and Angles of the east and the Celtic kindreds of the north were affected. It seems that the Saxon settlements of the south had little to do with their neighbours and enemies and perhaps the contagion did not spread everywhere. But what seems certain is a decisive shift in the military balance in Britain.

There is evidence to suggest that the extreme weather of 536 and 537 caused sea levels to rise worldwide. Eighty years before then, rising tides had forced those who lived on the low-lying coasts of Frisia, Angeln and Saxony to abandon their villages, to take to their ships and seek a home in England. It may be that a second wave of emigration across the North Sea was forced by the effects of the massive eruptions in the Sunda Straits.

If the British kingdoms were badly weakened and vulnerable to attack at the same time as more Germanic settlers were arriving, then a momentum would have built. In any event, a Saxon army triumphed at Deorham, modern Dyrrham in south Gloucestershire, near Bath. They had penetrated a long way west, effectively ending Gildas' period of 'our present security', having taken over territory in the Thames Valley. Three native kings were killed at Deorham and, soon afterwards, the Roman towns of Cirencester, Gloucester and Bath fell to the Saxons and their rich farming hinterland of large villa-estates fell with them. It was a turning point. The Saxons had reached the Severn Sea. Some time later, around 610, a holy man known as Beuno was walking on what is now the Welsh bank of the River Severn when he

---

Wansdyke

Southern England is criss-crossed by a complex pattern of ancient boundaries and almost all are ditch-and-bank earthworks. In Hampshire, an impressive ditch encloses an area of sixteen square miles, most of it lush farmland. There are shorter boundaries in Berkshire and Oxfordshire but the most spectacular was the Wansdyke. Named by the invading Saxons after their god, Woden, the frontier runs from Maes Knoll in Somerset eastwards for fifty miles to the Savernake Forest near Marlborough in Wiltshire. It was undoubtedly intended to mark a political divide between the retreating Britons of the kingdom of Dumnonia and the Saxon victors of the Battle of Dyrrham in 577. The Wansdyke seems to have been revetted with wooden beams or stone. Patrolled in places, it had clear crossing points. There is recent evidence to suggest that it extended westwards from Maes Knoll to the Severn shore. The Easter Wansdyke is, surprisingly, better preserved and in places still very impressive, the bank rising to four metres in height. Even though it was breached by Saxon incursions in the seventh century, the line of the Wansdyke divides modern southern England from the Celtic West Country.

heard a voice carrying over the water from the opposite side. It looked as though a man was calling his dogs but the saint did not understand what he was saying. At that moment Beuno knew that the hated Sais had conquered the south. 'Listen,' he said to a companion, 'I hear the Heathens coming.'

In the north, there was less drama and less clarity. Three sources do, however, signal an important political shift. Bede noted that, in the year 547, 'Ida began to reign, from whom the Northumbrian royal family trace their origin'. His version accords with the slightly longer and more informative entry in *The Anglo-Saxon Chronicle* for the year 547: 'In this year Ida, from whom originally sprang the royal race of the Northumbrians, succeeded to the kingdom and reigned twelve years. He built Bamburgh, which was first enclosed by a stockade and thereafter by a rampart.'

And finally, in the *Historia Brittonum*, an important detail is added: 'Ida, the son of Eoppa, possessed countries north of the Humbrian Sea and reigned twelve years, and he joined Din Guairoy to Bernicia.'

The emergence of Ida and his dynasty of Northumbrian kings is of great significance for the history of southern Scotland. Din Guairoy is the Old Welsh name for what is now the mighty fortress of Bamburgh Castle. A singular but broad rocky outcrop on the otherwise flat and sandy coast of Northumberland, it was naturally defensible and a place of strength long before Ida looked out from its ramparts. Below them lies a gently sloping beach that is perfect for hauling up boats beyond the high tide line and, from their stockade, lookouts had wide views up and down the coast. The rock had made an imposing *dun* for native potentates before the middle of the sixth century.

Din Guairoy is not the only Celtic name in the passages above. Bernicia or Bernaccia or Berneich is a wholly Old Welsh place-name and the wording used in the entry in the *Historia Brittonum* probably reflects a now dimly understood political reality. Some scholars believe that Bamburgh was originally a base for Anglian pirates and that, before Ida made himself a king, it had expanded to the landward areas as immigrants arrived from Angeln or from other parts of eastern Britain. It looks very much as though an Anglian military elite seized power in the native British kingdom of Bernaccia and established themselves as kings. Perhaps as few as scores of warriors were involved. But that is not to say that a native aristocracy was entirely effaced. In fact, the subsequent tremendous success of the Northumbrians and their hegemony over all Britain in the seventh century probably owed much to the involvement of British warriors and a political accommodation which left the new united kingdom of Bernicia relatively undamaged by war.

Archaeology supports this sense of takeover by a small group. In the 1950s and early '60s, Brian Hope Taylor dug the fascinating royal site of Yeavering as well as elsewhere in Northumberland and could find little trace of Ida and his immediate descendants. He made a comment which dated him and the Anglians as well: 'One au-pair girl would have made and broken in a week all the Anglo-Saxon pottery in Bernicia before and during the reign of Edwin [616 to 633].'

The name of Bernicia offers some sense of its location – and of its relevance here. The root of *berneich* means something like 'the gap people' or, more loosely, 'the people of the valley'. The area of the lower Tweed Basin is sometimes still called 'The Merse' and it may be an echo of Berneich. In Scots, a *merse* was a fertile area of ground to be found between hills, in this case the Lammermuirs to the north and the Cheviots to the south. The modern Anglo-Scottish border can seriously distort our view but the merse of Tweed includes much fertile farmland now lying in England. To join Din Guairoy or Bamburgh to such a rich area made a powerful kingdom and the name of Bernicia soon reached southwards.

Place names are important indicators of language survival. Rarely securely datable, they nevertheless usefully show processes rather than events and the survival of Old Welsh in the kingdom of Bernicia and its successors tends to support the notion of a British population under Anglian leadership. In his magisterial *Celtic Place Names of Scotland*, W.J. Watson counted forty-two native names on the map of modern Berwickshire and fifty-two in Roxburghshire.

If Bernicia should properly be seen as a unique Celtic-Anglian fusion, then the ambitions of its later kings can be interpreted as harking back to another past. Rome still cast a mighty shadow, and in the energetic and charismatic dynasty founded by Ida and imperial ambition quickly began to smoulder. But before that could ever catch fire, the native kingdoms of north Britain had to be confronted. They were powerful and none more so than Rheged and its greatest king, and his heir, the Son of Prophecy.

Emerging into the historical half-light towards the end of the sixth century, Rheged no doubt waxed and waned. Kingdoms were defined by the effective reach of powerful rulers and the web of loyalties and obligations they and their war bands could sustain. It may be that at its zenith Rheged stretched as far west in Galloway as was possible, all the way to Dunragit, formerly Dun-Rheged, near modern Stranraer, and hinging on Carlisle, down as far south as Rochdale. It was known as Recedham in the Domesday Book. Other sources hail a Rheged king as Lord of Catterick and perhaps for a time his power penetrated the Pennines, the spine of northern England. The name of the kingdom itself probably meant something unhelpful like 'the Kingdom'.

The earliest dated event to take place in sixth-century Rheged is listed in the *Annales Cambriae* for the year 573. It appears in sections of the annals which scholars believe are fragments of a lost North British Chronicle compiled in the eighth century. They noted a battle at a place called Armetrid, while later references (and there are many) in epic Welsh poetry use the variant of Arderydd. All agree that it was fought near Carlisle, just outside the village once known as Arthuret and now called Longtown. It stands on a bluff of high ground on the eastern bank of the Esk. There the river is broad and fast flowing but it runs over a flat bed of rock and was an ancient fording place, the lowest on the Esk. Travellers and armies moving north or south used it for between Arthuret and the outfall of the river into the Solway stretched the treacherous wastes of the great Solway Moss. Those who did not want to risk the tides and wade any of the three fords across the firth crossed at Arthuret or Arderydd.

Battles were often fought at fording places, where roads converged, where it was convenient. In the summer of 573, two

---

Armes Prydein Fawr

Composed in the ninth or tenth century, 'The Prophecy of Great Britain' recalls the extent of the lands of the Old Welsh-speakers, from the Clyde to Brittany, and predicts that the Saxons will be driven into the sea. Allied to the Vikings, the Cymry will rule in London once more. Here are some extracts:

> *From Alt Clut will come reckless men*
> *To drive the Saxons out of Prydein;*
> *From Brittany a mighty army*
> *Warlike warriors who spare not their foes.*
> *On every side Saxons will fall,*
> *Their day ended, their stolen lands foresworn.*
> *Death, brought hither on warriors' blades,*
> *Will pay for the thieving courtiers.*
> *May a hedge be their only haven,*
> *May the sea be their counsel,*
> *And may blood be their companion.*
> *Cynan and Cadwaladr, leaders of the war band,*
> *Will be praised forever, praise be theirs.*
> *Powerful lords, prudent in council,*
> *Crushing the Saxons in the sight of God . . .*
>
> *From Manau to Brittany our lands will stretch;*
> *From Dyfed to Thanet will be ours,*
> *From the Wall to Gweryd, right to the sea*
> *Our sway over Rheged,*
> *The Saxons won't return.*

---

armies faced each other on an area of undulating fields south of the modern village. Overlooked by the parish church and what may have been a place sacred to pagans – there is an ancient holy well nearby – the war bands of Gwenddolau ap Ceidio and his allies mustered. Almost certainly King of Carlisle, Gwenddolau, was a pagan – in all senses, a country and not a city dweller – and not far from the battlefield stood his glowering fortress. Near Carwinley, the modern rendition of Caer Gwenddolau, is a spectacular mound, raised high on a river cliff above the Esk. Known as Liddell Strength, it became a motte-and-bailey castle in the early medieval period, first on record in 1174. But the massive earthwork, much eroded into the river far below, whispers of much earlier origins.

When Gwenddolau and his warriors rode to the fords at Arderydd, they will have passed by the ruins of former glory. Less than a mile to the south of Liddell Strength stood the Roman fort at Netherby. Known as Castra Exploratorum, 'the Fort of the Scouts', it was built at the same time as Hadrian's Wall, in the period after 122. The early garrisons were large. Manned by a cohort of part-mounted Spaniards a thousand strong, the garrisons' role along the troubled frontier of the times was as a base forward of the great wall which collected intelligence and could send out sorties in some strength. After the death of Septimius Severus at York in 212, the fort's function was probably scaled back to scouting and the monitoring of any significant movement of native war bands and that required many fewer men. But the Castra Exploratorum was a substantial stamp of Roman power. Many units from all across the empire passed through its gates and dedications to both Celtic and Germanic war gods on soldiers' thanksgiving altars have been unearthed. There was a small civilian settlement beyond the walls.

As a pagan, a worshipper of more than one god, Gwenddolau may have recognised some of the deities such as Belatucadros and Cocidius. Nearby, the other Hadrianic outpost fort in the west at Bewcastle was known as Fanum Cocidi, 'the Shrine of Cocidius'. The nature of these gods and the details of the ceremonies surrounding their worship were never written down and are lost. But one rider in Gwenddolau's retinue will have understood for he held a vast store of religious knowledge in a prodigious memory. Myrddin was a druid, perhaps one of the last of his kind, and an aristocrat who wore a gold torc around his neck. All the sources say that he fought at Arderydd.

When Gwenddolau and his war band passed the old Roman fort in 573, it will still have been impressive. The gateway towers will perhaps have tumbled and, even though there were no large settlements at hand, stone from the ramparts will here and there have been robbed out where it was easy to remove. Few who lived in southern Scotland and northern England could be unaware of Rome, its reach and the stories of its former power. Many saw its relics every day.

On their way to Arderydd in the summer of 573, another band of warriors remembered the empire when they passed through Hadrian's Wall, probably through the massive gates of one of the large forts. Roads led to the likes of Birrens or, more likely, Castlesteads, old Camboglanna. At the head of their war bands, where their standards fluttered, rode the kings of Ebrauc. Shadowy figures, they ruled at the place Nennius called Caer Ebrauc, Roman Eboracum, modern York. And they ruled against a background of some splendour. Under York Minster lie the collapsed drums of a massive column. It helped hold up the roof of the basilica of the army headquarters building at the centre of the fort. A vast and impressive complex of buildings, it housed army command north, provided the quarters of several emperors campaigning in Britain and was a centre of power for centuries. The multangular tower at one corner of the fort stills stands close to its original height and the archaeologists who examined the collapsed column have found evidence that the buildings remained 'standing in good repair' until the ninth century and probably beyond.

In 573, more than 150 years after the last legionaries were stationed at York, two native kings and their war band occupied the old principia, its echoing basilica and the galleried courtyard beyond it. Towering like a cathedral, the huge hall had a tribunal at one end, a podium where commanders – and indeed emperors – stood to address officers. There were rows of eight columns on each side and the internal height of the building was more than 23 metres, only seven less than that of York Minster. No other structure remotely like it will have been seen for many miles, perhaps not in all Britain. The York kings borrowed the grandeur of Rome and gained authority thereby.

Peredur ap Elifer and his brother Gwrgi had ridden out of the *principia* and taken the roads to the north-west to wage war. They were Christian kings and may have controlled not only Ebrauc but also its hinterland. This was Deifr, 'the Land of Rivers', the fertile East Riding of Yorkshire and later the dynamic Anglian kingdom of Deira.

Conquest rather than conversion is likely to have supplied a motive for the strike across the Pennines and into Cumbria. What mattered to powerful rulers, whether native or Anglo-Saxon, was power. Despite Gildas' railings, British kings rarely made common cause against the Germanic invaders and, if it suited their purpose, Germanic kings would – and did – make alliances with natives. Not until much later was there any sense of a cultural or racial struggle for Britain between clearly defined enemies. In the ninth century, when the enclave of Wales was all that remained, a prophecy called the *Armes Prydein Fawr* exhorted the Welsh to ally with the Danes, the Irish and the Scots to drive the Anglo-Saxons back into the sea. There was a deep sense of loss, that Lloegr, the lost lands of England, had been submerged by the Saxons, a people 'so lacking in lineage'. And the later myth-history of Arthur the king fighting against the tide of barbarism threatening to engulf Britain has added much to that sense of a national war. In reality there was no Britain, only British kingdoms. And they often fought each other. That was why King Peredur and King Gwrgi and their warriors saddled their ponies and rode out of the citadel at York.

The outcome of the battle they fought at Arderydd is re-membered only in the uncertainties and conventions of later

The Thirteen Treasures of Britain

The very early Welsh epic, Preiddeu Annwfn *(The Spoils of Annwfn),*
was composed some time before the ninth century, possibly as early as the
seventh century. It tells the story of a raid to the Otherworld led by the hero,
Arthur, to steal a magic cauldron. This features in a list of the Thirteen
Treasures of Britain gathered by Myrddin or Merlin and kept safe on the
island of Bardsey off the Welsh coast. It is not a list of obvious treasures,
gemstones, silver and gold, but a collection of everyday objects with magical
properties. The Thirteen Treasures appear in many Arthurian myths and
what is striking are the clear northern origins of several:

1. Dyrnwyn *('White Hilt') – the sword of Rhydderch Hael, king of*
   Strathclyde, which burst into flame when one of the Well-Born drew it.

2. The Basket of Gwyddno Garanhir *(Gwyddno with the Crane's*
   Legs) – if food for one man was put in the basket, food for a hundred
   could be taken out.

3. The Horn of Bran, the Miser from the North – *whatever drink*
   most desired would be provided.

4. The Chariot of Morgan the Wealthy – *the driver had only to think*
   of where he wanted to go and the chariot would take him there speedily.

5. The Halter of Clydno Eiddyn *(Clydno of Edinburgh) – if a sleeper*
   tied it to the end of his bed, he would awake to find the horse he most
   desired in the halter.

6. The Knife of Llawfodedd the Rider – *it could serve twenty-four*
   men at one sitting.

7. The Cauldron of Diwrnach the Giant – *if you placed meat in it to*
   boil for a coward, it would never boil but, if you put meat for a brave man
   in it, the meat would boil quickly.

8. The Whetstone of Tydwal Tudglyd – *if a brave man sharpened his*
   sword on it, then the next stroke of his blade would kill a man but, if a

coward did so, his opponent would not suffer harm. (Tydwal appears in the Alt Clut genealogies.)

9. The Coat of Padarn Red-Coat – *if one of the Well-Born put it on, it would fit him but, if a common man did so, it would not fit. (This is a tantalising reference to one of Theodosius' prefects, Paternus Pesrut, who was set in authority over the southern Gododdin after the Barbarian Conspiracy in 367.)*

10–11. The Vat and Dish of Rhygenydd the Cleric – *these provided the food and drink most wished for.*

12. The Chessboard of Gwenddolau ap Ceidio – *the pieces played by themselves and they were made of silver and the board of gold. (Another historical figure – the loser at the Battle of Arderydd.)*

13. The Mantle of Arthur in Cornwall – *whoever wore it was invisible but the wearer could see everyone.*

bardic poetry, recensions of what was no doubt held in memory after 573. But it is clear that there was a great slaughter – perhaps 300 men died. One was Gwenddolau and it appears that the kings of Ebrauc added Carlisle, another half-ruined Roman city, to their domain. Such was the killing in the fields at Arderydd that Myrddin the druid was driven insane. Having cut down his own Christian nephew in the furious chaos of the fighting Myrddin, covered in his blood, fled into the wastes of the great wood of Celyddon. There, in the hills above the Ettrick, Yarrow and Tweed Valleys, he lived a fugitive life, tormented by his dreams. And he kept his weapons by him:

> I slept alone in the Woods of Celyddon
> Shield on shoulder, sword on thigh.

Most of all the old druid feared the vengeance of the king of Strathclyde, Rhydderch Hael. He had married Myrddin's sister and it was their son who was killed at Arderydd. Amongst the bardic devices and repetitions, these bleak stories contain glimpses of real historical personalities and they also follow traditions which were genuinely old – much older than the period when they were written down. It may well be that Myrddin, redrawn as Merlin in the twelfth century by Geoffrey of Monmouth and later united with King Arthur, was indeed one of the last of the druids and a scion of one of the few native courts to cling to paganism.

Peredur and Gwrgi's gore-spattered triumph at Arderydd was short-lived. In battle with the Bernicians, whose territory lay to the north of Ebrauc and Deifr, they were defeated and killed. Much weakened, their kingdom began to fray at the edges. A year after the brothers' death, Aella led his Angles in victory. Deifr fell under his control and became Deira. In 616 or 617, Aella's son, Edwin, took the citadel at York and the native kingdom of Ebrauc disappeared into the mists of history as the great basilica became the focus of a new royal power.

King Arthur in Merrie Carlisle

Cornwall, the West Country, South Cadbury and Glastonbury are the locations most closely linked with the legends of the mighty King Arthur but this was not always so. As the romance began to swirl after the publication of The History of the Kings of Britain *(which distilled much of the existing myth-history about Arthur) in the twelfth century, many writers chose an entirely different location. Throughout Europe and Britain Carlisle became famous as the home of Arthur, of Camelot. Sir Thomas Malory's* Le Morte D'Arthur *used Carlisle for many well-known episodes – Lancelot fighting his way out of Guinevere's bedchamber, his rescue of the queen from the stake and the ultimate reconciliation of Arthur and the errant Guinevere. Carlisle is also the surprising setting for many of the great French Arthurian romances. Why? Was there a shred of real history still attached to the tales of chivalry, round tables and damsels? Did some memory of Arthur as a northern figure in the Dark Ages still linger? Perhaps.*

The expansion and successes of the new Angle kingdoms of the east were answered by the emergence of a new name in the west – a king whose mystery and glory would outlive him in the praise poems of his bards. Urien, king of Rheged, turned out to be the eventual beneficiary of the slaughter at Arderydd. His name is derived from *urbgen* which means 'born in the city', almost certainly Carlisle. The old Roman city was the focus and hinge of Rheged, its walls, streets and civic buildings conferring the same sort of borrowed authority once enjoyed by the York kings. Hailed as Lord of Luguvalium, Master of the Forest of Luel and Lord of the Cultivated Plain, all references to Carlisle and its hinterland, Urien also established himself over a much wider territory.

Archaeologists have found evidence of late sixth-century occupation at three royal fortresses in Galloway – at Trusty's Hill near Gatehouse of Fleet, Tynron Doon in Dumfriesshire and Mote of Mark near Rockcliffe. All the sites show traces of trade with the Mediterranean in luxury goods, the sort of thing needed by powerful men to use as gifts to back their authority and to create the sense of conspicuous wealth, of continuing success. Although Rheged certainly developed out of the western territories of the Novantae, no bard mentioned Rerigonium, 'the Very Royal Place', Cairnryan or any fortress in that part of the kingdom, aside from whatever citadel gave Dunragit its name. All of which points to a ruler with his roots and base in Carlisle. With those of the Novantae, the lands of the Anavionenses and the Carvetii formed the three major regions of Rheged.

Amidst all the uncertainties and assumptions there is an unmistakable atmosphere of real power and a hunger for glory swirling around the mighty figure of Urien. No other native king of his era, or for many generations to come, could match his fame. Not only did he sit in high authority in the halls of Carlisle, he was a Christian king, one of Y Bedydd, 'the Baptised'. But he was also a Celtic warlord who rewarded his *teulu* with gifts of horses, gold, precious objects, weapons, armour, privileges. Like all great men, Urien needed others to record his deeds and broadcast his fame and, through their words, preserve it for posterity. He was fortunate to hear Taliesin, one of the greatest of bards to sing in Welsh, compose poetry to immortalise him:

> Urien of Echwyd, most liberal of Christian men,
> Much do you give to men in this world,
> As you gather, so you dispense,
> Happy the Christian bards, so long as you live,
> Sovereign supreme, ruler all highest,
> The stranger's refuge, strong champion in battle,
> This the English know when they tell tales.
> Death was theirs, rage and grief are theirs,
> Burnt are their homes, bare are their bodies.
>
> Till I am old and failing,
> In the grim doom of death,
> I shall have no delight,
> If my lips praise not Urien.

Although Taliesin paints Urien as the scourge of the English, the great king also campaigned to the north of Rheged, fighting native kings in Manau, Gododdin and Aeron (modern Ayrshire). In the 590s, the war bands of Urien began to confront the other major power in the north, the Bernicians. One of Ida's successors, Aethelric, was said to have led four expeditions across the Pennines into Rheged and no doubt there were native British warriors at his back. But at a place called Argoed Llwyfein, the Baptised at last defeated the forces of the heathens, 'the Gentiles', Y Gynt. Urien fought in the front rank beside his famous son on that glorious morning. Owain ap Urien grew to become as well known as his father in later Old Welsh myth-history.

As the Saxons in the south and the Angles in the north overran native British kingdoms in the seventh and eighth centuries, bards used their imaginations to hold evil at bay, keep the past alive and encourage belief in a resurgent future. Welsh-speaking kings would rule once more in London and the hated *Sais* would be expelled. With the Armes Prydein, another messianic tradition took root and grew strong. There would be 'a Redeemer', sang the bards – Y Mab Darogan would emerge to lead the Welsh in triumph back into Lloegr and reclaim the lost lands of their forefathers. The Sons of Prophecy would win victory after victory, drive the Sais to the coasts, the cliffs and into the depths of the cleansing sea. For almost a thousand years, people gathered in churchyards and on hillsides to hear prophecy, the tales of the great Welsh heroes and battles of the glorious past and how Y Mab Darogan would return and triumph.

There were eight Mabyon Darogan, eight sons of Wales and the lost dominions of Old Welsh-speaking kings, who would rise up and lead their people. Owain of Rheged was one and also Hiriell, Cynan, Cadwaladr and Arthur from the mists of post-Roman Britain. Much later Owain Lawgoch, 'Owain of the Red Hand', was added. A mercenary captain in the Hundred Years' War, he seems an unlikely addition to the ancient list. But it seems that he was the last direct male descendant of Llewyllyn the Great, the last Prince of Wales, and he led his men in the service of the French kings and fought against the English. That he was hailed as a Son of Prophesy is thought to have contributed to his death. The English had him assassinated. Owain Glyn Dwr and King Henry Tudor were the last names to be added.

When Owain and Urien led the charge of the Rheged war bands at Argoed Llwyfein, they drove back and destroyed the armies of an Angle king they called Fflamddwyn. He was Theodoric, another heir of Ida, and his name meant 'Firebrand'. The battle took place in the Lyvennet Valley in the fells above the Eden, not far from Appleby. It is a windy and lonely place with a few farmhouses and the bleat of ewes on the bleak hillsides. But, in the 590s, a now-invisible Roman road passed through it and was still in use. It connected Ribchester, the Lancashire forts and Chester with Carlisle. Only five miles to the east ran the road which cut through the Pennines from what is now Scotch Corner. Warring armies often clashed near these old arteries and they used them for centuries as the conduits of long-range strikes against enemies.

After the defeat of Fflamddwyn, Urien was determined to press home an advantage. In an unusually clear passage in the *Historia Brittonum*, Nennius begins with mention of another scion of Ida's house:

> Hussa reigned seven years. Four kings fought against him, Urien and Riderch Hen ['Riderch the old'], and Guallac and Morcant. Theodoric fought bravely against the famous Urien and his sons. During that time, sometimes the enemy, sometimes our country-men were victorious, and Urien blockaded them for three days on the island of Metcaud.

Riderch (or Rhydderch) Hen was also known as Riderch Hael, 'Riderch the Generous'. He was the Strathclyde king who was much feared by Myrddin and it seems that he rode south with his warriors to join Urien in a grand coalition. Gildas would have approved. Guallac was one of the last native kings to rule in Yorkshire. Elmet, who may have been a remnant of Ebrauc, and Guallac's son, Ceretic, was toppled when the Angles swept to power in 616 or 617. Guallac's doomed kingdom has surprisingly survived in modern place-names and his principal fortress may have stood at Barwick-in-Elmet, east of Leeds, where substantial defensive earthworks can still be seen. Morcant, sometimes Morcant Bulc, is the most mysterious of the allied kings – and also potentially the most interesting.

The most learned scholar in the historiography of Britain between 400 and 700, what still might usefully be called the Dark Ages, was John Morris. With a humbling and dazzling grasp of texts in Old Welsh, Irish Gaelic, Latin and Anglo-Saxon, he wrote a controversial book, *The Age of Arthur*. Morris' academic contemporaries attacked it and the author with uncommon savagery – even for the tetchy, jealous world of academic scholarship. Not only did they object strongly to his use of the name of Arthur in the title and all the mystical, new-age baggage that came with it (to say nothing of naked commercialism – the very idea!), they also believed that Morris was much too trusting of his sources, too credulous. After a lifetime of hard work, delving where few other researchers had bothered to look, it must have been hard to bear.

The central difficulty for sources for this period was, as ever, the reliability of material caught up in the rhyme and metre of bardic poetry or stuck in the webs of complex and semi-mythical genealogies. Almost all compiled centuries after the events they describe, these sources were and are thought to be without much value. Where most scholars place their trust is in written sources, preferably contemporary with or close to events, and in archaeology and its tangible, concrete results. Forensic, even scientific, most historians feel they must approach their period or their 'field' with clear-eyed objectivity and take nothing at face value.

The *reductio ad absurdum* is to suspect everything and believe nothing, not even beyond a reasonable doubt. Much that has been generally accepted for generations is now rejected, famous names and traditions cast into an outer darkness of discredit. In order to make their names, new generations of historians, especially those specialising in the Dark Ages, feel compelled to dismiss the work of those of the generation before them. They must make the old new, formulate a 'new' approach, for the reputation and finances of their university department may depend on it.

This sort of approach makes for bleak reading and, in the time between the end of the Roman Empire in Britain and the takeover of England and part of Scotland by the Anglo-Saxons, almost no reading at all. Many of the iconoclasts, the re-interpreters, have cast doubts without the benefit of John Morris' skills. Some current historians of Scotland, for example, feel comfortable in pronouncing and condemning without knowing a word of Gaelic or Old Welsh. Morris understood the essence of this period better than any other historian because he could hear its distant voices, sense its cultural nuances and feel passion for its great events. This was the time Britain was unmade, when

---

What Have the Romans Ever Done?

There are few more distinguished historians of Wales than John Davies and his excellent one-volume history has no peers. Generously, he lists the influences of Latin on Welsh – these are fascinating, showing the difference between a literate and non-literate society – and the number of Roman names which have become common in Wales (Emrys from Ambrosius, Tegid from Tacitusand, Iestyn from Justinus are only the most relevant here). But his critique on the empire is devastatingly eloquent:

> *The demise of the Roman Empire has been mourned to excess. Its essence was violence and its accomplishments were fundamentally second-rate. Its achievements in the world of science and technology were few; what need was there for new inventions in a society which had an abundance of slaves. Its literature and fine arts were a pale reflection of the splendours of classical Athens. As Mortimer Wheeler, among the most distinguished of the interpreters of the Empire, put it: 'I suffered from a surfeit of things Roman. I felt disgusted by the mechanistic quality of their art and by the nearness of their civilisation at all times to cruelty and corruption.'*

But nevertheless raw political and military power can be dazzling.

Scotland, England and Wales emerged, when their languages settled and when the word of God was everywhere heard. Morris' great text may need, on occasion, to be treated with caution but his achievement as a historian is immense.

He refused to reject the work of the bards out of hand because he grasped the importance of their role in a non-literate society. They were historians, propagandists as well as poets in the modern sense. They recited the genealogies as political texts, as underpinnings to authority. But they wrote nothing down. Why should what was held in memory be more unreliable than a written source? Both sorts of record have survived by accidental process and the whole picture for the period must be patchy. Morris argued that it made sense to take everything into account in compiling the jigsaw of early British history. Many pieces were missing and there would of course be blanks no amount of conjecture could fill. But surely what men believed, the stories they told themselves through their bards and genealogists, was as important as what a very few, self-selecting commentators reported, at second, third or fourth hand, that they did.

If taken in this spirit, *The Age of Arthur* is like an Aladdin's cave of glittering treasures, some of fool's gold or paste, but there are real nuggets to be found, especially in the vast appendices or where the footnotes and references direct the curious.

One of these nuggets is the story of Germanianus. Old Welsh-speaking bards knew of him and the genealogies reckoned him a 'son of Coel Hen', 'Old Cole', probably the last imperial general appointed by Rome in the north. Roughly contemporary with Cunedda, in the first half of the fifth century, Germanianus was the commander of a war band who preferred to adopt a Roman title. Like Claudius Britannicus or Commodus Britannicus and other emperors eager for an association with a conquest or military victory, this man celebrated his defeat of Germanic warriors. It may be that he led his men against raiders who had landed on the North Sea coast or come up from the south. In any event Germanianus is closely associated with the kings of the Votadini, the kindred which later morphed into the Gododdin. The king lists place him in the lineage of Morcant Bwlc, perhaps at a distance of five generations. But where did these men hold power?

Quoting bardic sources, John Morris made an uncharacteristic blunder. He believed that Catraut or Cadrawd of Calchvynydd's kingdom lay to the south of Powys on the mid-Wales borders. Evidently it was vigorous with an active war band but Morris insists that its men fought the Saxons in the English Midlands. In the great death songs for *The Gododdin*, composed around 600 by Aneirin in Edinburgh, the author sang of a prince, a sub-king, known as Catraut of Calchvynydd. He joined the royal war band as it rode south out of Edinburgh to Catterick in Yorkshire and battle with an Anglian host. Calchvynydd is the original Old Welsh name for Kelso and monastic records of the twelfth century still call it Calchou or Calco. One of the streets in the modern town preserves the old name in Scots in Chalkheugh Terrace. Calchvynydd, or Kelso, means 'Chalky Hill' and it was the focus of a shadowy sixth-century kingdom.

Morcant Bwlc was the heir of Germanianus and the ancestor of Catraut – and the ruler of a kingdom based on Kelso and perhaps the great fortress at Marchidun across the Tweed. When he joined Urien's coalition at the siege of Metcaud, Lindisfarne, he had the most immediately to gain and the most to lose. Calchvynydd lay on the borders of Bernicia and the attack on the island was a critical political moment.

The British kindreds knew Lindisfarne as Metcaud because of the herbs which grew in profusion in this beautiful, windswept place. They were famously medicinal and toponymists believe that the island was known as Medicata Insula, hence Metcaud. Only an island twice a day when the tides ripple over the broad sands between it and the mainland, it is a unique, atmospheric place which would become much beloved by Cuthbert, Aidan and countless generations of monks in love with the contemplative life and the isolated peace that the tides gave them.

Theodoric, Fflamddwyn the Firebrand, was likely the Anglian king besieged by Urien, Morcant and their allies. He valued Lindisfarne for its stunning, singular rock at the east end and the beach lying below it. Now the site of a romantic castle ingeniously designed by Sir Edward Lutyens, a building which seems both to cling to and grow out of the rock it sits on, it was no doubt seen by Theodoric as an impregnable stockade which would repel the armies of the British as they massed on the mainland shore. Islanders still know that the fairy castle of the nineteenth century stands on Bebloe's Rock, named after an Anglian queen, Bebba. From the ramparts of the sixth-century stockade, those who looked out over the sea to the south could see another fortress named after her. Bamburgh was 'Bebba's burh', the queen's stronghold. And on the southern horizon Theodoric could see that it had fallen to a furious assault. Perhaps smoke plumed above the stockade.

The Irish chroniclers wrote of Fiachna, a king in Ulster who joined Urien's coalition. He reigned after 589 and was in Britannia in the 590s with his warriors. No matter that a wooden palisade and ditching below it was all that defended Bamburgh, the rock was sheer in places and archaeologists have recently discovered that the only weak point, the gate at the northern end, was well defended with a double rampart. But Fiachna's men burst in, took hostages and then almost certainly hurried north around the sand flats of Budle Bay to take part in the siege of the island.

What made both Bamburgh and Lindisfarne excellent bases for the Angles was the accident of geography which put a high and defensible rock next to a shoreline good for beaching ships and dragging the keels above the high-tide line. Both fortresses also acted as clear seamarks visible from long distance in good weather. And, on an otherwise flat and sandy coast, the value of this combination was much enhanced. Below Bebloe's Rock there were beaches close at hand and when the British camped at the mouth of the River Low opposite the island, Theodoric and his desperate defenders will have seen their ships as the only means of escape. This time the Germanic invaders would be driven into the sea.

Morcant Bwlc understood the significance of the moment and that he and the British kings stood at the hinge of history, certainly in the north. The *Sais* might have overrun Gloucester, Bath, Cirencester and the other cities of the Roman south but the Gwyr Y Gogledd, 'the Men of the North', would not suffer the same fate. But Morcant also knew that the victor in this struggle would quickly grow more powerful – the High Kingship of the North, perhaps of all Britain, waited. And Urien, not Morcant, would be hailed by the bards and acclaimed by his allies as the victor. Here is the conclusion of the entry in the *Historia Brittonum*: 'But while he was on the expedition, Urien was assassinated, on the initiative of Morcant, from jealousy, because his military skill and generalship surpassed that of all the other kings.' And perhaps because Morcant had been made other promises. Native British warriors, Bernician aristocrats, may have stood defiantly on the ramparts of Bebloe's Rock with Theodoric. These men would have been known to Morcant and perhaps there were ties of blood for his kingdom on the Tweed was close by. And then there was Fiachna and the Irish war band. They had taken Bamburgh and Urien had allowed them to keep it even though the fortress and its hinterland should have naturally been joined to Morcant's domain. Perhaps it was indeed jealousy that drove home the assassin's dagger – ruthless politics and nothing to do with generalship.

When Urien was murdered, the coalition broke apart, the British kings and their war bands saddled their ponies and rode into the west. And the history of Britain and Scotland shifted decisively. The war between Rheged and Bernicia did not end with the treachery amongst the sand dunes of Northumberland, but there were no more reports of battles in the east. Bamburgh was retaken but Theodoric met the war band of Rheged again, for the last time.

Somewhere in the north, the bards offer no clues in their wonderful paeans, the Angle king was cut down in the charge of the Rheged cavalry:

> When Owain slew Fflamddwyn,
> It was no more than sleeping.
> Sleeps now the wide host of England,
> With the light upon their eyes,
> And those who fled not far,
> Were braver than was need . . .
> Splendid he was, in his many coloured armour,
> Horses he gave to all who asked,
> Gathering wealth like a miser,
> Freely he shared it for his soul's sake,
> The soul of Owain, son of Urien,
> May the Lord look upon its need.

Taliesin's celebration of the defeat of Theodoric is also the death song for Owain and, after that, there were no more victories for native kings in the north. The bards mourned internecine warfare, much informed by hindsight, and they whispered that Rheged was brought low by its neighbours as much as the Angles in the east. Gildas' dire warnings on disunity were coming to pass. There is much poetic convention in what follows but there is little doubt that the deaths of Owain and his brother, Elfyn, and the decline of Rheged fatally weakened the native hold on the north:

> This hearth, wild flowers cover it.
> When Owain and Elfyn lived,
> Plunder boiled in its cauldron . . .

> This hearth, tall brambles cover it.
> Easy were its ways.
> Rheged was used to giving.

> This hearth, dock leaves cover it.
> More usual upon its floor,
> Mead, and the claims of men who drank . . .

> This pillar and that pillar there.
> More usual around it,
> Shouts of victory, and giving of gifts.

Carlisle's halls did not fall to the Angles immediately. It is much more likely that Urien and Owain's authority fractured and its pieces were squabbled over by rival native factions. The house of Urien did not fall extinct for his son, Rhun, was still alive in the 620s. He took a crucial role in later developments but his calling as a monk may have disqualified him from kingship.

The pace of political change accelerated after the siege of Metcaud and whatever power remained with the royal house of Rheged was soon to be overtaken by events. The hegemony of the north passed to the Gododdin kings in Edinburgh but their time in the front rank was brief. Aneirin composed the great poem which bears their name, the earliest example of sustained literature to survive in Britain:

> The men went to Catraeth,
> Shouting for battle,
> A squadron of horse.
>
> Blue their armour and their shields,
> Lances uplifted and sharp,
> Mail and sword glinting . . .
>
> Though they were slain, they slew.
> None to his home returned . . .
>
> Short their lives,
> Long the grief
> Among their kin.
>
> Seven times their number,
> The English they slew,
> Many the women they widowed,
> Many the mothers who wept . . .
>
> After the wine and after the mead,
> They left us, armoured in mail.
> I know the sorrow of their death.
>
> They were slain, they never grew grey . . .
> From the army of the mountain court, grief unbounded,
> Of three hundred men, but one returned.

In other recensions of the great epic of *The Gododdin*, the composer, Aneirin, claims to have been the sole survivor, the bearer of the news of disaster at Catraeth, Catterick. Even though bards would have accompanied war bands as witnesses of their deeds, this is, of course, a poetic convention. Nevertheless the overall truth of the tale is that there had been a terrible slaughter and that the warriors of the kings of Edinburgh and their allies had been utterly defeated.

Bards sang or recited their compositions while using a small harp, known as a *clarsach* in Scots Gaelic and a *crwth* in Old Welsh, to add drama and shape. With its carefully made metrical structure, the poetry had its own music and it drove the narrative using a mixture of devices like alliteration, assonance, repetition and rhyme. Chords on the harp were probably plucked to point

---

Lords of Catraeth

The epic of death songs known as The Gododdin *has been open to many interpretations. Sometimes ambiguous, sometimes opaque, the Old Welsh used to transcribe it had certainly changed since the songs were first composed. The king of the eponymous kindred of the Gododdin is said to have been Mynyddog Mwynvawr but the words could plausibly describe a place as well as a person. Since there is no mention of Mynyddog at the Battle of Catraeth or Catterick – and, if he had been there and been killed, there surely would have been – scholars have preferred to see the name as a reference to the citadel of the Gododdin, Edinburgh's Castle Rock. Mynyddog Mwynvawr could mean something like 'the wealthy mountain court'. It seems likely that Yrfai map Golistan led the host but Gwlyget of Gododdin is also cited. He was the steward of the king – or the wealthy mountain court. Even more complications begin to pile up with the contention that, at Catraeth, the Anglian host was led by a British king, who was none other than Urien of Rheged, and his war band. In a description of an overwhelming victory at Gweith Gwen Ystrat, 'the Battle of the White Valley', Urien is described as Lord of Catraeth. Some scholars have conjectured that the two battles are in fact the same but seen from opposite sides and that Catraeth/Catterick was essentially a conflict between Rheged and Gododdin with the Angles involved as allies. That, in turn, would imply an earlier date than 600 but it is not an impossible interpretation. The underlying value of these contradictory views is that they further break down the easy ethnic division of native British against Germanic invaders by showing a potentially very complex picture – maybe too complex in this case.*

Above. The Catrail, near Galashiels

Left. Callanish, Lewis

The Lochmaben Stane

The upper Solway Firth at low tide

The site of Flanders Moss

Traprain Law, East Lothian

Addinston Fort, the site of the Battle of Degsastan, and probably where Aedan's men corralled their plundered cattle

Burnswark Hill

Dumbarton Rock

The Antonine Wall at Rough Castle

Hadrian's Wall, showing the Whin Sill (left)

Bennachie, the site of Mons Graupius

The Farne Islands, looking towards Bamburgh Castle

Bamburgh Castle

Lindisfarne Castle

Roxburgh Castle

From Roxburgh Castle, looking east

The site of the monastery of Old Melrose (centre)

The Eildon Hills

Bewcastle Church, Cumbria

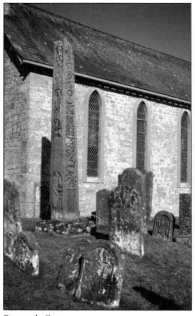

Bewcastle Cross

St Gordian's Cross, Manor Valley

Manor Valley

Stirling Castle

Edinburgh Castle

up climactic moments or punctuate changes in mood, pace, time or place.

Bards needed audiences and most sources set the recitals of eulogies, epics and elegies at a feast. In the circles of rushlight and firelight and the dark shadows beyond, the imaginations of the listeners took flight. Bards could conjure armies, the din of battle, the war cries and screams of dying men, the gore and the glory. War-gear, horses and tack and all the rituals around the *teulu* and its heroes were celebrated and its gorgeous detail dwelt upon.

When Aneirin had composed the horrors of Catraeth into the first version of Y Gododdin, he told a tale of heroism and shattering defeat, a series of baleful death songs for the fallen. Led by Yrfai map Golistan, Lord of Edinburgh, the host clattered out of the fortress on the Castle Rock. Northern allies had mustered – warriors from the kingdom of Rhydderch Hael in Strathclyde (Ystrad Clud) and from Aeron to the west. Unlikely comrades-in-arms for Y Bedydd, heathen Picts had ridden from 'beyond Bannauc', the Bannock Burn. This is the earliest explicit reference to the barrier of Flanders Moss and its function as a boundary between kindreds. Other Picts came to Edinburgh from beyond Merin Iudeu, the Firth of Forth.

After reaching the fortress at Calchvynydd and joining with the war band of Catraut, the growing host rode south, almost certainly down Dere Street. Men sent by the kings of Elmet and Gwynedd met Lord Yrfai and they massed near Cataractonium, the Roman fort which watched over the crossing of the rapids, the cataracts of the River Swale, by Dere Street. As at York and Carlisle, the Roman buildings may have survived more or less intact and Catraeth stood at a pivotal strategic position. Astride Dere Street, the fort also lay near the junction with the Roman road which led west over Stainmore and on to the lands of the Carvetii and Carlisle. Some Gododdin allies, perhaps the war bands of Strathclyde, may have travelled it and joined the host just before the battle. Catraeth was now threatened or possibly even occupied by the war bands of Deira and Bernicia. It was a takeover which would consolidate the Anglian gains east of the Pennines.

Often portrayed in black and white, as a straightforward battle between Celtic Britain and its Germanic invaders, Catraeth was in fact more complex. The Lord of the Celtic host was an Angle. Yrfai map Golistan is a version of 'the Son of Wulfstan', not an aristocrat but a professional soldier. His name betrays his origins. And in the Germanic army, especially if many Bernicians had ridden to Catraeth, there would have been native warriors.

Aneirin's great death song was not an account of the battle, how it ebbed and flowed, what the tactics were, the weapons used and the causes of defeat and victory. His purpose was to tell a tale of tragedy and glory, of valour and sacrifice, and to make a lament for the fall of the Gododdin and their allies. But amongst the adjectives and the metaphors, there are hints of what really took place near the old Roman fort in the summer of AD 600.

When Aneirin counted 300 in the host of the Gododdin king, it likely that he saw only the horsemen, the cavalry warriors. They stood in the front rank, the place of honour, circling their skittish ponies, checking their gear and their tack, eying the Anglian army opposite. They were almost certainly all noblemen or leading members of the war bands of underkings, like Catraut of Calchvynydd, or allied kings, like Rhydderch Hael of Strathclyde and the kings of Elmet and Gwynedd. Standards will have fluttered in the breeze – except for the red dragon of Gwynedd, their devices and totems are all now lost to history. And, as Christians, the Baptised may have also brought relics or icons onto the battlefield, just as Arthur was said to have ridden with the image of the Virgin on his shield at the battle at Guinnion.

Behind the squadron of great men stood their retainers, infantry war bands of varying size, men who owed their lords military service. And while they will have had some training for battle, most were not professional soldiers, not men whose deeds will have prompted verses from a royal bard. They were farmers who carried spears and shields and wore whatever protection they had inherited from their fathers or had been given. Amongst the less experienced the stink of fear will have been pervasive. Before that day few will have stood anxiously in the ranks and waited for battle, some will have been little more than boys and others will have soiled themselves or vomited.

Pictish symbol stones of the seventh century offer some sense of how the armies at Catraeth formed up and faced each other. Albeit stylised in design (and needing to be crammed into the limited sculptural surface of a stone), Sueno's Stone. And the famous depiction of the battle at Dunnichen in 685 set up at Aberlemno show cavalrymen leading ranks of infantry. If each of Aneirin's 300 brought a modest average of ten men to Catraeth, the host led by Lord Yrfai will have numbered close to 3,000. Not a huge army in modern reckoning but undoubtedly vast for the times.

Taken together, the epic of *The Gododdin* and the Aberlemno Stone offer some sense of what happened when 'the Baptised', Y Bedydd, fought 'the Heathens', Y Gent. Like those immortalised in the Great Cattle Raid of Cooley and other ancient Celtic sources, loud and taunting challenges to single combat may have been issued, perhaps even agreed beforehand. Champions may have ridden out to fight in no-man's-land, urged on and cheered or jeered by those standing in the ranks. Or perhaps the rituals harked back to a heroic age, to Calgacus and Mons Graupius. At the beginning of one stanza, *The Gododdin* poem sang of 'a champion in a war chariot'. The outcome of single combat could be important and decisive for morale. Victory for King Robert the Bruce over the English knight, Sir Henry de Bohun, certainly put heart and belief into the smaller Scottish army at Bannockburn in 1314.

Noise was also important. Roman commentators often noted the blaring of war horns, the screaming and taunting, men working themselves into what the Irish epics called the 'rage-fit' and the rattle of spears against shields made by Celtic opponents. Like single combat, it was another tradition which endured. While the Zulu impis clashed their weapons as they ran in on Rorke's Drift in 1879, the defending soldiers are said to have sung hymns.

Once a crescendo of noise was reached at Catraeth and the

war horn sounded a signal note, it is likely that the cavalry charged. This was not the thundering, earth-shaking gallop of heavily armoured medieval knights on their huge destriers but a charge of light cavalry. Riding small ponies, without much in the way of body armour, and wedged into saddles with high pommels and cantles but no stirrups attached, warriors carried a lance, a sword and a small, round parrying shield. Because they could not brace themselves by pushing their feet forward in stirrups, it is unlikely that riders couched their lances like a medieval knight. If they had and had managed to make a solid contact with an enemy, they would probably have been pitched backwards out of the saddle and injured. Lances are more likely to have been used for thrusting, throwing and delivering backward blows in passing. At the foot of the Aberlemno Stone a Pictish cavalryman takes back his arm and prepares to jab his lance at the Anglian riding towards him. The Pict's shield is held high in front of his head and upper body (the pony's head and neck protected him below the chest) as he attempts to deflect the lance about to be thrown by his enemy. In the melee and ruck of battle, the nimbleness and balance of cavalry ponies will often have made the difference between life and death.

Lances usually splintered and it was important to be able to unsheathe a sword quickly. Experienced men greased their scabbards to avoid jamming and to make them faster on the draw. At the top of the Aberlemno Stone, a victorious Pictish cavalryman raises his sword and rides down a fleeing Angle who has thrown away his weapons and shield.

Once the opening cavalry engagement had run its course and if it had not been decisive, foot soldiers formed what Aneirin called 'a alder palisade', a shield wall. Made from wood fitted around a metal handgrip, a boss, shields were often made from alder. It was tough – and magical. In the ancient Irish tree language known as Ogham, alder symbolised resistance. When a rank of foot soldiers were ordered to make a shield wall, they locked their shields together in an overlapping pattern with the edge of one man's touching the boss of the soldier's next to him.

'Rim to Boss' was the call. Standing sideways on, braced and with a spear in his right hand bristling out from the alder palisade, well-drilled men could make a tight and formidable formation.

The Aberlemno Stone shows a shield wall in some detail. Attacked by an Anglian cavalryman, three ranks stand in close order in classic Roman fashion. If they did indeed follow the practice of the legions in battle, as seems likely – given how their kings aspired to Romanitas in so many other ways – the armies of Dark Ages Britain will have stood to in first and second ranks equipped with javelins. On a signal from a war-horn – and carnyxes have a similarly penetrative note to bagpipes – both ranks will have launched a volley of javelins against enemy cavalry or charging foot soldiers. And then the front rank, the *hastati* in Latin, would draw their swords and engage. This appears to be the moment captured by the sculptor of the Aberlemno Stone. A cavalryman lies dead, impaled by a javelin, and the man in the front rank has his sword drawn and raised to strike.

In a variant on Roman tactics, the man behind him in the second rank holds ready a heavy war spear with both hands. He pushes its tip past his comrade but angles it below his shield and sword arm so as not to impede. In a shield wall, experienced men sometimes swung low and hacked at unprotected enemy legs to bring down a man and it appears that the second ranker at Aberlemno is attempting to counter that tactic. Behind him, in the third rank, stands a warrior with his spear held upright – one of the *triarii*, a reserve ready to plug gaps in the front line or rush forward if wide breaches opened in the enemy formation and commanders judged it could be splintered decisively.

When opposing ranks of infantry smashed into each other, momentum was everything. If the men in the leading line of a shield wall could get on the front foot, begin to pump their legs and push hard, shoved on by their comrades behind, then there could be a rapid outcome. When men were forced backwards over rough, tussocky ground, it only took one or two to trip or be beaten down before gaps opened. Men who fell were as good as dead. As the front rank of their enemies trampled over the top of them, the second rank hacked at and butchered men wriggling on the ground, trying to get up before blows rained down on them. Most did not die quickly. Early swords and axes quickly grew blunt on a battlefield and most who went down were bludgeoned into unconsciousness or bled to death. An infantry battle of this era could be little more than a savage, gory scrummage and, when formations broke, rout usually followed. And it seems that at Catraeth, there was the sort of wholesale slaughter associated with the headlong pursuit of a shattered army. In a moment of poignancy, pining for a heroic past and remembering the valour of a great leader, Aneirin sang:

> He struck before the three hundred bravest,
> He would slay both middle and flank,
> He was suited to the forefront of a most generous host,
> He would give gifts from a herd of horses in winter,
> He would feed black ravens on the wall
> Of a fortress, though he were not Arthur.
> Among the strong ones in battle,
> In the van, an alder-palisade was Gwawrddur.

The Aberlemno ranks may have been a self-conscious imitation of Roman models and if warriors did indeed fight in this way in the centuries after the fall of the empire in the west, then some drill will have been needed. Well-organised farmer armies were not always a disordered rabble depending for success on one tactic – the furious charge.

The Gododdin host at Catreath fought for honour, for the extravagant praise of Aneirin in the mead hall and the fame it would bring and for the extraordinary reputation of the sort that clung to the figure of Arthur – by the year 600, his name was a byword for bravery. But they also fought for riches and, while in the Dark Ages gold, treasure and war gear were valued, real riches meant land. After the rout by the River Swale, the Angle kings knew that the great prize of the fertile fields of the realm of the

Gododdin lay defenceless. And they moved quickly to seize them.

Dated 10 July 1910 in the right-hand corner, a fascinating photograph records almost fifteen centuries of continuity on a Borders hillside. Under the high summer sun, more than a hundred sit amongst the bracken, the men wearing straw boaters, the ladies under wide-brimmed hats or white umbrellas and two schoolboys in the foreground staring uncertainly at the photographer. At the centre of the scene is a small white, conical tent shading a minister of the church. The tenth of July 1910 was a Sunday and he appears to be preaching an open-air sermon next to a tall Celtic cross. But this is not a field conventicle, the sort of service sometimes held in southern Scotland to commemorate the Covenanters of the seventeenth century. Instead the minister and his hillside flock remember an ancient Christian saint from the fourth century.

The Celtic cross is new, raised in 1873, but it marks the place once known as 'the sanctuary of St Gordian'. Martyred in Rome in 362 during the murderous reign of the Emperor Julian the Apostate, Gordianus was a magistrate who was so moved by the faith of the saintly priest, Januarius, that he himself converted. Brutally tortured and finally beheaded, Gordianus was buried with another martyr of the time, St Epimachus, and quickly forgotten – except in the Manor Valley, near modern Peebles.

In all probability the sanctuary of St Gordianus was established soon after his death, perhaps as early as the late fourth century, in the decades immediately before the fall of Britannia. Perhaps relics of this obscure Roman had somehow found their way to the Border hills. The stories of men like him could credibly have spread amongst communities of Christians while the empire still held and a garrison on Hadrian's Wall was still in contact with Rome. What supports the notion of a very early church or sanctuary in the Manor Valley was the discovery of the Coninia Stone. Found in a large cairn in 1890 by Robert Anderson, the son of a shepherd at Kirkhope Farm, it was brought down the hillside and placed within the small enclosure where St Gordian's cross had recently been erected. Confirmed as late fifth or early sixth century by the style of its lettering, the Coninia Stone also carried a precisely incised Christian cross. It is one of the earliest tombstones to be found in Scotland for a native, a woman and a member of a church, someone who revered St Gordian. Coninia reads like a Latin version of *cynin*, which in Old Welsh simply meant 'little dog' or 'puppy'. The second line of the inscription, Etriria, was in all probability a local place-name, now lost.

What is very much alive is the reverence for St Gordian. The spiritual descendant of Coninia is Janet Stoddart. At the open-air service in July 1899, she was baptised and given Gordian as a middle name. It may be that the holy water was held in a stone receptacle mistakenly described as 'an ancient font'. Almost certainly not that but a socket for a sculptured cross of the sort set up in many sacred places in Britain in the sixth and seventh centuries and beyond, it is another fragment of a fascinating story. The sanctuary of St Gordian was created and consecrated by an established Christian community, one aware of a much wider world and ready to venerate the memory of a Roman martyr of the fifth century. Perhaps it was the fact that Gordianus had been an imperial magistrate that added lustre to his now-forgotten name – Romanitas by association.

It was also an organised community and something of its nature and structure in southern Scotland in the Dark Ages can be glimpsed in the modern landscape. Manor is a rendition of the Old Welsh term *maenor* and it carries a specific meaning. Eighth-century sources supply a good deal of detail. In the margins of a devotional work called the *Book of St Chad*, compiled in Wales around 740, there is a clear description of a *maenor*, one which fits very precisely what can still be seen on the ground in the Manor Valley. While there survives nothing so detailed as the *Book of St Chad* in southern Scotland, several telling traces of a society organised along very similar lines can be found in the *Yr Hen Ogledd*, 'The Old North'.

Another Jerusalem

The growing power of the papacy certainly borrowed authority from Rome's former imperial glories but it had, from the outset, a central role in the origins of the Christian faith. Beyond the city walls and by the side of the Appian Way, the main road to the south, a warren of catacombs was rediscovered in the sixteenth century. Dating as early as the first century AD, these tunnels contained thousands of notches cut out of the rock where corpses were laid. For a long time, it was believed that the Second Coming was imminent and the dead would rise more easily from the catacombs. Next to the Church of the Catacomb of Basileo*, Rome's most famous Christian legend is believed to have taken place. As St Peter fled from persecution down the Appian Way, he met Christ on the road and asked the famous question* 'Domine, quo vadis?' 'I am going to Rome,' *Christ replied,* 'for a second crucifixion.' *Peter realised what he meant and turned back to the city to suffer his own martyrdom. Early Christians believed that Jerusalem, the site of Christ's death and resurrection, was an earthly gateway to Heaven, where God was close at hand. Rome saw the appearance of Christ and the crucifixion of Peter and had a similarly magnetic attraction for the faithful.*

In essence a *maenor* was an estate run by an official known as a *maer* from the Latin *maior*, more colloquially 'the superior'. The old title still survives in Scotland as the surname Mair and in England as the office of mayor. And in the later Dark Ages, there were *mormaers* in the north, a title for great magnates. Where this apparent administrative tidiness begins to blur is over the question of the source of that authority. By the tenth century, *maers* were probably sometimes royal officials who managed an estate belonging directly to a king and sometimes these men were themselves aristocrats, with traditional title to the land they controlled, or they were the agents of a particularly powerful aristocratic family. Perhaps even a prototype *mormaer*.

In any event, *maenors* tended to comprise twelve or thirteen farms in upland areas and six or seven in the more fertile lowland districts. In the Manor Valley, this ancient pattern is clear. Bounded by the watershed ridges of hills on three sides and entered where the Manor Water tumbles into the Tweed, the valley supported thirteen farms in 1845, according to the Statistical Account, and now has twelve. It contains all the other elements present in a classic seventh-century *maenor*. As Christianity spread northwards through the high valleys of the Southern Uplands, almost certainly radiating from the ancient church at late Roman Carlisle, the estates began to acquire their own churches, a religious focus for a clearly defined community. St Gordian was the now apparently eccentric choice for the lords of Manor and the survival of the *eccles* place-name shows how early Christian churches were speckled over the map – *eccles* derives from the Old Welsh *eglwys* which, in turn, comes from the Latin *ecclesia* 'church'. Ecclefechan in Annandale means 'the Little Church' (probably in contrast to 'the Great Church' at the lost monastery at Hoddom), Eccles in Berwickshire retained its early sanctity and became the home of a medieval nunnery and Eaglescairnie in East Lothian, Eaglesham in Renfrewshire and several other sites can still be found. It is likely that all of them were sixth century or perhaps even earlier foundations associated with *maenors*.

The *maerdref* was the central farm and the residence of the *maer*. In Wales, these were often found in the shadow of great fortresses such as those at Dinorben, Dinas Powys and Aberffraw, the principal seat of the powerful kings of Gwynedd. In the sixth century, below the halls of Maelgwyn Fawr, a famous victim of Justinian's plague, there lay a church, a law court and the house of a *maer*. At the foot of the Manor Valley, near where the Manor Water meets the Tweed, the hill forts of Cademuir rise. Ancient, protected by the prehistoric ditches and stone obstacles known as *chevaux de frise*, these impressive fortifications continued to be garrisoned into the Dark Ages. St Gordian's sanctuary stood some way to the south, further up the valley, but the cluster of buildings at Manor Hall, Manor Church and Kirkton suggest the presence of a *maerdref*. It may be that St Gordian's served the upper valley and another church the people who lived at the mouth.

In the stock-rearing society of the seventh century, the farms on the lower ground by the Manor Water and its feeder streams were known as the *hendrefi*, 'the winter towns'. This name remembered the ancient journey of transhumance, when herdsmen drove their beasts up the hill trails in the spring to the high pastures. To allow the lowland fields to recover and the tender shoots of new crops to grow untrampled and unnibbled, flocks and herds summered in the unfenced grasslands up on the plateaux. The shielings where the herd laddies and their helpers slept and sheltered were known collectively as the *hafod*, 'the summer town'. With its self-contained geography, the Manor Valley is perfect for transhumance as the hills above Manorhead over towards the Megget Valley offer good and extensive grazing. Even when the wind blew over Black Cleuch and Sting Rig, shelter for men and beasts could be found in the steep-sided hopes and deans between the green and pillowy hills. Their names recall the timeless tradition of summering out – Hog's Knowe, Shepherd's Cairn. And two others remind the map reader of one of the dangers faced by the flocks, the herdsman and their dogs – Wolfhope Law rises near the farm of Langhaugh and Wolf Rig stands over towards the Yarrow Valley.

Close to where a shepherd found the hoard of Bronze Age metalwork at Horsehope Craig, the Glenrath Burn joins the Manor Water. The narrow valley of Glenrath Hope reaches into the hills to the east and, even though it is only ten miles to Peebles, feels very remote. Perhaps for that reason, an early Dark Ages settlement has been preserved on its northern slopes. The most extensive yet found in Scotland, the outlines of its fields are clearly visible and the foundations of a cluster of four small houses can be made out.

Protected by a series of elegantly curved enclosing walls, each had a courtyard, a series of pens where animals could be brought inbye for milking, where a midden of their muck might be piled up and where firewood and peats could be stacked. The houses were round and built in a long-lasting and sophisticated style seen in many parts of Scotland. Using only materials close at hand, their construction was simple and efficient. Once shallow founds had been dug and a drystone wall built up to waist height or higher, a conical set of roof trusses was assembled and jointed at the apex, often using only the weight of interlocking beams secured with cords. Bracken still grows in profusion on the steep sides of Glenrath Hope and this or turf was used for roofing. A beaten earth floor with some stone flags set at the only entrance (to keep the winter mud manageable) was made and perhaps strewn with more bracken. Archaeologists have found the remains of sweeter smelling herbs mixed in with floor debris in roundhouses. In the centre, a hearth of flat and raised stones was set out. There were no windows and the only light came from the doorway. Often this was placed in the east for the first rays of the morning sun or, if advisable, in the lee of the prevailing wind.

Most light and heat came from the downhearth in the middle of the house. It was used for cooking in the winter months and families sat and slept around its glow. Sparks floating up to the roof might be thought a hazard but the perpetually burning fire soon created a layer of carbon monoxide which extinguished them. Smoke filtered through the roof but the interior will have been eye-watering, encouraging people to squat or sit on low benches.

In the blast and ice of the winter these roundhouses will have been snug enough but there can be no doubt that, in the summer and periods of better weather, their inhabitants spent most of their time outdoors. The light was of course much better for the delicate work of weaving, for example, and a beautifully decorated spindle whorl was found on the site. It was used as part of the apparatus for spinning yarn from the wool pulled out of the fleeces of the sheep which grazed around Glenrath Hope.

The inbye fields were marked off by stone dykes whose footings have survived and earth banks which are less clear. Most were laid out on the northern slopes of the narrow valley so that they were canted southwards to catch as much of the warming sun as possible. Crops will certainly have included grain but not the range of other produce which comes out of modern fields. Milk, cheese, bread, meat (from game as well as domesticated animals) and a wild harvest of berries, fruits, nuts and fungi formed the staple diet of the farmers who lived in Glenrath Hope in the seventh century.

Who were they? A combination of Welsh and Scottish sources offer answers. In the society of southern Scotland around the time of the fateful battle at Catraeth, the most fundamental distinctions were between those who were free, those whose freedom was circumscribed and those who had none. The *Bonheddwyr*, the 'Well-born', were the sort of men who rode to battle with the Angles at Catterick on the banks of the Swale. They had what their enemies lacked – lineage – and, because they could trace their genealogy, they also had title to land and privileges. That was why a list of impressive ancestors mattered and why the generations sometimes wound back into myth-history and borrowed authority, like Coel Hen and the Roman prefects of the fourth century. When the bards of the *Bonheddwyr* sang of their lineage, they also reminded listeners of what they owned and controlled. Just as kings could maintain a *teulu*, a war band, the more powerful of the Well-Born could sustain a household which probably included a small cadre of professional soldiers or at least well-armed men trained in the arts of war. On occasion, lineage itself will not have been sufficiently assertive.

The farmsteads at Glenrath Hope were the homes of a lower class of people, the *taeogion*. These men and women were bound to the land they cultivated and tended and owed a series of rents and obligations to the Bonheddwyr. But every *taeog* on an estate had a right to farm and, depending on the nature of the ground to be worked, it could be a good life. There was a system of rotation known as the *tir cyfrif* and it was in the gift of the *maer*. *Caethion* were slaves – men and women who had no rights whatsoever and were the property of whoever had bought or acquired them. It is likely that many *caethion* were war captives.

Society appears to have been rigidly stratified and, while *taeogion* could be productive, they were bound always to remain

---

The Law of the Innocents

One of the most outstanding figures of the Dark Ages was St Adomnan. Much more than merely the biographer of St Columba, he was a politician and intellectual of considerable power. Perhaps his most notable initiative was the Law of the Innocents. At the Synod of Birr in central Ireland held in 697, he proposed that women, children and clergy be protected from the brutal realities of Dark Ages warfare. Nothing else like it had been promulgated in Europe. It was underwritten by an impressive list of Irish, Dalriadan and Pictish kings. Adomnan's protection of women extended further with penalties for sexual assault – 'If a hand is put under her dress to defile her . . .', a fine was to be paid – and an attempt to improve their lowly status as cumalaich *or 'little slaves'. As a balance, women were not to be treated too leniently if they themselves were guilty of a crime – 'For a woman deserves death for the killing of a man or woman . . . that is to say, she is to be put in a boat of one paddle as a sea-waif upon the ocean to go with the wind from the land.' Unusual.*

---

farmers. By definition, they were not Well-Born and were automatically excluded from the priesthood, from being trained as a bard – or a blacksmith.

This last prohibition is striking and may be an inheritance from prehistoric times. When metals were first worked in Britain, almost four millennia before the *taeogion* toiled in the little fields of Glenrath Hope, those who had the skills to convert lumps of ore into bright, shiny objects were probably considered to be in possession of magical powers. Certainly they were seen as people of very high status. One of the richest prehistoric graves ever found in Britain, that of the man known as the Amesbury Archer, contained much gold and bronze, and other items showed clearly that he had been a smith.

In the Manor Valley, six leading smelting sites have been found. The carbon dating of the charcoal places their use more than a thousand years ago. Lead has a low melting point and small furnaces were built to extract pure metal from the ore picked up on the valley bottom. Peat and charcoal were used as fuel. Inside a low, square drystone structure with gaps to allow the wind to act as a bellows, the fuel was layered with ore which had been broken down into fragments. Under this structure a clay-lined pit collected the molten lead. Easy to work, it was used to fashion both everyday objects and exotic ones, like jewellery. When combined with tin, it made lustrous pewter. All of these activities will have been the work of smiths, men of high status in the Dark Ages in the Manor Valley and no little skill.

A Scottish historical document dating back to the tenth century and probably reflecting society long before that, provides fascinating insights into how the society of southern Scotland functioned. Known as the *Leges inter Brettos et Scottos*, it recognised an enduring cultural distinction between the Britons of the south and the Scots of the west and north. The Old Welsh-speaking cultures of the kingdoms of the Gododdin and Strathclyde were still sufficiently vigorous to merit a different and detailed legal status and resist homogeneity.

A central concept of the *Leges* was blood-price. Called *cro* in Gaelic and *galanas* in Old Welsh, it consisted of a table of precise amounts to be paid in cattle as restitution for the killing of a man. From kings to slaves, the tariffs were tabulated with great clarity but it cannot have been as tidy as it seems. The notion of *galanas* developed for sensible reasons – as an attempt to avoid bloodshed and feud – but, no matter how many cattle were offered, some men will still have thirsted for and taken vengeance.

Women were heavily discounted in the tables of blood-price and generally reckoned as worth half of a man of equivalent social status. For the price of one king, two queens could be murdered. But, even if they were cheaper, women were not without legal rights. Perhaps harking back to the uncertain customs of a pre-Christian past, marriage was seen more as a contract than an absolute sacrament. If a husband was not faithful and constant or was unreasonably severe, even cruel, divorce was permitted and the injured wife could expect to be legally compensated in any settlement.

The Welsh Alphabet

Celtic languages do not sit easily in the mouths of monoglot English speakers and pronunciation is made even more difficult by a different alphabet. All those consonant clusters can be alarming and Welsh crossword puzzles have larger boxes so that dd or ch letters can be accommodated. Most letters of the alphabet are similar to English but there is no k, q or z in Welsh and y is a vowel. Here is a list of the letters not used or heard in English:

ch *like the Scots* loch, *a sound the English affect to be unable to pronounce although many manage the name of the German composer, J. S. Bach, well enough.*

dd *sounds like* **th** *in* the *so that* Dafydd *for David ends rather more attractively.*

f *sounds like a* **v***. The Welsh for little is* fychan *which gives the surname* Vaughan *and* Dafydd *is pronounced* davuth.

ff **f** *as in* off.

ll *the toughest Welsh letter, it is best managed by clamping the tip of the tongue to the top palate and hissing the English letter* **l***.*

rh *another difficult sound, this is an aspirated* **r** *which does not occur at all in English – similar to the difference between the* **w** *in* when *(aspirated) and the* **w** *in* went *(not), although sadly this distinction continues to fade.*

y *like* **i** *as in* sit. *Usually.*

There are significant differences in usage between South and North Wales and all sorts of accents are used – the grave, acute and diaeresis are the most common. Both Welsh and Gaelic are very beautiful to listen to, especially in poetry and song, and their rhythms are designed to be remembered.

Amongst the *taeogion*, there were more everyday obligations and those owed to kings were detailed. A food rent known as *cylch* was due to the royal war band, presumably when it rode into the *maenor* or was somewhere nearby. By their nature, food rents were seasonal and had to be collected and consumed on a peripatetic basis. Until modern times and the advent of easier transport and refrigeration, royal courts were in the habit of eating and drinking their way around the countryside, like a swarm of Well-Born locusts.

Hunting appears to have become a royal passion in the Dark Ages. When kings wished to chase the deer and other game, *taeogion* were obliged to feed their pack of hunting dogs, carve paths through the forest (this sounds as though it might be a reference to beating out game rather than finding a way through a primeval and long gone wildwood) and to house members of the royal party. To the Well-Born, the farmsteads of the *taeogion* were bound to render a food rent known as *gwestfa*, a portion of which could, in turn, be handed on to the ever-hungry royal household.

The *Leges inter Brettos et Scottos* was not a unique apparatus. In the late seventh century, the law codes of King Ine of Wessex made exceptional provision for the Old Welsh-speaking communities in the south of England. What is surprising about the Scottish *Leges* is their longevity. Up to the tenth century and on into the medieval period, long after the Celts of England had all but vanished from the historical record, there persisted a need for the recognition of native British legal status.

The differences between the Anglo-Saxon settlers and the native Celts were of course also cultural. In what is now eastern and southern England, the conversion of the Germanic peoples happened very gradually, only beginning with the papal mission of St Augustine to Kent in 597, more than 150 years after the first arrivals, what historians used to call the *Adventus Saxonum*. Elsewhere in the post-Roman west, it was very different. The process of conversion was completed very rapidly indeed. Only fifteen years after the fall of the last Roman ruler of the province of Gaul, King Clovis effected the mass entry of the Frankish nation into the church of Christ. But, over much of Britannia, the Baptised natives faced the armies of the Heathen invaders for many generations, long enough for deep enmities and divisions to solidify. This fault line was also emphasised by power politics and it may explain why the emerging dialects of English borrowed only a tiny dusting of vocabulary from the Celtic language of near neighbours. These were people who had developed an ancient, accurate way of describing the detail of a climate, a landscape and its flora and fauna. Colonists often gratefully adopt native terms for things foreign to their experience but, in Britannia, this simply did not happen. The reasons are almost impossible to fathom but perhaps the fact of a long-lasting religious divide offers a partial explanation.

What is certain is that a northern dialect of English was established in the south-eastern quadrant of Dark Ages Scotland and it gradually became the language of the Lowlands. Old Welsh

---

What Happened to Welsh?

Perhaps the most intractable of all the mysteries swirling around the history of the Dark Ages concerns language. Around the year 400, the fading Roman province of Britannia had a population of between three and four million. It appears that most of them, the overwhelming majority who lived in the countryside, spoke dialects of Old Welsh but could probably get by in Latin when they visited markets in towns or had any dealings with the army or the provincial government. In the next 150 years, the Angles, Saxons, Jutes and other Germanic peoples came, conquered and settled. And, despite holding on to its Celtic language throughout the Roman occupation (unlike France or Spain where languages based on Latin developed), most of Britannia quickly became English-speaking. Why? The new settlers cannot have been very numerous – small groups of men in small boats, perhaps as few as 50,000 and no more than 200,000, tiny percentage of the existing Celtic population. What happened? Did all of the natives flee to the west or die of the plague or fall at the hands of the invaders? Surely not? Bernicia may offer a hint of an answer. Where political and military fusion took place, cultural fusion followed and, amongst the different dialects of Old Welsh, Early English became a lingua franca. Or perhaps the answer is even simpler. Colonised populations often have to adopt the language of the colonisers whether they are Romans on Hadrian's Wall or the tiny number of soldiers and managers employed by the East India Company to govern a vast subcontinent. Where a spear or a gun pointed, words followed.

---

shrank back into the hills and high valleys and, although it lingered for many centuries, the English of the low country and its fertile farms and fields was without doubt the language of the future. And the political and cultural phenomenon of Bernicia was the catalyst which forced most Scots to adopt it.

7

Bernicia

✵

S UMMER WAS THE battle season. War was best waged
when the grass grew and could feed grazing cavalry ponies,
when the weather was better and when men could sleep out
around their campfires without a winter chill numbing their bones
after the embers had ceased to glow. And, on long summer days
when the light died only slowly in the west, armies could advance
great distances quickly, appearing as if from nowhere, surprising
their unprepared enemies with sheer speed. Farmers could fight in
the summer. Between the times of sowing and harvest, they could
take up their spears and join the retinue of their lords, the well-
armed, horse-riding Well-born. Politics brought armies to the
summer battlefields of Dark Ages Scotland. When rival kings
contested control of territory or settled a disputed succession, they
rode out with their war bands and those who owed military service
followed. The chroniclers relate that the green grass of June, July
and August was often spattered with gore.

Raiding was another matter. Certainly summer soldiers plundered but, for a society which counted its wealth and measured
its prestige in livestock, especially cattle, winter was the time to
saddle ponies and set out on raiding expeditions. Even though
rain, wind, snow and mud will have dampened much of the
excitement and discouraged extravagant displays of prowess,
winter was better because the cows, sheep and other beasts were
more readily available. The ancient rhythms of transhumance

took the flocks and herds up into the high pastures from April to October and they scattered widely over the unfenced moorland. It was only when herdsmen brought their animals down off the hills at the end of autumn to the inbye fields of their farms and settlements that they were corralled in one place – and could be stolen.

As the summer days of 603 shortened, one of the greatest kings of the west was planning a raiding party. The rock of Dunadd rises almost sheer out of the Moine Mhor, the flat, sodden wastes of the Great Moss. On the banks of the meandering River Add, which flows into the Atlantic at Crinan, at the northern end of the Kintyre Peninsula, the citadel of Dunadd was one of the principal seats of the kings of Dalriada – and surely their most impressive stronghold.

Now Dunadd is a windswept, bare outcrop. But at the summit there are traces of departed grandeur. Cut into a flat stone is the shape of a footprint. Often puddled with rain, it once had a powerful, venerable and central importance in the inauguration of kings. Perhaps symbolising royal control of the land, it was where a king probably stood when he took an investiture oath. Nearby is a rock-cut basin for libations, a carving of a boar which was perhaps an animal totem for the prehistoric peoples who lived around Dunadd and an inscription in the magical tree-language known as Ogham. When a new king stood on the footprint rock, he looked out at a deeply sacred landscape, a place where men had communed with their gods for millennia. At nearby Kilmartin there lies a series of burial monuments and standing stones which still dominate. Mysterious rock carvings can be found in the hills around these valleys, marking the margins of a sacred landscape and the remains of henges and an earthwork known as a *cursus* will have been even more obvious in the early seventh century. Those who watched the ceremonies will have understood that the kings of Dalriada were part of traditions which stretched back beyond mere memory, to a time of gods and heroes.

Into the Christian era, the links between sacred and temporal power emerged in the historical record. Writing only fifty years after the reign of Aedan macGabrain, Adomnan compiled a hagiography of St Columba. Almost without exception the cults of popular early saints were established by biographies which listed their miracles, prophesies and the important details of their exemplary lives. Later canonised himself, Adomnan was the ninth abbot of Iona after Columba and his claims for 'the praiseworthy man' will have greatly enhanced the prestige of his monastery.

One of the most striking assertions in the *Life of St Columba* is that Aedan was consecrated as King of Dalriada by the saint. In a ceremony of anointing and blessing, probably modelled on biblical accounts of the priest, Samuel, and kings David and Solomon of Israel, the early church appears to have insisted upon, or at least aspired to, a central role in the power politics of the day. Almost two centuries before Charlemagne was surprised to be crowned Holy Roman Emperor by Pope Leo III as he rose from praying at Christmas Mass in 800 in Rome, Adomnan wrote of a similar ritual in Dalriada. It may be that Aedan regarded the ceremony with the same scepticism as Charlemagne but he may also have valued the additional buttress of ecclesiastical – and sacred – support for his authority.

Archaeologists have discovered the remains of a large strong-hold on Dunadd with buildings perched on a series of terraces below the footprint stone at the summit. In one of these, in 603, King Aedan macGabrain sat with his captains and his allies, and they talked of a great raid, a foray far to the east into the lands of the south-east, the plump lands of Bernicia and its Anglian kings. It is likely that Aedan held a feast. Fragments of fine glass vessels made in Gaul have been found at Dunadd and they will have been unloaded from merchant ships with containers of wine from Europe. On the eastern edges of the rock, a great deal of debris was found which spoke of metalworking. Moulds, crucibles and even traces of gold, silver and precious stones have turned up and they date to the seventh century. These are the traces of prestige and the exercise of power. The moulds were used to make a classic design of brooch, one shaped like a small torc and with a pin through it. These were probably badges of rank given by King Aedan to his warriors and noblemen. Also found were the remains of an Anglo-Saxon buckle, almost certain proof that craftsmen came north to work in Dalriada.

Gifts and luxury goods were more than usually important to King Aedan as he planned his expedition. As the war band mustered, princes came from afar. From Ireland, Mael Umai macBaetain led his men to Dunadd and, most importantly, the Dalriadan host would fight with Hering, the son of Hussa, former king of the Bernicians. Perhaps it was Aedan's intention to do more than plunder. If the raid went well, Hering may have expected to be installed as the new king of Bernicia, one who would be helpful or maybe even subject to Dalriada.

The chroniclers wrote of Aedan as a great warrior, an audacious general who led his men on ambitious and long-range campaigns, from Orkney to the Isle of Man. Certainly the muster list known as the Senchus Fer na h'Alban reckoned the military strength of the kindreds of Dalriada in naval terms. Oarsmen for seven-benched seagoing curraghs must also have fought as marines and the expeditions to Man and Orkney will have been launched from their beaches and bays. But the raid to the east was to be predominantly overland. Curraghs may have ferried men and ponies down sea lochs and perhaps into the mouth of the River Clyde but, from there, Aedan's men moved across country. Perhaps their scouts directed them along the military way which ran immediately to the south of the Antonine Wall. In 603 much will still have been extant and no better road linked the Clyde with the Forth.

The Roman fort at Cramond almost certainly continued to be occupied long after the departure of the imperial army and indeed well into the seventh century and beyond. Built over the *principia*, the military headquarters building at the centre of the fort, Cramond Kirk is a very early foundation and very suggestive of continuity. Inside the crumbling walls and gateways, native peoples could enjoy both an enhanced sense of security and whoever of the Well-Born was powerful locally could bask in enhanced prestige, an inheritor of Rome's mighty legacy. The importance of Cramond for Aedan's war band was that it marked the northern terminus of Dere Street, the road south, the road to glory and plunder.

Winter raiders always avoided wet ground if they could and the hard paving of the old Roman highway will have been welcome, even if it was fraying in places. The war bands may have forded the Water of Leith at the ancient crossing below where the Dean Bridge now soars. Dere Street is thought to have then followed the line of Lothian Road before skirting the western edge of the Meadows and beginning its climb out of what is now Edinburgh at the junction with Nether Liberton. Still clearly visible on the northern flank of Soutra Hill, some distance to the west of where the modern A68 takes a traverse up the gradient, the old Roman road passes close to the ruins of a medieval hospital.

When Aedan's scouts breasted the rise at the southern edge of the Soutra plateau, Lauderdale opened before them, the route down into Bernicia, the Tweed Basin and herds of cattle and other beasts fat from a summer's grazing. No details of the raid have survived but it is likely that little attempt was made at stealth. According to Bede's *Ecclesiastical History of the English People*, the Dalriada captains and their allies led 'an immense and mighty army'. Perhaps like the lords of the Border Reivers a thousand years later, Aedan simply used his overwhelming force to intimidate any farmers or local landowners who might have – only for a moment – considered resistance. In the reiving centuries, large raids established temporary headquarters and sent out smaller forces to ingather plunder.

What is recorded is the reaction. Even though it was only three years after the Gododdin defeat at Catterick, it appears that the defender of the Tweed Basin was not a prince like Catrawt of Calchvynydd or an alliance of the Well-Born. Aedan had passed through the heartland of the Gododdin without report of any battle or hindrance. Perhaps Catterick broke utterly the power of the kings who ruled from Din Eidyn, Edinburgh's Castle Rock and Traprain Law. Perhaps some of the remnants of the Gododdin's war bands rode with them. For when a response to the Dalriada raid came, it was from an Anglian king, perhaps the greatest ever to rule Bernicia.

Aethelfrith's reign began in 592 and the genealogists counted him as the grandson of Ida, the first to rule from the stronghold at Bamburgh. Here is how Bede introduced him:

> About this time [AD 603], Aethelfrith, a very powerful and ambitious king, ruled the kingdom of the Northumbrians. He ravaged the Britons more cruelly than all the other English leaders, so that he might well be compared to Saul, the King of Israel, except of course that he was ignorant of true religion. He overran a greater area than any other king or ealdorman, exterminating or enslaving the inhabitants, making their lands either tributary to the English or ready for English settlement . . .
>
> Alarmed at his advance, Aidan, king of those Irish who lived in Britain, came against him with a large and strong army, but was defeated and fled with very few, having lost almost his entire army at a famous place known as Degsastan, that is, Degsa's Stone.

No longer famous, the exact location of Degsastan is a matter of conjecture. Historians agree that the battle must have been fought in the Borders and a traditional, and little interrogated view was that the armies met at Dawston, a place-name that still clings to a burn flowing through the high and windy valley of Liddesdale. This must be unlikely. For raiders, the pickings are slim in the Cheviot ranges and the country rough and difficult for large numbers of warriors to move through and sustain themselves. Moreover Aethelfrith's victory at Degsastan secured for him and his lords the Tweed Valley and Dawston is simply in the wrong place for that to have happened so quickly and completely. Writing in the fourteenth century, the Scottish chronicler, John of Fordun, has no hesitation in stating that the Dalriadan army and their allies attacked the Borders from the north and by far the most likely route was the Old Roman road of Dere Street. It passed very close to a place with a prime claim to be the location of the great battle.

Above the modern farm at Addinston are two very well preserved prehistoric, ditch-and-bank fortresses. They glower over Lauderdale and protect the steep-sided valley of the Cleek-himin Burn directly below – and they make a perfect location for a raiders' base camp. The fortresses sheltered men and perhaps ponies while the steep-sided glen corralled stolen beasts and watered them while they waited to be herded away north up nearby Dere Street and over Soutra Hill.

Not only is the name of the farm at Addinston in upper Lauderdale a clear toponymic descendant of Degsastan, the full seventh-century version of Aet Aegdanes Stan shows the link more precisely. 'Aedan's Stone' is the meaning and it is intriguing. Why was the place of battle named after the defeated king if it had not been near a base fortified by his war band? At seventy, he was an old man to be leading an army and perhaps he was killed at Addinston. Certainly so little is heard of Aedan after 603 that some believe that he was forced to abdicate. The chroniclers reported his death in 609. In any event, the stone is a monument of some sort to the man who took part in a battle which was a signal event in the flood-tide of Bernician, and later North-umbrian, advance.

Here is the remainder of the passage form Bede:

In this battle, Aethelfrith's brother, Theodbald and all his followers were killed. Aethelfrith won this fight in the year of our Lord 603, the eleventh of his reign, which lasted twenty four years . . . From that day until the present, no king of the Irish in Britain has dared to do battle with the English.

Bede saw Degsastan as an unequivocal turning point and, throughout his great history, he never misses an opportunity to underline the inevitable advance of English power – and the fact that it was morally right. Even though Aethelfrith was a pagan and

Aedan a Christian, Bede nevertheless enlists the Anglian king on the side of history as he saw it. And the frequent references to nationality, to the English overcoming the Irish or the Britons, lends a definition to the wars of Aethelfrith and Aedan which was almost certainly inappropriate. Plunder, raiding, the ability to exert power over regions and their inhabitants – all of these mattered much more than the ethnic identity of those who fought at Degsastan and the battles and campaigns of the time. It seems very likely that the English-ing of south-eastern Scotland, making lands tributary or ready for English settlement, as Bede has it, was achieved with the collusion of many who were not English. And it was also a contest between military elites. A closer analysis of the events around Degsastan will support this view.

The Anglo-Saxon Chronicle described Aedan's force as a 'raiding army', even though all accounts said it was large. No farmers followed on foot with their spears. Rather, this was likely to have been an alliance of war bands and their lords brigaded together under the leadership of King Aedan. Reports of the fighting confirm this. The Irish prince, Mael-Umai, was said to have killed Eanfrith, Aethelfrith's brother and perhaps even more seriously another brother, Theodbald, also died 'with all his followers'. These casualties reinforce the sense of lords and princes at the head of their war bands clashing in the winter hill country above Lauderdale. And also qualifies somewhat Bede's assertion that Aedan was routed rather than merely defeated at Degsastan.

Momentum was nevertheless firmly with Aethelfrith and, a year after his victory in the north, he turned his warriors south and his attention to the neighbouring Angle kingdom of Deira. After the death of King Aella, his son and heir, Edwin, was driven out by Aethelfrith and, by 604, Bernicia and Deira united to become what was later called Northumbria.

Twelve hundred monks were said to have been slaughtered at a battle fought in 613 at Chester. They were praying for victory for the kings of Powys and the defeat of the pagan Aethelfrith. Bede reported this appalling act without comment, no word of criticism for the slaughter of so many of the faithful, even blaming their British guards who fled at the Bernician assault. The attack on the monks may have been a tactic, a means of diverting the warriors of Powys, perhaps flanking them. In any event, Aethelfrith appears to have been an inventive general and he attracted the Old Welsh nickname, Am Fleisaur. Meaning 'the Trickster', it may have been conferred by his British allies, impressed at his resourcefulness. Just as Hering, son of Hussa, and Yrfai map Golistan could be found in the war bands of British kings, so native princes could have sided with the most successful and wide-ranging Anglian king of the early seventh century. Perhaps the speed of Bernician takeover in the Tweed Valley should be attributed to the making of astute alliances. Although Aneirin insisted that, along with the entire Gododdin host, Cadrawd of Calchvynydd perished, his son may have thought it wise to ride with Aethelfrith and his men. History appeared to be running with them.

Politics as well as military skill would soon combine to make Northumbria even more powerful in the north. Edwin of Deira had sought refuge at the court of King Raedwald of East Anglia, the man probably at the centre of the spectacular ship burial found at Sutton Hoo. Having managed to have another Deiran rival poisoned when he fled to the kings of Elmet, Aethelfrith offered gold to Raedwald if he would give up Edwin. Instead a battle was fought on the banks of the River Idle in Nottingham-shire and there the Trickster ran out of ideas and luck as the East Anglians cut him down.

Edwin quickly established himself as King of Northumbria, of both Deira and Bernicia, and it was the turn of the heirs of Aethelfrith to flee into exile. These periods of enforced absence were important, defining and had clear political and cultural consequences. Northumbrian exiles were taken in by neighbouring kings who hoped to gain advantage by offering what could be a dangerous shelter. When Edwin was installed on the Northum-brian throne by Raedwald's army, the East Anglian king wielded great influence in the north and perhaps even claimed overlordship.

The heirs of Aethelfrith went further north, to the Atlantic coastlands. Oswald and his brother, Oswiu, sought the protection of Eochaid Buide, the successor of Aedan macGabrain and their seventeen-year stay in Dalriada was enormously influential. Both young men were converted to Christianity on the holy island of Iona and they became fluent speakers of Gaelic, a detail which would be important later.

While the Aethelfrith princes were raised in a thoroughly Celtic milieu, the much more English Edwin (from Deira, his instinct had been to flee south while the Bernicians of the Tweed Basin always seemed more comfortable in the north) began to wax powerful. Here is part of Bede's account:

> At this time [625], the people of the Northumbrians, the English living north of the Humber, under Edwin their king received the Faith through the ministry of Paulinus, whom I have already mentioned. As a sign that he would come to the Faith and the heavenly kingdom, King Edwin received wide additions to his earthly realm, and brought under his sway all the territories inhabited either by English or by Britons, an achievement unmatched by any previous English king.

Writing in Latin about a king with imperial, or at least expansionist, pretensions, Bede adds the aura of Rome to Edwin's regime. The war band is called the *comitatus*, royal reeves or administrators are *praefecti* and the royal estates and fortresses are the *villae regiae* and the *urbes regis*. A royal progress through the countryside is also recorded by Bede and it reeks of Roman pomp and the panoply of the legions:

> So great was his majesty in his realm that not only were banners carried before him in battle, but even in time of peace, as he rode about amongst his cities, estates and kingdoms with his thegns, he always used to be preceded by a standard-bearer. Further, when he walked anywhere along the roads, there used to be carried before him the type of standard the Romans call a 'tufa' and the English call a 'thuf'.

And thirty years before Bede, Adomnan went further with the historical analogy when he hailed Edwin's successor, Oswald, as *Imperator Totius Britanniae*, 'Emperor of All Britain'.

At Yeavering, now a deserted and windy valley leading into the eastern ranges of the Cheviots, Edwin did more homage to the memory of Rome. With an earlier Old Welsh name of Ad Gefrin, meaning 'Goat Hill', Yeavering was already a power centre before the 620s. But Edwin added much to its lustre when he ordered the construction of a remarkable new structure. Known as the 'Grandstand', it was made in wood – its reconstruction conjectured out of the pattern and depth of its post holes – and it resembled a wedge or a section cut out of a Roman amphitheatre. There may have been extant examples for the designers to copy at Catterick or York. The tiered seating was arranged so that everyone on it had clear sight and hearing from a dais built at the foot of the structure.

The idea was to create an open-air meeting place where one man could talk to many at once. In a preliterate society, kings and their senior men laid down the law by speaking it out loud in a large group so that there could be no doubt and little room for interpretation. This ancient form of law-giving is still practised in the British Isles when, each summer, at St John's on the Isle of Man, the Deemsters or Judges declaim aloud in Manx Gaelic any new legislation. It cannot be accepted and codified until this ceremony is enacted.

The Grandstand may have been used for moots or meetings but the excavators at Yeavering believed that it also had a religious purpose. Behind the dais on the flat ground, in front of the tiered seating, there was a large post hole unrelated to any structure close at hand and whatever had been erected in it had not been removed but allowed to rot where it stood. Was it a large wooden cross?

In the first passage from Bede, welcoming Edwin's reign, the missionary, Paulinus, is noted. Sent north by Augustine's church at Canterbury, he undertook the mass conversion of the Angles at Yeavering and elsewhere. Baptism was the central ritual and

Paulinus' mission is remembered in the place-name of Pallins-burn near the modern border between England and Scotland.

Also excavated at Yeavering were the classic timber halls well known from poems such as *Beowulf*. When Bede related the story of the conversion of the Anglian kingdom of Edwin, he wrote of a meeting of leading men and counsellors. Perhaps it took place on the Grandstand. In any case, he employs a telling image which seems to make the life of the time come alive for a moment:

Another of the king's chief men signified his agreement with this prudent argument [that the kingdom should convert to Christianity], and went on to say:

'Your Majesty, when we compare the present life of man on earth with that time of which we have no knowledge, it seems to me like the swift flight of a single sparrow through the feasting-hall where you are sitting at dinner on a winter's day with your thegns and counsellors. In the midst there is a comforting fire to warm the hall: outside, the storms of winter snow or rain are raging. This sparrow flies in swiftly through one door of the hall, and out through another. While he is inside, he is safe from the winter storms; but after a few moments of comfort, he vanishes from sight into the wintry world from which he came. Even so, man appears on the earth for a little while; but of what went before this life or of what follows, we know nothing. Therefore if this new teaching has brought any more certain knowledge, it seems only right we should follow it.'

While Edwin and his counsellors sat around the winter fire and debated the adoption of a Christianity sent from Rome, hundreds of miles to the west, on the island of Iona, another group of Angles was also entering into the arms of Holy Mother Church. Oswald and Oswiu, the exiled sons of Aethelfrith, were baptised by the monks of Columba's famous monastery. And their teachings had a profound effect.

At the Battle of Hatfield Chase in 633, Edwin was killed by the warriors of Cadwallon, King of Gwynedd. Commentators have sometimes described Hatfield as a rare and late victory for the native British over the English but the reality was probably much more complicated with war bands from both ethnic groups fighting on both sides.

Nevertheless names and origins were beginning to matter. In the seventh century, a curious dichotomy developed. Many different groups of Germanic settlers had come to Britain after the end of the Empire – Angles from Angeln, Saxons from Lower Saxony, Jutes from Jutland in northern Denmark, Swedes (Raedwald of East Anglia may have been the most famous), Franks from what is now France and others from Northern Europe. But only 150 years after the *Adventus Saxonum*, these Germanic groups began to acquire a common name.

The instigator of the famous mission of St Augustine, Pope Gregory I, called King Aethelbert of Kent *Rex Anglorum* even though he was almost certainly of Saxon origin. The term quickly gained currency. In the early eighth century, Bede wrote his *Ecclesiastical History of the English People* – not the Saxon or Jutic People – and, in the version of Old English spoken by his generation, the Germanic groups had come to know themselves as the Angelcynn or 'Angle-kin'. By AD 1000, a nation had been named. Englaland meant 'the Country of the Angles' and they spoke various dialects of English.

It may be that the early dominance of the Bernician and Deiran kings had a powerful influence beyond the lands they controlled directly. They were the true Angelcynn and it may be that others wished to be included or associated with the prestige of kings like Aethelfrith, Edwin and their successors.

But what is immediately striking is the name conferred on them by the Celtic natives of Britain. Without exception, they declined to call the Germanic incomers the Angles. In Welsh, they are still the Sais, in Scots Gaelic the Sasunnaich and in Cornish the Sostenagh. And these Saxons live not in England but in Sasunn or Saxony. All of these terms speak of the Saxons and it may be that this is an accident of early contact – the Saxons came first and people like them, the Angles, came later. But they were similar, spoke similar languages and were also land hungry. In a further poignant historical twist, the Welsh word for England is not a version of Saxony but Lloegr, 'the Lost Lands'.

The misnaming was mutual. In Welsh the Cymry live in Cymru. Wales is an English word and comes from *wealas*, a word meaning 'a foreigner'. The natives were the foreigners and the incomers an undifferentiated tide of Saxons, no matter what they called themselves. This dichotomy describes an atmosphere of cultural apartheid, a time when the much more numerous natives simply had as little to do with the rampant and ruthless military elite who would eventually force their language on all but the Celts who clung to their independence in the west and the north.

When the frustrations of exile ended with Edwin of Northumbria's death at the hands of Cadwallon in the autumn of 633, the sons of Aethelfrith made their plans. The medieval chronicler, John of Fordun, related that their protector and sponsor, Domnall Brecc, King of Dalriada, sent a war band to accompany them south and ensure the succession. It was a wise precaution. After the slaughter at Hatfield Chase, Cadwallon's warriors and those of his ally, Penda of Mercia, plundered Deira and Northumbria was once again divided. With Dalriadan backing, Eanfrith took an uncertain control of Bernicia but, when he attempted a diplomatic settlement with the ferocious Cadwallon, the result was conclusive. Eanfrith was taken and beheaded.

The news of this outrage galvanised the new king, Eanfrith's brother, Oswald. He mustered an army in the Tweed Basin and, probably supported by the war bands of both Dalriada and Pictland, the Bernicians crossed Hadrian's Wall near Hexham. At Denisesburn, they clashed with Cadwallon, broke through the royal war band and killed him. The effect was dramatic and immediate. Like Aethelfrith and Edwin before him, Oswald moved quickly to re-establish himself in Deira and reunite Northumbria. His decisiveness catapulted him into the exalted status of *Bretwalda*. Meaning 'Britain Ruler', it was a term coined later but the political reality was less ambiguous. After the victory at Denisesburn, Oswald was the most powerful king in all Britain.

Like his predecessors, the Bretwalda pursued his rivals relentlessly, driving Edwin's heirs into exile. Elsewhere he followed an aggressive policy, always moving forward, always seeking to extend his reach and strength. But, in the midst of all that campaigning, politicking and planning, Oswald never forgot the peace and spirituality of Columba's monastery at Iona. And he sent messengers to the west.

So that the conversion of the English begun by St Paulinus might continue, the new king asked the Abbot of Iona for missionaries. He did not seek help from Canterbury or, by extension, from Rome but from where Oswald had himself been baptised with his exiled family. Based as it was in the Tweed Valley, Bernicia's instinct was again to look northwards rather than south as Deira had done. After the failure of the first mission, Aidan made the long and arduous journey across Drumalban, the range of high mountains which runs north from the head of Loch Lomond, what Adomnan called the *montes dorsi Britanniae*, the 'mountains of the spine of Britain'. When he at last reached Bernicia, Aidan began the work of creating a Christian community, a bishopric. For its centre, he chose somewhere peripheral. Following his hermetic, Celtic instincts and with the example of Iona in mind, Aidan came to the beautiful tidal island of Lindisfarne. Only two generations before, Urien had besieged the English here and been murdered in his tent by assassins sent by Morcant Bwlc.

Like Iona, Lindisfarne retains an unmistakable air of sanctity, a spiritual place dominated by sea and sky, somewhere on the edge of the land but somehow not of it. It was a *diseart*, less storm-tossed and harsh than the extraordinary foundation on the island of Canna but without doubt in the same tradition.

As he travelled around his new bishopric – on foot in imitation of Christ and not on horseback like the aristocrat he was – Aidan set up at least four other communities whose geography was thought to encourage the contemplative life. Far inland, the new monasteries depended not on the waves of the ocean for their seclusion but on the bends and loops of Border rivers.

Continuity of sanctity is a clear theme in early Christianity in Scotland. Up on Eildon Hill North, a long circle of ditching was dug around the summit, not for defence but to mark off a sacred precinct. Hills and particularly prominent hills like the Eildons, which were not part of a range, were thought of as being magical, perhaps closer to the sky gods. The ditching around many in southern Scotland was the beginning of an ancient idea – the holy of holies, the *sanctum sanctorum*, the consecrated ground where men might commune with their gods.

Aidan and his followers chose a place within sight of the pagan sky-temple on Eildon Hill North. The Celtic monastery at Old Melrose was probably founded in 635 or soon afterwards. On three sides, it is enclosed by a lazy loop of the River Tweed and on the fourth by a ditch, the monastic vallum. What may have attracted Aidan to bends in rivers was a sense that they represented a boundary made not by mud-spattered monks hacking at the ground with mattocks and piling up earth with baskets but by the hand of God. Just as He made the Palestinian deserts surrounding the hermitages of the Desert Fathers and the waves of the Atlantic which cut off Iona, Canna and other island monasteries from the temporal world, so He put the protective arm of a river around His monks at Old Melrose.

Similar instincts may have guided Aidan and his missionaries elsewhere in the Borders. There are tantalising remains found at Jedburgh which point to an early foundation. Fragments from five stone crosses have been recognised as well as parts of a shrine with beautiful carvings of vine scrolls and birds. Bishop Ecgred of Lindisfarne certainly founded a community at Jedburgh in 830 but there was probably an earlier church. Traces are unlikely ever to come to light since they likely lie under the magnificent ruins of the medieval abbey. It stands in a bend of the River Jed but the remains of any monastic vallum will have long since been obliterated by the surrounding town.

At Dryburgh Abbey, this time on a site almost made an island by a loop in the Tweed, a fragment of another early stone cross hints at a long past. And a sixth-century figure, St Modan, was listed as being the abbot of a community of monks at Dryburgh. Tradition places him as a missionary around Falkirk and Stirling and there are several ancient dedications to him in the area. Perhaps he came south to found a community. At Kelso, in another bend of the Tweed, there was a pre-existing church on the site of the medieval abbey, although no archaeology has emerged to suggest an early date. It may be significant that all of the medieval dedications of the four Border abbeys were to St Mary, maybe an echo of an earlier cult of the Virgin.

As often in the story of Dark Ages Scotland, place-names offer flickers of light and that of Old Melrose is illuminating. In Bede's writings, the spelling of Mailros makes the derivation clearer. The second element *ros* is a Gaelic word and it means 'a promontory' or 'peninsula', a straightforward description of the tongue of land almost encircled by the River Tweed. The first part of the name is harder to understand. In imitation of Christ's crown of thorns, monks had themselves tonsured, that is, the crown of their heads shaved to leave only a fringe of hair. Aidan's followers had also been tonsured but in a different way. Known as the *ceudgelt*, this Irish style was thought to have druidic origins and, not only had it signified a holy man for many centuries before the coming of Christianity, it was perhaps more dramatic than what was known as the Roman tonsure. Hair was shaved back from the front of the scalp to a line from ear to ear and left to grow long at the back. In any event, the Gaelic word *maol* came to signify someone who was not only bald but a shaved or shorn monk or more precisely 'the holy man's servant'. This last is a reference to Columba and it survives in the popular Scottish Christian name of Malcolm. As *maol-chaluim*, it originally meant 'a servant of Calum or Columba' – in other words, 'a monk'.

What all of this shows is how a place-name can carry a great deal of historical freight and that Melrose means 'the Promontory of the Monks' – specifically, monks from Iona. When King

David I refounded the monastery in the twelfth century, he had both the church and the name removed to the site of a village called Fordel two miles upriver. Part of the reason was Old Melrose's long association with one of Britain's greatest saints whose cult centre lay beyond the king of Scotland's control. But all these concerns lay far in the future.

When Aidan's missionaries began work at Old Melrose, their first task was probably the marking-off of the sacred precinct. The vallum across the neck of the promontory is one of the few features of the monastery still detectable. Against its banks monks may have built their cells and, like them, the church will have been built out of wood. Similar structures from the same period which have been excavated had an A-frame at each gable and stanchions and beams on the long sides to tie them together. The walls would have been made from clay daubed on to woven screens or hurdles or planking driven into the ground. Kings and high lords feasted and slept in wooden halls of the same shape and scale and, when Bede wrote that Benedict Biscop had had the church at Monkwearmouth built in 'the Roman manner', he meant that, very unusually, it had been made with dressed stone. Perhaps such stone was robbed out of the nearby Roman fort at Trimontium but no trace of it remains on the site of the old monastery.

Old Melrose was small and its buildings rudimentary, and its comforts were few. In fact discomfort was something the monks actively sought. In a rare flash of genuine colour and character, Bede tells the story of Brother Drythelm:

This man was given a more secluded dwelling in the monastery, so that he could devote himself more freely to the service of his Maker in unbroken prayer. And since this place stands on the bank of a river, he often used to enter it for severe bodily penance, and plunge repeatedly beneath the water while he recited psalms and prayers for as long as he could endure it, standing motionless with the water up to his loins and sometimes to his neck. When he returned to shore, he never removed his dripping, chilly garments, but let them warm and dry on his body. And in winter, when the half-broken cakes of ice were swirling around him which he had broken to make a place to stand and dip himself in the water, those who saw him used to say, 'Brother Drythelm (for that was his name), it is wonderful how you can manage to bear such bitter cold'. To which he, being a man of simple disposition and self-restraint, would reply simply: 'I have known it colder'. And when they said: 'It is extraordinary that you are willing to practise such severe discipline', he used to answer: 'I have seen greater suffering.' So until the day of his summons from this life he tamed his aged body by daily fasting, inspired by an insatiable longing for the blessings of Heaven, and by his words and his life he helped many people to salvation.

Such lives of constant prayer and extreme privation seem extraordinary now, even faintly ridiculous, but, by enduring severe hypothermia, like Drythelm, monks hoped to induce euphoric, trance-like states as they edged ever closer to death. It was as though they stood in the ante-chamber of Heaven,

---

Mortification of the Flesh

The phrase means, literally, 'putting the flesh to death'. In Christian teaching, it is an idea which appears early, with references in the gospels and from St Paul – 'Put to death what is earthly in you: fornication, impurity, passion, evil desire and covetousness,' he said. And the way to achieve purity was to deny the body comfort, most commonly food. Fasting became part of most monastic rules. The repeated and deliberate inflicting of pain and discomfort was also practised early and Drythelm's immersion in the freezing River Tweed was mild compared to some examples. St Dominic Loricatus was said to have given himself 300,000 lashes. Self-flagellation also became common and sometimes it was done publicly. Others, such as St Thomas More and St Ignatius Loyola wore hair shirts and heavy chains. It all seems extreme to us now – holiness measured in blood and pain – and there were certainly those who suffered in order to induce trance-like states of religious ecstasy.

within touching distance of glory, almost on the point of meeting their Maker. These episodes were very dangerous and groups of monks almost certainly kept vigil (literally vigilant, on the lookout for signs of danger) with their brothers as they underwent extraordinary suffering in search of purity and a greater knowledge of God. Those watching will have been ready to end these trances before they went too far.

What manner of men were willing to submit themselves to a life of such severity? It appears that many were aristocrats, well-born people of varying degrees. St Columba was perhaps the best connected – a prince of the royal house of the Cenel Conaill, the rulers of lands in north-west Ireland. When he left in 563 to found a monastery, he took twelve companions with him. A conscious imitation of Christ and his Apostles, it was also a group which included at least two aristocratic relatives – his cousin, Baithene, and his uncle, Ernan. Like them, Columba could trace his lineage from the semi-legendary Irish king, Niall of the Nine Hostages (one for each of the sub-kingdoms he had dominion over) and most of the abbots who ruled in the seventh and into the eighth centuries at Iona were descended from the same line. St Aidan came from the same part of Ireland and, when he came to Bernicia at the request of King Oswald, he may well have brought relatives with him.

Although they seem like family affairs, the early Celtic monasteries were also cosmopolitan and certainly quickly grew famous. Amongst the founding community at Iona after 563, there was a British monk (that is, a man who came from one of the Old Welsh-speaking kingdoms of southern Scotland), a Pictish monk and two Englishmen, Pilu and Genereus. It is important, in this secular age, not to underestimate the magnetic power of saintliness and a place made ever more sacred by the lives and prayers of the holy men who lived there. And islands like Iona and Lindisfarne added to a sense of spirituality, of otherworldliness.

When Aidan founded Old Melrose around 635, his monks will have needed a sponsor to sustain them as they set up the new community. Since King Oswald invited them, it is likely that they enjoyed royal patronage from the outset. But like Iona and Lindisfarne, Old Melrose will have aimed at self-sufficiency. Aristocrats some of them may have been but they needed to do all sorts of menial jobs for the community to thrive and not require the constant intervention of those not in holy orders. At Iona, there were blacksmiths, woodworkers and a gardener and, at harvest time, the abbot toiled with his brothers in the fields.

Almost all trace of Columba's monastery at Iona has disappeared except for the vallum and the free-standing stone crosses. They were originally painted in vivid colours and used not only as a focus for worship but also for biblical instruction. Raised in the early eighth century, the beautiful Anglian cross at Ruthwell in Dumfriesshire has four scenes from the gospels and, carved in runic script, a vivid poem about the crucifixion. No remains of the monastery's crosses have yet been found at Old Melrose but the five discovered at Jedburgh may not all have been placed inside the vallum. These new foundations quickly became a magnet for pilgrims and sometimes crosses were erected as waymarkers and signs that a sacred area was being approached. Around the ancient church at Coldingham on the Berwickshire coast, place-names – at Applincross, Whitecross and Cairncross – remember this habit.

Once pilgrims and more exalted visitors arrived at the gateway through the vallum, their ardent wish was simply to enter the monastery and walk where holy men and saints had walked. Shrines could be visited and touched while praying hard but, by the late seventh century, a fascinating belief had developed. Kings in Scotland began to request burial inside the precinct of the monastery at Iona and other aristocrats followed suit. More specifically, they believed that their impure bodies would be cleansed by burial in the sacred soil and thereby dramatically improve their chances of reaching Heaven. Kings may have had more on their conscience than most and, until the early medieval period, many were buried on Iona. And all significant monasteries, including Old Melrose, will have taken the sinful and well-connected laity into their cemeteries.

More than most, Christianity is a religion of the Word. Through both testaments, believers hold that God speaks and bibles and gospels are therefore in themselves sacred objects. And one of the most impressive legacies of the early Christians in Britain and Ireland, what is known as the Age of the Saints, is the great corpus of illuminated manuscripts. The Lindisfarne Gospels is one of the most glorious. Commissioned by Bishop Eadfrith at the beginning of the eighth century, it was a sumptuous and expensive undertaking. Some of the work may have been done at Old Melrose and tradition holds that materials for the binding and the covers came from the banks of the Tweed.

When Aidan founded the monastery around the year 635, the opulence of the Lindisfarne Gospels lay in the future. More immediate political concerns occupied the mind of Melrose's patron, King Oswald. With the catastrophic defeat of the Gododdin at Catterick in 603, it appears that their lands quickly fell under Anglian control. The seizure of much of the Tweed Basin, what might be seen as Greater Bernicia, probably allowed Oswald to extract tribute from the native lords in the Lothians. But the decisive event was not long in coming. For the year 638, the Annals of Ulster record the siege of Etin, more conventionally Dun Eidyn, now Edinburgh.

With the fall of the great stronghold on the Castle Rock, the Lothians saw an influx of English-speaking lords and settlers. Place names mark their progress, especially in East Lothian. Those which contain the elements *ingas, ingaham, ingatun* or *ing* are reckoned by toponymists to be early and there is a clutch of them along the banks of the River Tyne, a pattern which strongly suggests arrival by sea. Tyninghame means simply 'the settlement of the people by the Tyne'. Nearby was the lost name of Lyneryngham, what East Linton used to be called. It incorporates an Old Welsh word, *linn*, for a pool. And Whittinghame recalls the name of one the leaders of the early Anglian colonists. It was 'the settlement of the people of Hwita'. Another magnate left his name in Haddington, the old county town. He was Hoedda. There are many other, possibly later, English elements in East Lothian place-names such as *ham* in Morham, Auldhame and Oldhamstocks and *botl*, meaning 'a hall', in Bolton and Eldbotle, a medieval settlement now deserted.

What is also striking is how quickly the newly converted Anglian settlers acquired their own saint. Now largely forgotten, the cult of St Baldred or Bealdhere was once popular and his feast day on 6 March was celebrated widely. Now, only place-names hint at his old renown – near the mouth of the Tyne is a rock formation known as St Baldred's Cradle, off North Berwick is an outcrop called St Baldred's Boat and at Auldhame Farm, reputed to have been the holy man's birthplace, there is a St Baldred's Well. At some point in the seventh century, he is said to have founded communities of monks at Tyninghame, Preston Kirk (where there is another St Baldred's Well) and at Auldhame. When the Vikings began to raid the eastern coasts of Britain in the eighth, ninth and tenth centuries, Baldred's church was reported as a target. It must have been wealthy to attract such unwelcome attention. But the life and work of Baldred himself (even the date of his death, sometimes given as late as 756) lack substance and much of his story may have been safely ignored as myth-history or, at best, a series of whiskery traditions – until a remarkable archaeological find came to light.

In May 2005, a dig at Auldhame Farm uncovered the remains of a very old church. Small, with rounded corners and several other telltale signs of great antiquity, the building may have dated as early as the seventh century – according to tradition, precisely the period of Baldred's ministry. And around the founds of the church lay a cemetery with more than two hundred grave sites.

The finds at Auldhame not only appear to confirm Baldred's birthplace, they also occur in the midst of the small group of other place-names which remember him. One of these is very intriguing. From the old church at Auldhame, it is possible to look directly out to sea and the looming mass of the Bass Rock. Perched on the outcrop are the medieval ruins of St Baldred's Chapel – was this the site of a *diseart*, a Celtic hermitage like that on Skellig Michael which rises dramatically out of the Atlantic off the Irish coast? A saint with an English name founding a *diseart*? There may well be more layers to Baldred's story than first appear.

Particular to East Lothian, this central figure in a highly localised and intense cult may have closer links to the area and its Celtic past. Like a landlocked version of the Bass Rock, Traprain Law dominates the landscape east of Haddington. It was certainly a principal stronghold of Gododdin kings, and archaeologists have established a long sequence of occupation. But no excavator was prepared for what came to light on Monday, 12 May 1919.

After the turmoil of the First World War and having himself been badly wounded on the Western Front, George Pringle must have longed for the relative peace and slow pace of archaeology. But, when he set his workmen on digging at the western end of

---

St Ethernan

Also known as Itarnan, a name derived from the Latin word for 'eternal', St Ethernan is remembered on the Isle of May in the Firth of Forth. Like St Baldred at the Bass Rock and the holy men on Inchkeith, the islands in the Forth made good disearts – they were apart from the world but in sight of it. St Ethernan died around 669 and was buried on the Isle of May, which soon became a place of pilgrimage. Many early Christian burials, dating from the fifth to the tenth century have been found and, in the ninth century, a drystane chapel for a shrine to St Ethernan was built. In the twelfth century, a priory of Benedictine monks was established and, near the high altar, in a place of great sanctity, a young man was buried sometime in the fourteenth century. Excavators found something remarkable. Wedged into the mouth of the skull was half a scallop shell. It was the badge of pilgrims to the shrine of St James at Santiago de Compostela in northern Spain. The young man had been there and the shell was buried with him so that St Peter might more easily recognise his piety. And his family had redoubled his chance of reaching Heaven by having him buried on one of Scotland's most sacred islands. Now St Ethernan is almost completely forgotten and the Isle of May no more than part of a picturesque view.

---

the spectacular hill fort of Traprain, Pringle's hopes for a quiet life evaporated. On that Monday afternoon, a pit full of treasure was discovered. Buried beneath what turned out to be the floor of a house, workmen found more than a hundred items of fine Roman silverware. There were tableware, cups, spoons, bowls, flagons and coins. Little value appears to have been placed on the craftsmanship for many of the objects had been cut up or folded in such a way as to suggest they might be melted down. These were not *objets d'art* but bullion. Perhaps it was tribute paid by the government of Britannia towards the end of the life of the province. The eclectic nature of the pieces certainly suggests an improvised exercise, valuables raised in ad hoc taxation from wealthy individuals. The territory of the Gododdin lay in a strategically vital position, between the Pictish kings on the northern shores of the Forth and beyond and the sparse garrison of Hadrian's Wall. The coins found amongst the spoons and cups were datable to the reign of the Emperor Honorius, from AD 395 to 423. It was a huge and immensely valuable hoard.

It was also an archaeologist's dream, what almost everyone who delves into the soil of an ancient site hopes to find. The official director of the dig on Traprain Law was Alexander Curle, who ran the National Museum of Antiquities in Edinburgh and his weekly visit was not due for another five days. George Pringle judged that Curle ought to be informed immediately of this extraordinary find and a workman was sent down off the hill to nearby East Linton to make a telephone call. This was 1919 and privacy on the phone was not always assured as operators connected callers so Pringle advised his messenger to be discreet – too discreet for Curle waited until the following day to make his way east from Edinburgh. But, once he climbed the hill and looked into the uncovered pit, the impact must have been jaw-dropping. Treasures like Tutankhamen's were the stuff of archaeological legend and, while the Gododdin king who sat on Traprain Law was no pharaoh, Curle could see that this glittering hoard meant that he was no grunting savage either. Silver gathered together on this scale meant power and, in the Dark Ages, military power.

But what was its precise significance? Something as precious as the Traprain treasure is likely to have been buried only in time of peril and it must be significant that a new rampart was thrown up around the old stronghold at about the same time as the coin dates. And then, sometime after 400, the occupation of the site appears to have come to an abrupt end. The silver was left in its pit and forgotten for 1,500 years.

Recent excavations on the summit of Traprain Law have come across evidence of early Christian burial and, like the emergence of Baldred and his church from the mists of tradition and conjecture, these new finds may hint strongly at something more. Despite his English name, Baldred is believed to have been a Celtic priest, or at least a priest trained and ordained in a Celtic atmosphere, and to have been sent from the west by St Kentigern to convert the heathen Angles who had settled in East Lothian. Kentigern, or Mungo, has a more substantial historical personality and his principal fame is as the apostle of Strathclyde, the old kingdom of Alt Clut. But his beginnings were said to be at Traprain.

At this point, the story begins to blur into incredibility. Kentigern's medieval biographer, Jocelyn of Furness – an abbey in South Cumbria – appears to have understood Old Welsh and possibly Gaelic. The great scholar, K. H. Jackson, believed that the life of the saint was adapted and translated in Latin by Jocelyn and that it may preserve features of a much older tale. In any case, it seems that Kentigern was born of royal Gododdin blood and conceived in or around Traprain Law – but not legitimately. His illicitly fornicating mother, Princess Thenu, was condemned to be thrown off the cliffs of the law as a punishment handed down by her pagan father. But after prayers to the Virgin Mary, presumably for a soft landing, she was cast adrift in a coracle in the Firth of Forth. After having fetched up at Culross, the seaside sanctuary of St Serf, Kentigern was born. And his exemplary life followed. Stripped of its Old Testament overtones, the tale may reflect the reality of banishment to the periphery of the Gododdin kingdom. And, as with Columba, it may confirm the aristocratic origins of one of the north's most famous saints.

Whether or not the legend that Baldred was sent by Kentigern to East Lothian to convert the Anglian settlers has any substance, the reality was that the new arrivals appear to have organised themselves into parishes and attracted priests to minister to them. The churches at Auldhame, Tyninghame, Haddington and East Linton may have had their fabric frequently changed and renewed but they are all very ancient foundations, perhaps predating the expansion of Bernicia into the Lothians in the seventh century.

To the south of the Lammermuir Hills the more famous church at Old Melrose was flourishing. And the atmosphere of piety around it began to attract young men who believed they had a vocation. One of these would become Britain's greatest medieval saint, a man whose holiness was revered all over Western Europe, the most famous Bernician who ever lived, who would inspire one of the world's greatest cathedrals and whose powerful, charismatic personality still inhabits a beautiful and otherworldly island.

Some time around 651, Cuthbert appeared at the gates of the monastery of Old Melrose:

By chance Boisil was standing at the monastery gates when he arrived and thus saw him first. Cuthbert dismounted, gave his horse and spear to a servant (he had not yet put off secular dress) and went into the church to pray. Boisil had an intuition of the high degree of holiness to which the boy he had just been looking at would rise, and said just this single phrase to the monks with whom he was standing; 'Behold the servant of the Lord,' imitating Him who, at the approach of Nathaniel, exclaimed: 'Behold an Israelite indeed, one in whom there is no guile'. An old veteran, Sigfrith, priest of Jarrow monastery, told me the tale; he was there with Boisil at the time, a mere youth in the first steps of monastic life. Now he is living the life of perfection. He has only a few feeble breaths in him and is thirsting for the joys of the future life.

Boisil said no more. He welcomed Cuthbert and when he explained the purpose of his visit, namely to leave the world behind him, Boisil received him with great kindness into the community.

This passage from Bede's *Life of Cuthbert* has the quality of reportage, gilded a little perhaps but undoubtedly made the more authentic by old Sigfrith's recollections. Riding a horse, carrying a spear and accompanied by a servant, Cuthbert was clearly an aristocrat of some degree, like most of the leaders of the early church. And his name is English, meaning 'famous' and 'bright'. The latter element is clear in the Galloway place-name, Kirkcudbright, which means what it sounds like, 'Cuthbert's Kirk'. The young man's name passed into common currency as both a surname and a Christian name and, like the seventy-two church dedications to him, it is concentrated in the north of England and Scotland, broadly in the expanded territory of ancient Northumbria.

Traditions vary but, much to the continuing distaste of some at Durham Cathedral, it seems likely that Cuthbert came from Lauderdale, the valley which saw the bloody battle at Degsastan fifty years before. In his magisterial *Antiquities of Roxburghshire and Adjacent Districts*, Alexander Jeffrey recorded the belief that the young man rode only a short distance to Old Melrose, from the disappeared settlement of Wranghame, at the foot of Brotherstone Hill. It appears that he had been fostered out to a family there and raised by a woman called Kenspid. Bede wrote that he often visited 'the house of his old nurse, indeed he always called her "mother"'. Aristocratic boys were often sent away from home in this way and fosterage was a tradition which persisted amongst the Highland clans until the eighteenth century.

Although much of Bede's hagiography is formulaic, consciously drawn from biblical examples and designed to establish Cuthbert, the man of God, as a great saint, the author includes a remarkable passage in the prologue addressed to Bishop Eadfrith and the community of monks on Lindisfarne:

While the book was still in note form, it was often looked over and revised by our very reverend brother, the priest Herefrith, whenever he came here, and by others who had lived a long time with the man of God, and who were, therefore, more conversant with the details of his life. On their advice I made several amendments. I have tried to avoid all ambiguity or hair-splitting and write a clear investigation of the truth in simple terms. I have already taken care to let you yourselves examine what I have written, so that what was false could be amended, what was true confirmed.

When, with the help of the Lord, the book was finished, and had been read for two days before the elders and teachers of your community, and its every detail had been considered, they then approved all I had written, declaring it fit to be read and transcribed by all whose holy zeal moved them to do so. The discussions you held among yourselves have brought to light many other facts, just as important as those I record here and well worth writing down, except that it hardly seems right to make insertions and add to a carefully planned and completed work. Furthermore, since I have been quick to carry out the task you thought fit to impose on me, may I suggest that you crown your kindness by not being slow to reward me with your prayers. When, in reading my book, your hearts are raised to a more burning desire for the Kingdom of Heaven, by the memory of our holy father, do not forget to intercede with the divine mercy on behalf of one so small, so that I may be found worthy on earth to long for and hereafter in perfect bliss to see 'the goodness of the Lord in the land of the living'. And, when I am dead, pray for my soul and say mass for me as though I were one of your own household, and be so good as to inscribe my name on the roll with your own.

Few scholars before modern times took such trouble as Bede to verify his information from trustworthy sources where it was possible. But there is more than a faint echo of tetchiness in the second part of this extraordinary extract. Bede was not modest and knew he was scrupulous – it appears that he had been forced to cry 'enough' and defend his work from never-ending meddling from Lindisfarne. Cuthbert was a figure of vast importance – powerful Northumbrian churchmen knew it – and this unmistakable evidence of squabbling over the detail of his saintly life only serves to underline that importance. But Bede was not to be moved. Echoing clearly across thirteen centuries is the stamp of man putting his foot down. The *Life of Cuthbert* became the definitive text, the basis of a tremendously popular cult, and its author's name was indeed inscribed on the roll of the pious. In Durham Cathedral, the tomb of St Bede keeps company with that of his hero.

Bede Himself

Most of the writers of the textual sources for the Roman period and the Dark Ages have little or nothing to say about themselves. Tacitus was the son-in-law of Agricola and a Senator, Aneirin survived the battle at Catterick and Nennius apologised for his poor Latin. Uniquely, Bede of Jarrow offered posterity more than a passing sense of his life, his preoccupations, occasional irritations and his temperament. Here is his own potted autobiography at the end of the Ecclesiastical History of the English People*:*

> *I was born in the territory of this monastery. When I was seven years of age I was, by the care of kinsmen, put into the charge of the Reverend Abbot Benedict and then of Ceolfrith, to be educated. From then on I have spent all my life in this monastery, applying myself entirely to the study of the Scriptures; and amid the observance of the discipline of the Rule and the daily task of singing in the church, it has always been my delight to learn or to teach or to write. At the age of nineteen I was ordained deacon and at the age of thirty priest, both times through the ministration of the reverend Bishop John on the direction of Abbot Ceolfrith. From the time I became priest until the fifty-ninth year of my life I have made it my business, for my own benefit and that of my brothers, to make brief extracts from the works of the venerable fathers on the holy Scriptures, or to add notes of my own to clarify their sense and interpretation.*

Cuthbert's life story is related as a series of miracles, pro-phecies and pious acts woven together into a chronological sequence. Exorcisms, the power of prayer to prevent disaster and the ability to see into the future are all essential in compiling the sense of an exemplary life, one touched directly by the hand of God and one upon which a cult can begin to build. But amongst the marvels are strewn fascinating glimpses of seventh-century Bernicia.

The wide extent of Anglian control of the Tweed Basin is hinted at when Cuthbert was visited by a man in great distress. His wife had been possessed by a demon and he begged for the saint to send him a priest so that she might have comfort in her last tormented hours. But Cuthbert said that he himself would come and, more, that the man's wife would be cured at his approach and the devil completely cast out when she touched the bridle of his horse. And so it happened.

Bede begins the passage with: 'There was a sheriff [shire-reeve] of King Ecgfrith, called Hildmer.' It appears that this man lived fairly close to Old Melrose and that Cuthbert knew the couple. Like him, they were part of a local elite and Hildmer administered a royal shire on behalf of King Ecgfrith. This reference dates the incident to some time between 670 and 685 but, more particularly, the use of the phrase 'a sheriff' suggests several royal estates along the banks of the Tweed. In a territory only recently incorporated into Bernicia, such a degree of royal ownership is perhaps not surprising. Hildmer's shire may have been at Sprouston where aerial photo-graphy has revealed the outlines of several Anglian halls of the relevant period. Or perhaps the possessed woman touched the bridle of Cuthbert's horse at Philiphaugh, near Selkirk, where another hall stood. The scatter of Anglian place-names – Midlem, Bowden, Ashkirk – around the latter is suggestive. Four centuries later, much of the central Tweed Valley was still in royal hands when King David I of Scotland famously endowed three abbeys at Selkirk (later moved to Kelso), Jedburgh and Melrose.

In addition to exorcism, it appears that apostasy was another of Cuthbert's many cares:

[A]nd outside, in the world, he strove to convert people for miles around from their foolish ways to a delight in the promised joys of Heaven. Many who had the faith had profaned it by their works. Even while the plague was raging some had forgotten the mystery conferred on them in baptism and had fled to idols, as though incantations or amulets or any other diabolical rubbish could possibly avail against a punishment sent by God the Creator. To bring back both kinds of sinners he often did the rounds of the villages, sometimes on horseback, more often on foot, preaching the way of the truth to those who had gone astray. Boisil did the same in his time. It was the custom at that time among the English people that if a priest or a cleric came to a village everyone would obey his call and gather round to hear him preach.

A very early preacher's bell was unearthed at Ednam, a village with an Anglian name near Kelso, and it seems that, when he arrived at a settlement, a preacher would use one to summon the faithful. While Bede's account is a useful record of how the word of God was spread in a countryside without churches, it is also puzzling. The archaeological record, inscriptions, scraps of evidence from written sources and Bede himself attest a native British population who had been Christian for some time. They were, after all, Y Bedydd, 'the Baptised'. The Angles were recent converts and Bede specifically mentions 'the English'. At least two readings are possible. Either Cuthbert was preaching only to the communities of Anglian settlers in the Borders or native Christianity was shallow, possibly only securely established amongst the Well-Born and in need of regular reinforcement. Here is another extract from the same chapter which inclines to the latter interpretation:

He made a point of searching out those steep, rugged places in the hills which other preachers dreaded to visit because of their poverty and squalor. This, to him, was a labour of love. He was so keen to preach that sometimes he would be away for a whole week or a fortnight, or even a month, living with the rough hill folk, preaching and calling them heavenwards by his example.

The Old Welsh language hung on in the hill country of the Borders for many generations after the coming of the Bernicians and it may be that Cuthbert had the gift of tongues, having been raised in a bilingual community.

Once his congregation had listened to his stories and pious examples, 'they confessed every sin openly'. This reference catches a moment in the development of a particularly powerful aspect of early Christianity. Much influenced by Irish example, monks began to seek someone to be an *anam-cara*, a Gaelic term meaning 'a soul-friend'. Usually a fellow monk, this was a person to whom it was possible to confess sins and thereby entrust with the welfare of the soul in the afterlife. Gradually confession became a transaction between two people, private and confidential – and frequent. In Cuthbert's time, sins were, it seems, for public consumption. In small communities, they probably were anyway.

Despite his forays out into the world to spread the gospel, Cuthbert hankered after the hermetic life but with qualifications. In his last days, Boisil had prophesied that the young monk would become a bishop and Cuthbert struggled to reconcile two competing and very different religious impulses:

> 'If,' he would lament, 'I could live in a tiny dwelling on a rock in the ocean, surrounded by the swelling waves, cut off from the knowledge and sight of all, I would still not be free from the cares of this fleeting world nor from the fear that somehow the love of money might snatch me away.'

Clearly the attraction of the *diseart* was very strong but Cuthbert knew that complete isolation was probably unrealistic. Out in the fleeting world, politics was shifting and the Bernician kings were waxing immensely powerful.

In his *Life of Columba*, written a generation before Bede,

Adomnan of Iona recounted the story of a vision which came to King Oswald before the battle at Denisesburn in 634.

> That same night, just as he had been told in the vision, he marched out from the camp into battle with a modest force against many thousands. A happy and easy victory was given him by the Lord according to his promise. King Cadwallon was killed, Oswald returned as victor after battle and was afterwards ordained by God as emperor of all Britain.

Imperator Totius Britanniae – these were grand, resonant words, a very deliberate harking back to the glories of Rome and the time when Britannia was a united province and not a squabble of small kingdoms. Still standing close to its original height in many places and with many of its formidable forts largely intact, Hadrian's Wall ran through the midst of Oswald's territory and profoundly informed his aspiration. Around the year 600, his contemporary, Oswin of Deira, was said to have been born inside the walls of the old fort at Arbeia, at South Shields. The great wall was a daily reminder of the ancient might of Rome and a relic of the immense power of the imperators, as well as a persistent prompt to ambition.

Bede made much of Oswald's brief reign, claiming that he held hegemony over 'the four nations of Britain' and, at the time of writing, the Bernician king had been canonised. A saintly ruler, touched by the hand of God, was always likely to be awarded a heroic and determinant role in the *Ecclesiastical History of the English People* but it seems, in hindsight, that Bede was overstating Oswald's actual achievements.

In 641, the saintly king needed more than the aura of lost empires to save him. Here is the entry from *The Anglo-Saxon Chronicle*:

> Here Oswald, King of Northumbria, was killed by Penda the Southumbrian at Maserfield [probably Oswestry – Oswald's Tree – in Shropshire], on 5th August, and his body was buried

at Bardney. His holiness and miracles were abundantly made manifest through this island, and his hands, undecayed, are at Bamburgh . . .

And in the same year that Oswald was killed, his brother Oswy succeeded to the Northumbrian kingdom, and he ruled 28 years.

Like his brother, Oswiu became king at the age of thirty, a mature and experienced warrior in the prime of his life, but, unlike Oswald, he reigned for a long time before dying not on the battlefield but in his bed in 670. Despite Adomnan and Bede's attachment of the title of Emperor of All Britain to Oswald, it was Oswiu, the hard-bitten pragmatist who came after the saint, who turned a big name and claim into a clear political reality.

Oswiu's opening challenge lay on the southern borders of his kingdom of Bernicia. Occupying the modern counties of Durham and much of Yorkshire, Deira had been Edwin's base and, in the 640s, had fallen under the control of Oswin, the baby born in the ruins of the Roman fort at Arbeia which stood at the mouth of the Tyne. Bede wrote that Oswiu 'could not live at peace with Oswin' and the new king of Bernicia wasted little time in moving to establish himself as overlord of Deira. By 651, the way was clear. Betrayed by Deiran noblemen, Oswin had been captured, handed over to Oswiu and murdered. But instead of taking the throne himself, the new overlord installed his nephew, Aethelwald. It was to prove a dire miscalculation. Three years later Aethelwald allied himself with the pagan King Penda of Mercia, the killer of his father at Oswestry. Here are extracts from *The Anglo-Saxon Chronicle* and Bede which describe, almost as a matter of routine, the treachery and violence of seventh-century politics:

Here Oswy killed Penda at the River Winwaed and 30 royal children with him, and some of them were kings . . . And Peada, Penda's offspring, succeeded to the kingdom of the Mercians . . . But that king Peada ruled no length of time, because he was betrayed by his own queen at Eastertide.

And Bede sketched in more detail:

> But Oswald's son, Aethelwald, who should have helped them [at
> the battle at the Winwaed] had gone over to the enemy and had
> acted as a guide to Penda's army against his own kin and country,
> although during the actual battle he withdrew and awaited the
> outcome in a place of safety. When battle had been joined, the
> pagans suffered defeat. Almost all the thirty commanders who
> had come to Penda's aid were killed . . . This battle was fought
> close by the River Winwaed, which at that time was swollen by
> heavy rains and had flooded the surrounding country: as a result
> many more were drowned while attempting to escape than
> perished by the sword.

The Winwaed flowed through the district of 'Loidis', according to Bede, and it is the ancestor of the modern name of Leeds,
part of the ancient kingdom of Elmet and before that, the
Ladenses. The defeat and destruction of the thirty war bands
who rode with Penda to the Winwaed, if not an exaggeration,
probably swung the balance of power decisively in Oswiu's
favour and firmly established his overlordship of Mercia, which
stretched from the Humber to the Thames. And the victory at
the Winwaed made the Bernician king *Imperator Totius Britanniae*,
in control of almost all of the old Roman province. But it was not
to be enough. Oswiu's ambition turned his gaze westwards.

With the death of Owain, the Son of Prophecy, the Celtic
kingdom of Rheged seemed to fade into the shadows of history.
After the 590s, little is heard of the once-mighty dynasty of Urien
and his famous son. But, in 642, a remarkable echo and an
extraordinary name appear in the records. In a ninth-century
compilation, the *Liber Vitae*, kept in Durham Cathedral, a Rheged
princess called Rieinmelth is noted as the wife of King Oswiu of
Bernicia. This *Book of Life* lists a series of other names which
strongly suggest that it is a copy of a document written in
Bernicia in the seventh century, perhaps in the scriptorium at
Lindisfarne. Rieinmelth's name means the 'Queen of Lightning'.

Mercian Gold

'Spirits of yesteryear, take me where the coins appear.' Every time he fired up his metal detector, Terry Herbert uttered this his ritual prayer. In August 2009, it was answered and in spectacular fashion. While Terry was quartering a field near his house in Hammerwich, near Lichfield in Staffordshire, he came across a huge Anglo-Saxon hoard of gold – the largest ever found. There were more than 1,500 pieces, ranging from beautifully worked buttons to sword fittings and war gear of all sorts. In all, the Hammerwich hoard weighed in at a staggering five kilos of gold. Archaeologists have provisionally dated the pieces to the early decades of the powerful Mercian kingdom, some time between 675 and 725. Lichfield was an important royal centre but Gareth Williams of the British Museum does not believe that the hoard necessarily belonged to King Aethelbald or any of his predecessors. He sees the pieces as being the property of an aristocratic war band – perhaps the proceeds of successful warfare – and, more than that, the scale and value of the hoard strongly suggest a vast divide between a warrior elite who had fabulous wealth and the rest of society, farmers, bonded workers and slaves, who had nothing and were merely subsisting. It is a dazzling find and, on a most basic level, shows that Dark Ages potentates had tremendous resources.

She was a direct descendant of Urien, the granddaughter of Owain, and it seems that her marriage to Oswiu was a strategic dynastic union. And it also means that Rheged remained distinct and important until the 640s but the doings of its lords and princes went unnoticed in surviving chronicles. In any event, the great Celtic kingdom of the west began to disintegrate. In the *Life of St Wilfrid of Ripon*, it was recorded that Oswiu had been active on the western side of the Pennines, probably taking control of the fertile farmlands of Southern Rheged.

Settlers with Anglian names were also beginning to establish themselves around the neck of the Solway Firth. In what was Northern Rheged, a great monastery was built at Hoddom. Like Old Melrose it was sited in a loop of a river, the Annan, and there was almost certainly an earlier native foundation. The nearby place-name offers a tantalising hint. About a mile to the east lies the village of Ecclefechan. The name means 'the Little Church' – probably so called because of 'the Great Church' at Hoddom.

There exists a tradition that Oswiu endowed Hoddom in memory of Rieinmelth and it seems that the Queen of Lightning may have died young, perhaps in childbirth as so many women did. But, as ever, there were other royal motives. Hoddom was said to have been linked with St Kentigern, the child of the princess from Traprain Law. Conventionally associated with Strathclyde, whose dominion would later reach southwards as far as Cumbria, and appointed as the founding Bishop of Glasgow, he was, by the middle of the seventh century, a figure of great prestige amongst the Old Welsh-speaking population. By endowing Hoddom in memory of a native princess and adopting a native saint, his cult and a location closely associated with him and thereby elevating the importance of the monastery in the loop of the river, the Bernician kings were legitimising their political takeover of Rheged.

There was another, less direct, reason for Oswiu and his successors to include figures like Kentigern. The old saint had links with the Roman past – the genealogies connected him and his sponsors with the likes of Coel Hen, the last duke of the Britains – and, at one time, southern Scotland, Strathclyde, Manau and Gododdin had briefly been part of the Empire in the days of Agricola, Severus and the shadowy province of Valentia. If Oswiu claimed to be *Imperator Totius Britanniae*, the blessing of Kentigern added substance.

After the victory on the Winwaed and the establishment of his British hegemony, Oswiu received a rare approving notice from Bede:

King Oswy gave thanks to God for his victory and dedicated his daughter, Aelffled, who was scarcely a year old, to his service in perpetual virginity. He also gave twelve small grants of land, where heavenly warfare was to take the place of earthly, and to provide for the needs of monks to make constant intercession for the perpetual peace of his nation. Six of these lay in the province of Deira, and six in Bernicia, each of ten hides in extent, making one hundred and twenty in all.

It may be that, of the six estates in Bernicia, one was given to Hoddom, perhaps others to Old Melrose (such as Yetholmshire and the less identifiable shire of Melrose) and to Coldingham, a monastery on the Berwickshire coast associated with the king's sister, Aebbe.

Anglian penetration westwards is difficult to date and trace but a series of very early place-names in Dumfries and Galloway is suggestive. Beyond Hoddom and the Annan, it seems that colonisation (almost certainly following the eviction and displacement of native landowners) proceeded by sea. Many of the early place-names are close to the Solway shore – such as Southwick, Kirkcarswell, Twynholm, Penninghame and, most famously, a cluster around and including Kirkcudbright, 'the Church of Cuthbert'. These settlements are distributed in groups and it seems that, in Galloway, native *maenors* were taken over and renamed as shires. Place names offer strong corroboration. To the west of Gatehouse of Fleet and the impressive castle at Cardoness, the Skyreburn flows into Wigtown Bay and the Solway. The derivation is from the Anglian *scir-burne* and it meant 'the shire-stream' – that is, the western boundary of a shire. Beyond the Skyreburn, the Cairnsmore Hills reach right down to the edge of the Solway coast. The land is good only for stock rearing and the place-names are predominantly Old Welsh – Carsluith, Minnigaff and Kirroughtree.

Oswiu's arm is unlikely to have reached as far west as the Skyreburn and the naming of Kirkcudbright must postdate the death of the saint by a suitable distance but the successors of the Imperator certainly saw Galloway as part of Greater Bernicia.

Pressing matters closer to Oswiu's home were much on the king's mind. Christianity had come to Bernicia in at least two versions. Oswiu and his brother, Oswald, had been refugees at Iona and elsewhere in Dalriada during the reign of Edwin of Deira. When they themselves came to power, it seemed natural to invite Aidan and other priests from the west to convert their pagan countrymen but, in so doing, the Bernicians set up a conflict which Oswiu had to resolve.

Queen Eanfled was a Deiran princess who had been forced into exile in Kent after the death of her father Edwin at Denisesburn in 631. There she was exposed to a version of Christianity which was more Roman in its nature, which looked to the papacy for leadership and doctrinal guidance and which, crucially, calculated the date of Easter differently from the Ionan clergy sponsored by her husband Oswiu. This was no small matter of domestic difficulty or a footnote to history. Eastertide was the central festival in the Christian calendar and all others were dated from it. In the royal household and in different parts of Oswiu's kingdom, all feasts were therefore celebrated on different days, the whole year being out of kilter. Not only was this awkward, there was also a vital doctrinal matter involved. Early Christians believed that prayer was tremendously powerful and that it worked best when it was collective and simultaneous. At Easter, when God confronted Satan and his hellish army of fiends, believers could lend maximum support in the good fight when they all prayed together and worshipped at Mass on the same day. It was a quasi-military matter of numbers. The mathematical disparity between the Ionan and Roman traditions divided the forces of the Lord at the time of His greatest need. Something had to be done.

Queen Eanfled had gathered about her a band of pious supporters and one young aristocrat who had the gifts of oratory and argument and a command of the scriptures. When Oswiu convened a synod at Whitby in 664, Wilfrid would speak for the Queen's party and put the case for allegiance to Rome and the papacy, while Bishop Colman of Lindisfarne would present the argument for Iona.

The teachings of Columba, said the bishop, were derived directly from the Apostle John and were therefore both ancient and correct. Wilfrid appealed to greater authority by contending that the Pope, as Bishop of Rome and the successor of St Peter,

Easter Tables

Being a famously movable feast, Easter has been the subject of regular – and recent – controversy for almost 2,000 years. In 1923, the Eastern Orthodox Church called a conference in Istanbul to settle disagreements and, in 1997, the World Council of Churches met in Aleppo to decide the issue for once and for all – at least until the next time. Taking into account the latest astronomical data and the new sophistication, they decided to endorse the basic formula agreed by the Council of Nicaea in 318. Easter should fall on the first Sunday after the first full moon after or on the vernal equinox. To be absolutely unequivocal, the council set dates for Easter Sunday until 2020. Here they are:

> 2011 – 24 *April*
> 2012 – 8 *April*
> 2013 – 31 *March*
> 2014 – 20 *April*
> 2015 – 5 *April*
> 2016 – 27 *March*
> 2017 – 16 *April*
> 2018 – 1 *April*
> 2019 – 21 *April*
> 2020 – 12 *April*

the rock upon whom the Church was founded, should be seen as paramount. Moreover, the Gospel of St Matthew recorded Jesus' promise to Peter: 'I will give you the keys of the kingdom of Heaven.' This last appeared to be conclusive. Colman made no counter-argument and Oswiu ruled that the Roman calculation of the date of Easter be universally adopted.

While his domestic arrangements, to say nothing of his relationship with Queen Eanfled, will have improved, the Bernician king made his decision for political reasons. *Romanitas*, the idea of Roman-ness, mattered very much and, if Oswiu could draw closer to Rome as the focus of the Christian Church in the west, then his own pretensions to imperial prestige would be enhanced. In many ways, the Church was seen as the heir of the Empire. It spoke in Latin and ruled an empire of souls from the old imperial capital. For Oswiu, there was also the compelling imperative of political unity. In compiling his vast domain, which stretched in the east from the Forth to the Thames and was edging ever further westwards, the king knew that it was better to create a single, unified church. And so realpolitik defeated sentiment and, however sad Oswiu may have been to find against the religious traditions he grew up with, he did not hesitate.

Ionan monks left Bernicia. Colman quit the bishopric of Lindisfarne and returned to Iona. From Ripon a young Cuthbert accompanied the expelled Abbot Eata back to Old Melrose and, despite anomalies and objections, it appears that Oswiu's directive was widely adopted. It was eloquent testament to his power and reach.

At the Synod of Whitby in 664, Oswiu may have had occasion to translate. Bilingual in Gaelic and Early English (and very possibly in Old Welsh too) as a result of his upbringing, the king would certainly have understood both Colman and Wilfrid even if they did not understand each other. However, what both priests did have in common was the language of the Church and of the emperors and the legions. With the conversion of the Anglo-Saxons and its royal sponsorship, Old English imported hundreds of Latin words. Many are still familiar – monk, priest, bishop, angel, disciple, Mass, relic, shrine and others which directly describe the workings and institutions of the Church. Just as importantly, the arrival of these words also enabled and encouraged greater subtlety of expression. Old English was generally clumsy with abstracts (although good on observation) and as the new language of Christianity developed so did the range of discourse. Sometimes as a direct translation, occasionally as interpretation, new words and phrases were coined. Judgement Day became Doomsday, Spiritus Sanctus became the Holy Ghost and *feond* or 'fiend' was a synonym for the Devil. Over time, a process of translation would produce a wider and richer vocabulary – for example, the Latin *evangelium* means, literally, 'good news'. Old English rendered this as *god-spell* which became 'gospel'.

As the Northumbrian dialect spread over southern Scotland and all the way down the Humber and the Mersey, more welcome uniformity bound Oswiu's empire together. How quickly or emphatically Old English displaced Old Welsh is difficult to know but as the colonised are forced to understand the language of the conqueror (from the Roman to the British and American empires), it is likely that English was spoken and understood as far north as the Tay by the end of the seventh century. And Northumbrian, the ancestor of Scots, must be counted as one of Scotland's ancient tongues. And Oswiu must also rank as one of the greatest kings ever to rule in Scotland.

In 670, the Imperator died and was buried at Whitby. His son, Ecgfrith, appears to have succeeded without fuss or difficulty and the new king immediately signalled a continuity with his father's policies. After the dedication of a new church at Ripon, Ecgfrith and his noblemen gave to Bishop Wilfrid 'consecrated places in various districts which British clergy had deserted when fleeing from the hostile sword wielded by the hand of our own people'.

In 671, Ecgfrith fought and won a battle against the Pictish kings somewhere in the north. It seems he was able to extend Northumbrian hegemony beyond the Forth for the first time. A year later, he rode south with his war bands to confront Wulfhere, son of Penda of Mercia and leader of 'all the southern kingdoms', and again Ecgfrith was victorious.

Like his father and their historian, Bede, heavenly warfare was also on King Ecgfrith's mind and there were few greater warriors for Christ than Cuthbert whose reputation for piety had been growing. When the see of Lindisfarne fell vacant in 685, the ascetic monk seemed the obvious choice but there was a problem. Bede takes up the story:

Thus Cuthbert served God in solitude for many years in a hut surrounded by an embankment so high that he could see nothing but the heavens for which he longed so ardently. Then it came about that a great Synod was held under the presidency of Archbishop Theodore of blessed memory, and in the presence of King Ecgfrith. This assembled near the River Aln at a place called Twyford, or the Two Fords; and the whole company unanimously elected Cuthbert as bishop of the church of Lindisfarne. But although many messengers and letters were sent to him, nothing would induce him to abandon his hermitage. At length the king in person, accompanied by the most holy Bishop Trumwine and other devout and distinguished men, took boat to the island. There they were joined by many of the Lindisfarne brethren, and the whole company knelt before him and adjured him in God's name and begged him with tears to consent, until they eventually drew him, also in tears, from his dearly loved retreat, and brought him to the Synod. Still profoundly reluctant, he at length bowed to the unanimous decision of the whole assembly, and was persuaded to assume the burden of episcopal dignity.

There is an atmosphere of formula around this story – the ritual reluctance and protestations of unworthiness of newly elected popes is a modern echo but the substance of it is likely to have been authentic. At the time Bede was writing, there will have been people still living who witnessed the events he described.

Cuthbert was Bishop of Lindisfarne for only two years but, as soon as he accepted office, he behaved like a prince of the church, a powerful figure at the centre of contemporary politics. The contents of his coffin offer a sense of the worldly bishop and the splendour of his office. In 1540 Cuthbert's shrine in Durham cathedral was smashed by ruffians acting for King Henry VIII in the licensed land grab known as the dissolution of the monasteries. Relics were treated like rubbish and the gorgeous Lindisfarne Gospels removed to London (from where they have yet to return). The saint was hastily reburied in the cathedral precincts and, when antiquarians opened the grave in 1827, they expected to find that Henry VIII's men had robbed out everything of value. Instead they retrieved a beautiful pectoral cross made from gold and garnets, an ivory comb, a small travelling altar bound in silver and a copy of St John's Gospel. Cuthbert may have been dragged in his hermit's rags from the island of Inner Farne but, when he put on the episcopal cope, he looked the part.

The year 685 turned out to be fateful. Here is Bede again:

> Cuthbert set off to Carlisle to speak to the Queen [Eormenburh] who had arranged to stay at her sister's convent to await the outcome of the war. The day after his arrival the citizens conducted him around the city walls to see a remarkable Roman fountain that was built into them. He was suddenly disturbed in spirit. He leaned heavily on his staff, turned his face dolefully to the wall, then straightening himself up and looking up into the sky, he sighed deeply and said almost in a whisper, 'Perhaps at this moment the battle is being decided.'

And it was. Far to the north, King Ecgfrith had ridden to Dunnichen, near Forfar. It was a punitive expedition, intended to bring the Pictish king Bridei back into the Northumbrian empire – compel him into subjection. But Cuthbert, the hermit turned strategist, had advised against the war and his fears prompted a fit of dire prophecy against the city wall at Carlisle.

Bridei followed the strategy of his ancient Caledonian ancestors when they retreated in front of Agricola's legions in AD 83 but he was a great deal more successful when the inevitable battle came.

> [King Ecgfrith] rashly led an army to ravage the province of the Picts. The enemy pretended to retreat, and lured the king into narrow mountain passes, where he was killed with the greater part of his forces on the 20th of May in his 40th year and the 15th of his reign.

Despite Bede's scathing assessment, the expedition did show both the reach and power of the Northumbrians but not their tactical acuity. Historians have argued over the location of the battle and it seems very likely that it took place near Dunnichen. The English name was Nechtansmere, cognate with Dun Nechtan, or the modern Dunnichen. In Old Welsh, Ecgfrith and his war bands were slaughtered at Linn Garan, 'the Heron Lake'. At the supposed battle site, old maps show a moss or shallow lake – the sort of place where herons wade and fish. And it seems that, like the rout at the Winwaed, one army was trapped between the enemy and the water.

Only three miles away stands the remarkable Aberlemno Stone, the sculptural record of this signal conflict. Even though the carvings were made at least a century later, memories of the great Pictish victory at the Heron Lake will not have dimmed. And it is beyond credibility that the patron who paid the sculptor will have had the stone erected in the wrong place. In any event, defeat at Dunnichen marked an abrupt end to Northumbrian suzerainty in the north And it also prompted Cuthbert to advise his Queen to take urgent action and leave Carlisle in case her husband's death sparked a palace coup. Here is more from Bede:

> Tomorrow being Sunday you cannot travel. Monday morning at daybreak leave in your chariot for the Royal City [Bamburgh]. Enter quickly for perhaps the king has been slain. Tomorrow I have been invited to a neighbouring monastery to dedicate the chapel but as soon as the dedication is over I shall follow you.

It is known that Cuthbert and Queen Eormenburh travelled on the Stanegate, the Roman road to the south of Hadrian's Wall. By the time they had gained the safety of the fortress at Bamburgh, news may have arrived from the north that the king was dead and his army destroyed. In any case, it may have been Cuthbert who steadied the dynastic ship. Ecgfrith's brother Aldfrith had entered the monastery at Iona as a scholar rather than a monk and had travelled extensively in Ireland and the west – as far from Ecgfrith as possible for Northumbrian kings could be ruthless about the elimination of potential rivals. Cuthbert may have sent word recalling Aldfrith and, when the wandering scholar arrived at Bamburgh, he certainly enjoyed the Bishop of Lindisfarne's support in the crucial early stages of his reign.

Ecgfrith's defeat marked the end of Northumbrian domination in the north. Bede again:

Henceforward the hopes and strengths of the English realm began to waver and slip backward ever lower. The Picts recovered their own lands that had been occupied by the English, while the Irish living in Britain and a proportion of the Britons themselves regained their freedom, which they have now preserved for about 46 years. Many of the English were at this time killed, enslaved or forced to flee from Pictish territory. Among them, the most reverend man of God Trumwine, who had been appointed their bishop, withdrew with his people from the monastery of Abercurnig [Abercorn], which was situated in English territory but stood close to the firth that divides the lands of the English from those of the Picts.

This is a key passage to any clear understanding of the impact of the defeat at Dunnichen and the subsequent history of Northumbria. And, as he often does, Bede summed up the situation succinctly when he observed that, after 685, the new king Aldfrith 'ably restored the shattered fortune of the kingdom, though within smaller boundaries'.

Bede's support and obvious approval are scarcely surprising. As a scholar-monk Aldfrith was a royal version of the historian himself and Bede awarded him the superlative of *vir doctissimus*, 'a most learned man'. Others were also enthusiastic. The great European ecclesiastic, Alcuin of York, tutor to Charlemagne and one of the leading figures of the Carolingian Renaissance, called Aldfrith *rex et simul magister*, 'both a king and a teacher'. And it was true.

Having been educated in exile in the Celtic west, most notably under the pious and learned Abbot of Iona, Adomnan, Aldfrith was also known by the Gaelic name of Flann Fina mac Ossu. It

The Strasbourg Oaths

When the Deiran cleric, Alcuin of York, went to become head of a new academy of scholars at the court of Charlemagne, he became centrally involved in a fundamental language shift in Europe. Not only did Alcuin invent the difference between upper and lower case letters, he also produced a standard form of the pronunciation of Latin for all of the vast Carolingian Empire. This meant that different dialects were not used and that a distinction between Latin and what came to be called 'vulgar speech' developed. French, Italian and Spanish date the beginnings of their independent development from Alcuin's reforms. A moment in this fascinating process was caught in 842 when two of Charlemagne's grandsons had publicly to swear to support each other in front of their supporters. Charles the Bald spoke a very Latinised version of Early French whereas Ludwig the German and his men spoke Early German. Each man needed a crib sheet and they have survived. Here is Ludwig's and what he read out in Early French. Versions in Latin and English follow:

Pro Deo amur et pro Christian poblo et nostro commun salvament, d'ist di in avant, in quant Deus savir et podir me dunant, si salvarai eo cist meon fradre Karlo et in ajudha et in cadhuna coas, si cum om per dreit son fradra salvar dift . . .

Pro Dei amore et pro christiano populo et nostro communi salvamento, de hoc die in posterum, in quanto Deus sapientiam et potentiam mihi donabit, sic servabo ego hunc meum fratrem Carolum et in adiumento et in re quaque, ut quis iure suum fratrem servare debet . . .

For God's love and the Christian people and our common salvation, from this day forward, insofar as God gives me knowledge and power, I shall so keep this my brother Charles both in aid and in every thing as when a man in right his brother should keep . . .

says something of his parentage and means, approximately, 'a Prince, son of Fina, son of Oswiu'. Fina was an Irish princess and her lineage might well have been welcoming to the exiled Northumbrian prince. Taught to speak and write fluently in

Gaelic (there being little difference between Irish and Scots dialects in the seventh century), Aldfrith produced a collection of aphorisms which often hint at his Celtic heritage. Echoing the contemporary development of a soul-friend, a confessor, the king wrote:

> A teacher deserves honour,
> Wisdom should be revered,
> The beginning of wisdom is mildness,
> Wisdom is a good gift,
> Which makes a king of a poor man,
> And a wise one of the foolish,
> Good its beginning,
> Better its end.

The great scholar, Aldhelm of Malmesbury (an Irish foundation) carried on a correspondence with Aldfrith and sent him the *Epistola ad Acircium*, a treatise on numerology, specifically the power of the number seven. The depth of the king's curiosity and learning is demonstrated in a remarkable exchange. In return for an estate of eight farms, Aldfrith was given a book on cosmology by Abbot Ceolfrith of Bede's monastery at Monkwearmouth–Jarrow. No doubt Aldfrith gained spiritually but the story comes from a near-contemporary source and the substance may well be accurate.

While in exile in the Atlantic west, it seems that the future king had been a pupil of Adomnan of Iona, whose diplomacy was to produce another book for the royal library. In 688 the abbot travelled to Northumbria, to Jarrow, where Bede was a young monk. He came to plead for the release of captives taken in war in the north in the time of King Ecgfrith. Aldfrith agreed and was rewarded with a copy of Adomnan's *De Locis Sanctis (On the Holy Places)*, a gazetteer of places of pilgrimage in the Near East (the abbot was not discouraged by the fact that he had never visited any of them). It was becoming an expensive library. Aldfrith himself may have added to it for one of his surviving groups of aphorisms might serve as a commentary on his aspirations as – according to one scholar – his status as a philosopher-king:

> Learning merits respect.
> Intelligence overcomes fury.
> Truth should be supported.
> Falsehood should be rebuked.
> Iniquity should be corrected.
> A quarrel merits mediation.
> Stinginess should be spurned.
> Arrogance deserves oblivion.
> Good should be exalted.

However banal or everyday these saying might sound to a modern ear, they are the words of a very early king who ruled in Scotland and northern England and they do offer some sense of how he and his contemporaries thought. Aldfrith's literacy and learning may have dazzled fellow intellectuals like Bede and Alcuin but these talents will have meant nothing to rival claimants to his throne. And the transition after the sudden death of Ecgfrith appears to have been bloodless or at least no reports of conflict have survived. Aldfrith probably had the support of the Scottish and Irish Celtic kings, especially if he had agreed to renounce the aims of Ecgfrith's disastrous expedition in the north.

The kingdom of Northumbria seemed to settle within accepted boundaries, and despite Bede's barb about retreat and retrenchment, these still compassed a vast area of Britain, at least a quarter of the landmass, much of it fertile farmland. The Firth of Forth and the Lothian coastline were as far north as Aldfrith's writ ran while, to the west, the old realm of Rheged, from Dumfriesshire to Galloway, was falling under Northumbrian control. Greater Bernicia also included Carlisle, much of lowland Cumbria, and the Lancashire Plain down to the Mersey. In the east all of the Lothians, the Tweed Basin, Northumberland and Durham down to the Tees, and most of modern Yorkshire were part of Aldfrith's powerful kingdom. This period of stabilisation may well be underlined by the excavation and refurbishment of long boundary ditches which can still be clearly seen. Between Doncaster and Sheffield, in the Don Valley, the Roman Rig Ditch almost certainly divided Northumbria from Mercia. Its line was carried on westwards over the high moors, where the modern A628 now runs, and is picked up on the outskirts of Greater Manchester by a six-mile-long earthwork known as Nico Ditch. It still marks the boundary between Stockport and Manchester.

While Aldfrith's undoubted but unreported political skills pacified his kingdom, his intellectual interests appear to have set a fertile ground for the flowering of what historians have called 'Northumbria's Golden Age'. For almost a century after the new king's accession, great art was made in the monasteries of the north and the first masterpieces began with the death of a saint.

Bede's account of Cuthbert's last days is both moving and very atmospheric – and, as far as it is possible to tell, it is also accurate. Unusually the scrupulous historian made use of the testimony of a witness and introduced it verbatim into his text. Herefrith was Abbot of Lindisfarne at the time he was writing and, while much of Bede's irritation at interference in his *Life of Cuthbert* may have stemmed from the criticisms made by those monks who cared for the saint at his death, there can be no doubting their devotion and piety.

Sensing that he would not be long for the world, Cuthbert resigned his bishopric and retreated to his beloved hermitage on Inner Farne. Its cliffs rise out of the turbulent tide rips of the North Sea. One of a scattered archipelago, the island lies closest to the shore, directly visible from the royal fortress at Bamburgh. On stormy nights, as the waves lashed the black rocks of Inner Farne, the kings of Northumbria could look out eastwards over the sea and marvel at the faith and fortitude of their holy men and their willing suffering in search of perfect communion with God. Perhaps a guttering candle could be made out through the darkness. At the risk of introducing a sour note of cynicism, it may be that part of the attraction of Inner Farne was its visibility from the principal seats of the kings of Northumbria, faithful patrons of Holy Mother Church.

Cuthbert was rowed out to the little island in the January of 687, when the winter weather was at its worst and he endured a life of welcome solitude for two months before he fell ill. It seems that, in the bitter chill of the hardest months, Cuthbert starved himself to death. For five days, a storm prevented any of the Lindisfarne monks from reaching Inner Farne and, when Herefrith finally came ashore, he asked:

> 'But my lord, how can you live like this? Have you gone without food all this time?'
>
> He turned back the coverlet on which he sat and showed me five onions.
>
> 'This has been my food for the last five days. Whenever my mouth was parched or burned with excessive hunger or thirst I refreshed and cooled myself with these.'
>
> One of the onions was less than half nibbled away. He added: 'My assailants have never tempted me so sorely as they have during the past five days.'
>
> I did not enquire what kind of temptations they were but contented myself with asking him to let himself be waited on. He consented and let some of us stay . . .

During his long fasts Cuthbert had thought a great deal about his death and gave instructions that he should be buried near his oratory on Inner Farne, to the east of the cross he had himself raised. When Herefrith and his brother monks asked the saint's permission to take his body for burial to Lindisfarne, the dying man refused, saying:

> '[I]t would be less trouble for you if I did stay here, because of the influx of fugitives and every other kind of malefactor which will otherwise result. They will flee for refuge to my body, for,

whatever I might be, my fame as a servant of God has been noised abroad. You will be constrained to intercede very often with the powers of this world on behalf of such men. The presence of my remains will prove extremely irksome.'

It seems that Cuthbert knew he would become the focus of a cult and, as such, a place of sanctuary for criminals and fugitives and he recoiled from the worldiness and commerce attached to that likelihood. But, after many entreaties, he ultimately agreed to allow himself to be buried in the monastic church at Lindisfarne. At last the end came.

'I went to him,' Herefrith continued, 'about the ninth hour and found him lying in a corner of the oratory, opposite the altar. I sat down beside him. He said very little, for the weight of affliction made it hard for him to speak.'

But Cuthbert did manage to warn against schism in the church and to exhort his brethren to piety, kindness and obedience.

These and like sayings he uttered at intervals . . . He passed the day quietly till evening, awaiting the joys of the world to come, and went on peacefully with his prayers throughout the night. At the usual time for night prayer I gave him the sacraments that lead to eternal life. Thus fortified with the Lord's Body and Blood in preparation for the death he knew was now at hand, he raised his eyes heavenwards, stretched his arms aloft, and with his mind rapt in the praise of the Lord sent forth his spirit to the bliss of Paradise.

I went out and announced his death to the brethren, who were themselves spending the night in prayer and vigil . . . One of the monks went without delay and lit two torches and went up, with one in each hand, to a piece of high ground to let the Lindisfarne brethren know that Cuthbert's holy soul had gone to the Lord. They had decided amongst themselves that this should be the sign of his holy death. The brother in the watch-tower at

Lindisfarne, who was sitting up all night awaiting the news, ran quickly to the church where the monks were assembled for the night office . . .

In 698, eleven years later and on the anniversary of his death, Cuthbert's body was disinterred by the monks and, in the monastic church, they witnessed a miracle. The corpse was entirely uncorrupted, its joints flexible and skin unbroken. The winding sheets were pristine and, to the amazed brothers, it looked as though Cuthbert was not dead but only sleeping.

The news of the miracle was rowed across the water to Inner Farne. There Bishop Eadberht had passed Lent 'in prayer and severe fasting, shedding tears of devotion'. He ordered that Cuthbert's tomb be elevated – that is, not reburied but placed above ground by the altar of the monastic church. It was the first stage of canonisation. As Cuthbert had foreseen, pilgrims would come to visit his tomb and indeed to touch it. Closeness to sanctity meant closeness to God and, as the cults of saints developed, many came to pray by the tomb for intercession on their behalf or for others. Bede's *Life of St Cuthbert* lists several miracles which took place in the church at Lindisfarne. And, when Eadberht died, he was buried, according to his wishes, in a casket under the sarcophagus containing the saint's uncorrupted corpse.

More marvels were to come. Some time around 698, Bishop Eadfrith began work on the magnificent achievement known as the Lindisfarne Gospels. Several accounts of the life and teachings of Jesus had been in circulation amongst early Christian communities but in 325 the Council of Nicaea authorised four, the work of the Four Evangelists, generally recited as Matthew, Mark, Luke and John. Eadfrith set to work on the immense labour of writing them all into a single volume and illuminating their stories of Christ with gloriously coloured and conceived miniature paintings.

The copying of the text was done first. Paintings of two of the gospel writers bound into the book showed how Eadfrith and other scribes of the time worked. Having placed a board across their laps, they put their feet on a stool approximately half the height of their chair. This canted the board towards the scribe and allowed him to see his work square-on rather than looking at the letters obliquely as happens when writing on a flat desk. While this set-up produced very beautiful calligraphy, the long hours needed to complete all four gospels without help must have taken their toll on Eadfrith's back and posture. And, with only small and often unglazed windows to admit it, the quality of the light was poor in monastic buildings of the seventh and eighth centuries and most scribes preferred to work outdoors when the weather allowed.

The Lindisfarne Gospels were tremendously costly in more than time and discomfort. Known as a codex, the bound book was made up of pages of vellum or calfskin. The younger the animal the better the quality of the writing surface and the monastery at Lindisfarne must have had access to large herds of cows whose progeny they could afford to slaughter each year. Four years after the first sheets of vellum had been scraped, sized in lime and stretched out for Eadfrith, another tremendous project was undertaken in Northumbria – this time at the joint monastery of Monkwearmouth–Jarrow. Three copies of the entire Bible were commissioned by Abbot Ceolfrith and, to produce the vast quantity of vellum needed, land was granted to raise a herd of 2,000 cows. In the economy of eighth-century Northumbria, this represented a huge outlay.

Once a sheet of vellum was pinned to a writing board, tiny holes were made to delineate the area for text and then it was ruled with a pointed stick. Since vellum was organic and still springy, it was hoped that these ruled lines would become quickly invisible. In the portraits of Matthew and Mark (Luke and John are shown by Eadfrith working with scrolls, the predominant form of the book in the first century AD and so historically correct), the gospel writers are seen holding quill pens. The long tail feathers of geese or swans were preferred because they could be repeatedly sharpened and, in the illustrations, none of the pens appears to have been left fledged in classic style. For closer, finer work, reed pens could be used but the pressure from a scribe's fingers usually meant a short life. Ink sat in an inkhorn often poked through a hole in the writing board. Until the middle of the twentieth century, school desks were still being made with a hole for an inkwell and the design is a direct descendant from the methods of the Northumbrian scribes. The bible-black ink used by Eadfrith was probably made from a form of carbon – either soot or burnt bones. Irish scribes sometimes used iron-gall, a black ink made from oak apples and sulphate of iron.

The text in the Lindisfarne Gospels is very beautiful. Eadfrith wrote the Latin in a script called 'insular uncial'. This probably developed from Roman cursive but the smooth surface of vellum allowed greater flourish than was possible on much rougher papyrus. Letters had more rounded forms and these could be achieved without the risk of the pen nib catching and spattering ink over the page. Uncials are capital letters but, in the Lindis-farne Gospels, Eadfrith added some ascenders or upward strokes, such as b, d, h, or l, or descenders as with p and q. Letters with bowed elements, like the last two, are given wide flourishes and ascenders are often decorated with wedge-shaped finials, an opportunity for Eadfrith to add more colour.

The gospels were written in a diminuendo style with very large and gorgeously decorated capital letters at the beginning of sections. The size of the letters gradually shrinks until a standard script is reached and this carries on until the end of a chapter or passage. And unlike earlier Roman script and inscriptions, Eadfrith made each word distinct with the use of spacing and, borrowing from Tiro, Cicero's famous secretary and the inventor of shorthand, scribes used a number of standard abbreviations.

Once Eadfrith had completed the text, he began to paint. Using compasses, set squares and protractors, he almost certainly worked out his designs and compositions on wax tablets first. Then, with a series of dots and pinpricks, he transferred the outline to the vellum and began using his tiny brushes. Those made from the coats of pine martens were much favoured. Eadfrith's palette was wide and shows the network of trading contacts these apparently isolated Northumbrian communities had. Yellow, green, blue, black, gold, silver and white could be sourced from Britain's plant life and mineral resources but rich reds such as kermes or carmine came from the Mediterranean. Lapis lazuli was brought from Afghanistan and pulverised to produce ultramarine while folium, which yielded a range of tints from pink to purple, was extracted from the sunflowers of the Mediterranean littoral.

Once the pages of the Lindisfarne Gospels were complete, they were bound in fascicles or gatherings of double pages. This was a moment in the production process which shows how much planning was required. Because the hide of a calf provided a large area for writing (and when laid on its long side, the shape of the book), it meant that double pages could be bound in multiples of at least two. If a codex was thought likely to make 16 pages then numbers one and sixteen needed to be copied on the same double sheet and so on. Not all gospels were made like this but calfskin was very expensive and the advantages of fascicle binding became quickly clear.

A beautiful leather binding and cover, richly tooled but now lost, was made for the gospels by Aethelwald, Eadfrith's successor as Bishop of Lindisfarne. And an outer cover of gold, silver and gemstones was created by a man called Billfrith the Anchorite, another term for a hermit. Perhaps he worked alone in his forge but given the precious materials he was using, he cannot have been left in isolation.

The Lindisfarne Gospels have been acclaimed as a masterwork, a perfect synthesis of Celtic and Anglo-Saxon techniques, motifs and sensibilities. In the tenth century a dedication was added and it simply said that the great book had been made 'in honour of St Cuthbert'. And, between the lines of Eadfrith's immaculate Latin text, a translation into Old English was added. It is the earliest gospel in the vernacular in England.

The vast resources devoted to making the book should be

understood in the context of the eighth century. Above all Christianity was seen as the religion of the word and the Bible as the repository of the word of God. As such the gospels, placed on the high altar during Mass, were objects of veneration in their own right. This way of looking at Eadfrith's achievement places the book alongside the great altarpieces, devotional sculpture and icons of Christian art. Made to honour a very great saint, made in the monastery he knew and loved so well, near where he went to die, the gospels are absolutely of Lindisfarne in a spiritual as well as a historical sense. It is a matter of great regret that they are kept in the British Museum in London.

While the scribes worked in the peace and beauty of Lindisfarne, all was not quiet on Northumbria's northern front. In his 'recapitulation' of dates and important events at the conclusion of his great history, Bede noted that, in 698, 'Bertred, the royal commander of the Northumbrians, was killed by the Picts'. Perhaps this defeat took place around the Stirling Gap or was the result of a reassertion of Pictish control over Fife. The battle or skirmish happened well after the death of Bridei, the victor of Dunnichen and slayer of Ecgfrith, and it is evidence of a growing power in the north. The Anglian bishopric founded at Abercorn on the southern shores of the Forth was abandoned around this time and its bishop, Trumwine, 'withdrew with his people', finding refuge deep in Northumbria at the monastery at Hartlepool. Abercorn lay very close to the old ferry crossings to Fife – near the narrows where the modern bridges stand – and within easy reach of a hostile shore opposite. If Aldfrith and his generals could not sustain a bishopric at Abercorn, it may be that their reach had shrunk back to Edinburgh and the fortress on the Castle Rock and perhaps what is now West Lothian had been lost.

Pictish kings had close dynastic links with the rulers of Dalriada and the Old Welsh-speaking kingdom of Strathclyde and, as Bede concedes, all were released from Northumbrian overlordship when Ecgfrith and his war bands fell at Dunnichen. In the south, another great power rose up to confront Aldfrith and his successors. The name Mercia derived from the word for marches or borders because it lay on the southern frontier of Northumbria but, with the long reigns of three capable kings, it ceased to be marginal and became the central political focus in England. Aethelbald, Offa and Coenwulf ruled Mercia from 716 to 821, more than a century of continuity and expansion. Directed by them, Mercian armies enforced overlordship in the south and, while Northumbria remained more or less independent, it was as a junior partner. Kings who sat on the throne at Bamburgh were no longer *Imperatores Totius Britanniae*.

Monasteries had begun to multiply in the late seventh and early eighth centuries but Bede did not approve. Here is a passage from a letter to his old pupil at Jarrow, Bishop Egbert of York:

Others even more disgracefully, since they are laymen with no experience or love of life under a rule, give money to kings and buy for themselves, under the pretext of building monasteries, estates in which they freely indulge their lust: they have these ascribed to them in hereditary right by royal charters which are confirmed by the written assent of bishops, abbots and secular magnates as though they were truly worthy of God. Having thus usurped for themselves small or large estates, free from both human and divine service, they serve in reality only their own desires as laymen in charge of monks. Moreover they do not assemble real monks there, but rather wanderers who have been expelled from genuine monasteries for the sin of disobedience, or whoever they may have enticed out of them, or any of their own followers whom they can persuade to receive the tonsure and promise monastic obedience to themselves. They thus fill the 'monasteries' they have built with groups of these deformed people and – a very ugly and unprecedented spectacle – the very same men are now occupied with wives and procreating children and now rise from their beds and accomplish assiduously whatever needs to be done inside the monastic precincts. Moreover they obtain with similar audacity places for their wives, as they say, to build 'monasteries': as these are laywomen they authorise themselves to be rulers of the handmaids of Christ. To all these people the popular proverb applies: 'Wasps can indeed make honeycomb, but they fill it with poison, not honey.'

Bede's rant may have been justified but the habit of treating monasteries like family possessions was neither new nor did it prevent them from being exemplary. The sanctity and piety of Iona and its monks are rarely questioned but ten out of its first twelve abbots were relatives of St Columba. The monastery at Whitby, scene of the famous synod, was also a family concern in its early years. The root of Bede's anger was the use and abuse of monastic status for advantage and exploitation. Religious houses and those who ran them enjoyed exemption from military service and were entitled to a share of war booty, including conquered territory. Sometimes monasteries and their property were divided between the heirs of a founder and even converted back into secular estates over time.

What underpinned monastic privilege and attracted those who subverted it was something simple and easy to underestimate in this secular age – it was absolute belief. Early Christians believed that good deeds, generous gifts, prayer and devotion (even that done by proxies) in various combinations could be accumulated in sufficient quantity to guarantee entry into Heaven. With that firmly in mind, secular rulers moved to protect monasteries and their pious monks and some even believed that the name and form of monasticism, if not its spiritual substance, was sufficient to store up credit for the afterlife.

After 25 January 1990, it turned out that even more ancient beliefs were stirring amongst the modern population of Britain. A tremendous storm blew down a very old yew tree in the churchyard at Selborne in Hampshire. It had been made enduringly famous by the parish minister, the Reverend Gilbert White, when he published *The Natural History of Selborne* in 1789. Reckoning the tree to be at least as old as the ancient church, White wrote that 'it may be deemed an antiquity'. When the yew fell in the winter of 1990, the news produced an extraordinary reaction. Almost immediately thousands of people descended on Selborne, some of them to mourn the venerable tree's passing, most to beg or steal a piece of the wood. It seemed that the yew's death had drawn upon a well of old beliefs, that an ancient power was at work, a phenomenon which both appalled and astonished the watching villagers.

Often the heartwood of very old yews dies and the trees become hollow, and therefore impossible to date by counting the rings. The outer edges survive and growth continues through a ring of root systems. Girth is used to estimate age and when it crashed to the ground the Selborne yew measured 26 feet around. It seems that White had underestimated and his beloved tree was not coeval with the church but about 2,000 years old. When archaeologists examined the upended root systems, they found the remains of many skeletons. Since 1200 and probably long before, people had been buried hard up against the sides of the tree. As it slowly grew over their graves, its roots curled around the skeletons often moving them some way from their original resting place.

These early burials inside the precincts of old churchyards and close to their yew trees continue a very long tradition. In Celtic languages and tree lore they occupy a talismanic place. Because they can live for millennia in sheltered places, are densely evergreen and always lustrous and every part of them protectively poisonous, yews have long been bathed in the light of sanctity. The name is a direct survival from Old Welsh *ywen* or *pren ywen* for 'yew tree'. It is also known in both Gaelic and Welsh as 'the Everlasting One' and 'the Tree of Life'. It was believed that the sinuous and immensely strong roots and branches took a unique grip on the earth and the air, closing around the bodies of the recently dead and drawing out their essence, their 'dream-soul', and expelling it into the sky through their ever-living branches.

Most prehistoric yews are unlikely to have been planted by the hand of man. The gods placed them on earth and Celtic priests or Druids were attracted to groves of trees, particularly oaks, but also yews. Columba's island of Iona's name comes from a sacred pre-Christian association – it means 'Yew Island'. Britain's oldest yew stands at Fortingall in Perthshire. Measured at 52 feet in girth in 1769, now thought to be 3,500 years old, the tree has now lost its heartwood entirely (mainly due to people hacking off pieces) and it looks like a circular copse of smaller trees. But it still lives and casts its ancient shade.

Mourners on their way to burials at Fortingall kirkyard used to pass through the circle of the old tree and the pall-bearers would often stop for a moment in its centre. These glimmers of pre-Christian ritual are given substance by the tree's location. Nearby stands a grim monument. Carn na Marbh means 'the Mound of the Dead' and it is a prehistoric earthwork re-used after the scourge of the Black Death in the second half of the fourteenth century. There is an inscription:

> Here lie the victims of the Great Plague of the 14th century, taken here on a sledge drawn by a white horse led by an old woman.

The mound had more associations with the past. Until 1924 it was used as a prehistoric fire hill, a place where bonfires were lit at the turning points of the year. On Samhuinn Eve, now known as Halloween, the whole community climbed the hill, formed a circle around the fire and clasped each other's hands. Then they danced round it, first *deiseal* or 'sunwise' and then *tuathal* or 'against the sun' (what used to be called 'widdershins'). When the embers had died down, young men leaped through the fire in an echo of purification rituals. Around Carn na Marbh other mounds rise and there are several standing stones. Place names and archaeology are suggestive of a sacred landscape of the first millennium BC which looks as though it had the old yew as its centre.

Fortingall's tree is famous – not least for the spurious legend that Pontius Pilate was born in its shade – but it is not unique. All over Britain there are churchyards with ancient yews which predate their churches. Many of those which stand on low eminences also show traces of prehistoric earthworks. What all of this points to is continuity. When Christian missionaries arrived in an area they often chose to preach in places which were already sacred. Bede was unblushing about this practice. In his *Ecclesiastical History*, he repeated the advice of Pope Gregory in a letter to British churchmen dated around 600:

> [We] have come to the conclusion that the temples of the idols among that people [the English] should on no account be destroyed. The idols are to be destroyed, but the temples themselves are to be aspersed with holy water, altars set up in them, and relics deposited there . . . In this way, we hope that the people, seeing that their temples are not destroyed, may abandon their error and, flocking more readily to their accustomed resorts, may come to know and adore the true God. And since they have a custom of sacrificing many oxen to demons, let some other solemnity be substituted in its place . . . On such occasions they might well construct shelters of boughs for themselves around the churches that were once temples, and celebrate the solemnity with devout feasting.

Fortingall derives from *forterkil* which means 'the church at the fort', a reference to the prehistoric stronghold near at hand. Far to the south, another place-name based on a different sort of fort became important in the story of Bernicia. Bewcastle is from Bothecaestor, the Roman fort where shepherds had shielings, most likely lean-to huts, against the crumbling walls. Now isolated in the high moorland of the western Cheviot ranges, Bewcastle had both a strategic and spiritual importance 2,000 years ago. When the Emperor Hadrian ordained a mighty wall to divide Britannia, his more canny commanders advised a screen of outpost forts to the north. At that time, Bewcastle did not lie in the middle of nowhere but astride a cattle and stock droving route from the Border valleys to Cumbria. In the eleventh century, a medieval castle was built out of the stones of the Roman fort and in the sixteenth and early seventeenth centuries an English garrison was stationed at Bewcastle to discourage Border reiving.

The religious importance of the site is equally ancient. During the Roman period, Bewcastle was known as Fanum Cocidi, 'the Shrine of Cocidius' – Cocidius being a Celtic war god. His cult probably predated the arrival of the legions and it seems to have been enthusiastically adopted by them. The Latin *fanum* meant 'a shrine' or 'a sanctuary' and, in a Celtic context, this may well have been a grove of trees inside a sacred precinct rather than the temples visualised by the Roman pope. They are gone now but at least two ancient yews grew around Bewcastle Church (younger trees have replaced them by the churchyard wall) and the site appears to have been marked off at some point in a long history by ditching and a bank. This may be Roman but archaeology has yet to investigate. The shrine of Cocidius was well known in the second century AD and a place which attracted worshippers. Such sanctuaries usually had definition of some sort – a way of recognising what was holy ground and what was not.

When the tide of Northumbrian Christianity began to rise and wash westward, Bewcastle became an important focus. As Pope Gregory advised, it was 'an accustomed resort'. And at such a famously sacred place, Anglian churchmen chose to make a spectacular gesture. A magnificent stone cross was erected, probably towards the end of the seventh century. It tells a fascinating story about early beliefs and society in the North-umbrian west.

In the era of Christian conversion, churches, where they existed at all, were mostly modest structures. Small, built from wood and dark inside, they were not the soaring cathedrals of later times, nor did they have spires that reached heavenwards and could be seen and heard for many miles as their bells pealed. When a stone church was built, it was a matter for comment, as at Jarrow and Whithorn. The word of God was heard out of doors in the early centuries of Christianity and, at Bewcastle, a great preaching cross was raised amongst the sacred yew trees.

Like churches, most early crosses are likely to have been

wooden but these have left little trace. Stone crosses were more impressive and enduring but, looking up at their grey dignity, it is easy to forget that most were brightly painted. The scenes and decorations carved on the four faces of the shaft and on the cross-piece were picked out in vivid colour, no doubt renewed each year after the winter rains and before major festivals. The high crosses were intended as both a focus and a text. Worshippers, summoned by word of mouth or the tinkle of a handbell, gathered around the base and listened to a priest tell stories from the Bible, speak about the lives of the saints or use the symbol of the cross itself to explain the Christian message. Since many who listened could not read, the painted saints and scenes were an attractive illustration, probably something pointed to during a service.

Although its cross-piece is missing, the Bewcastle Cross is impressive, the shaft standing 4.4 metres high. Almost square, the four faces of the shaft must have been carved in situ, probably by masons sent from Bede's monastery at Jarrow or the sister house at Monkwearmouth. On three sides the sculptors have incised intricate decorative patterns known as 'inhabited vine scrolls'. Stems and foliage are woven together and support a series of animals such as birds and others more difficult to identify. Elsewhere there are patterns of interlace and dicing very reminiscent of the carpet pages of the Lindisfarne Gospels.

The oldest sundial to survive in Britain can be seen on the Bewcastle Cross. It shows the day quartered into four tides. Derived from the Early English *tid*, meaning 'time', the word survives in the slightly quaint usage of Christmastide or Eastertide. Because they had few reliable means of measuring it, apart from the sun and the moon, the people of the seventh and eighth centuries (and long after that) are thought to have had little interest in time and the mechanics of its passage. But Bede was fascinated. His *De Temporum Ratione* (*On the Reckoning of Time*), is a scientific masterpiece and has been enormously influential. In 664, the Synod of Whitby was much concerned with the correct dating of the feast of Easter and, to avoid dispute, Easter Tables projected the precise dates far into the future. Bede listed them up until 1063. He also compiled a chronology of world history and, to make it intelligible, he adopted the AD system. It was invented by Dionysius Exiguus or 'Little Dennis', a monk from the Black Sea coast living in Rome, and, through his widely disseminated writings, Bede helped make it standard throughout Europe.

In the measurement of the life of men and women, *De Temporum Ratione* was also influential. The number four seemed to hypnotise Bede as he listed the four ages of man, the four seasons and the four cardinal compass directions. He undertook a scientific programme of observation of the tides, working out the seasonal median level between low and high tides. Since Jarrow Slake, a huge tidal mudflat near the mouth of the River Tyne, lapped at the foot of the monastery precincts, Bede may not have had to exert himself greatly. And even though he did not publish any measurement of daylight, the division of it into four tides on the Bewcastle sundial is likely to have derived from the monk's researches. Accessible to everyone, including the illiterate, these divisions are likely to have had some general meaning beyond the academic.

Down the length of one of the faces of the Bewcastle Cross is a series of relief sculptures. At the top is St John the Evangelist, the writer of the fourth gospel. Depictions of biblical figures were usually not portraits (although there were descriptions of Jesus in circulation, these were all apocryphal) and they are usually identified by attributes. St John is holding an eagle, a symbol of the soaring heights he rose to when writing his gospel – and, incidentally, the reason many church lecterns are modelled on the great bird and its outspread wings.

Below John, Jesus treads on the beasts. This obscure motif is from Psalm 91 and it links the Bewcastle Cross (and the cross at Ruthwell which carries a similar sculpture) once again to Bede and Jarrow. He wrote a commentary on Psalm 91 and made much of the passage where Christ trampled the snake, the lion, the dragon and the basilisk. Symbolising the triumph over Satan, this image seems to have been powerful and popular with early Christian missionaries as they moved to convert pagans. Psalm 91 was sung at the monastic service of compline, the prayers at the end of the day. It sent monks into the fearful dark of the night, to the period of the long silence, to contemplation, to temptation and it fortified them with Christ's example.

At the foot of the cross is a carving of a mysterious figure, a man resembling a falconer with a bird on his gloved hand. It may be another illustration of St John but the rationale for showing the gospel writer twice and with the same attribute is hard to fathom. Above the falconer there is an inscription carved at a height where it can be easily read:

THISSIG BEACN THUN SETTON HWAETRED WAETH-GAR ALWFWOLTHU AFT ALCFRITH EAN KYNIING EAC OSWIUING + GEBID HEU SINNA SAWHULA

(This slender pillar Hwaetred, Waethgar and Alwfwolthu set up in memory of Alcfrith, a king and a son of Oswiuing. Pray for them, their sins, their souls.)

Translation is not difficult because the early English inscription contains clear ancestors of modern words: *thissig* for 'this', *beacn* for 'beacon' or 'pillar', *thun* for 'thin' or 'slender', *setton* for 'set up', *aft* for 'after', *ean* for 'one', *kyniing* for 'king', *sinna* for 'sin' and *sawhula* for 'soul'. What is mysterious – and striking – is the script used for these words.

Runes were clearly thought to be more intelligible than the Roman alphabet to the people who lived around Bewcastle. The letters were also much easier to carve, being straight chisel strokes rather than the rounded sort needed for the uncials used in the Lindisfarne Gospels. Based on an order of Roman letters that differs from that of the conventional Latin alphabet, the oldest form of the runic alphabet is known as 'futhark' because it was derived from the sounds represented by the first six letters of a Scandinavian-Germanic version of it – /f/ (ᚠ), /u/ (ᚾ), /th/ (ᚦ), /a/ (ᚨ), /r/ (ᚱ) and /k/ (ᚲ). The letters were thought to be intrinsically magical and that belief is echoed in the phrase 'reading the runes'. In *Germania*, the companion volume to his *Agricola*, Tacitus described how this was done:

> They break off a branch from a fruit tree and slice it into strips; they distinguish these by certain runes and throw them, as fortune will have it, onto a white cloth. Then the priest . . . or family father . . . after praying to the gods . . . picks up three of them, one at a time, and reads their meaning from the runes carved on them.

Twenty-five miles due west from Bewcastle, at Ruthwell, the other great Anglian high cross is also inscribed with runes. Around the vine scrolls on one face of the shaft there are fragments of a remarkable poem, probably the earliest work in English to be preserved. The full text is kept in Italy in a manuscript known as *The Vercelli Book*. Known as *The Dream of the Rood*, the narrative is told by the cross upon which Christ was crucified and, after thirteen centuries, its power is undimmed:

> Almighty God stripped himself,
> When he willed to mount the gallows,
> Courageous before all men,
> [I dared not] bend.
>
> I [lifted up] a powerful king,
> The Lord of Heaven I dared not tilt.
> Men insulted both of us together;
> I was drenched with blood poured from the man's side.

The shafts of the Bewcastle and Ruthwell crosses were carved as each lay on the ground supported by bearer beams. When it had been completed, the shaft was winched upright and slotted into a base socket cut from a large and heavy piece of stone.

Often all that survives of high crosses are these immovable sockets. Usually the cross-piece was made separately and fitted onto the top of the shaft with a tenon joint. Ruthwell's cross was cast down and broken by religious reformers in the middle of the seventeenth century. Left out in the churchyard under the ancient yews for almost 200 years, the pieces were collected by Henry Duncan, a local antiquary (and, incidentally, inventor of the savings bank) and the cross was re-erected in the small church. These two monuments are great treasures – the best-preserved examples of Anglo-Saxon high crosses in Britain and a testament to the vigour of Bernician Christianity.

Bernician politics of the eighth century made for a less impressive spectacle. After the death of Aldfrith in 705, civil war appears to have broken out. A series of kings came and went but the power, or at least the appearance of power, of the Northumbrian military machine protected their feuding kingdom

---

Caedmon

Bede told the story of Caedmon, a shepherd who tended the flocks of the monastery at Whitby. In a dream, he composed a hymn to God, embellishing it upon waking. When taken to the Abbess Hilda, he was allowed to learn from the scholars and musicians and appears himself to have taken holy orders. Caedmon is a native name but he may have been bilingual in Old Welsh and Early English. Along with The Dream of the Rood, *the hymn is one of the very earliest examples of English poetry to survive:*

> *Hail now the holder of Heaven's realm,*
> *That architect's might, his mind's many ways,*
> *Lord forever and Father of glory,*
> *Ultimate crafter of all wonders,*
> *Holy-maker who hoisted the heavens*
> *To roof the heads of the human race,*
> *And fashioned land for the legs of man,*
> *Liege of the worldborn, Lord almighty.*

from incursion from either the Pictish north or Mercian south. In fact, expansion westward continued beyond Ruthwell and Bernician bishops came to govern the old see of Whithorn. Their names were odd – Peohthelm means 'Leader of the Picts' and Peohtwine, 'Friend of the Picts'. Galloway is some way south of Pictland but perhaps the hill peoples spoke a dialect of Old Welsh which sounded Pictish to a Bernician ear or perhaps they were merely pagans.

By 759, Aethelwald Moll had made himself king of Northumbria. Not a descendant of Aethelfrith and probably a Deiran aristocrat and not a Bernician, he marched an army north to eliminate a rival claimant. In the heartland of Bernicia 'a severe battle', the Battle of Eildon, was fought by the River Tweed. *The Anglo-Saxon Chronicle* added that the armies clashed at a place called Edwinscliff and that Oswin, possibly a Bernician rebel, was killed somewhere in the shadow of the Eildon Hills. Dere Street crosses the Tweed near the old Roman fort at Trimontium and there the ground descends steeply to the river on either bank. The precise location of Edwinscliff is no longer known but it is likely that Aethelwald Moll had fought a battle to deal with a Bernician uprising in the Tweed Valley.

Hardship followed the victory at the Eildon Hills. Chroniclers only occasionally comment on the weather – most are concerned with war, royal succession and events affecting the Church. But the winter of 763–764 was bitter with heavy snowfall and an intense cold which kept the snow on the ground long into the spring. Such forage as there was for animals will have run out and those that could scrape down to the lifeless grass will have found little to sustain themselves. The consequent slaughter of stock will have staved off starvation in the early months of the year but stored up problems for the immediate future. A late spring and the likely effects of a rapid snowmelt as temperatures at last climbed will have delayed sowing and perhaps washed away such seed as was planted. Famine gripped the land for at least a year and disease followed malnourishment.

It may be that the brutal winter also had political consequences. A year later Aethelwald Moll was deposed and tonsured.
That meant being forced to become a monk and retire from
public life to the seclusion of a monastery. In the same *Book of
Life* at Durham which records the brief reign of the Rheged
princess, Rieinmelth, Aethelwald Moll is noted not as a king but
an abbot.

In the shape of King Alchred, a direct descendant of Ida of
Bamburgh, the Bernicians returned to power. There followed a
series of short reigns of kings who were deposed and tonsured,
exiled or murdered. Mercia and its long-lived rulers dominated
southern Britain in the second half of the eighth century. Offa
(757–796) was tremendously ambitious, wealthy and famous,
with economic and diplomatic contacts in both the Muslim
world and eastern Europe. In some of his charters, he appeared
to arrogate to himself the title, *Rex Anglorum*, 'King of the
English'.

In 789, a minor event signalled that the world was about to
change. Here is the entry in *The Anglo-Saxon Chronicle*:

> In this year King Beorhtric married Offa's daughter Eadburh and
> in his days there came for the first time three ships of the
> Northmen (from Horthaland) and then the reeve rode to them
> and wished to force them to the king's residence, for he did not
> know who they were; and they slew him. Those were the first
> ships of the Danish men which came to the land of the English.

Four years later the Northmen, seaborne war bands from
Scandinavia (Horthaland is in western Norway) who became
known as the Vikings, attacked Northumbria. *The History of the
Kings of Britain*, a chronicle continued and edited by Symeon of
Durham, recorded these shocking events:

> In the same year the pagans from the north-eastern regions came
> with a naval force to Britain like stinging hornets and spread on
> all sides like dire wolves robbed, tore and slaughtered not only

beasts of burden, sheep and oxen but even priests and deacons and companies of monks and nuns. And they came to the Church of Lindisfarne, laid everything waste with grievous plundering, trampled the holy places with polluted steps, dug up the altars and seized all the treasures of the holy church. They killed some of the brothers, took some away with them in fetters, many they drove out, naked and loaded with insults, some they drowned in the sea.

So began the era of the Vikings, the raiders described by terrified monks as 'The Sons of Death'. Their attacks and invasions transformed British history but the story of that process in what was to become Scotland is fragmentary. If the chroniclers are to be trusted, there were very few raids in Galloway, even fewer on the eastern coasts of Scotland north of the Forth and only one major incident in the late ninth century north of the mouth of the Tweed when the nunnery at Colding-ham was attacked and burned. Vikings seemed to have sailed to targets to the south.

While it seems that the early assaults on churches such as Lindisfarne were motivated by the availability of portable and valuable loot, there were other attractions. Some raids were timed to take place at Christian festivals when Vikings could be sure that gold, silver and gem-studded treasures would be on display and not hidden away. But the traditional image of horn-helmeted (the headgear is the invention of the nineteenth century, no such items have ever been found) berserkers carrying bags of swag out of burning churches is at best incomplete. What consistently attracted Viking raids, long after the valuables had run out, was something much less dramatic, much less eye-catching for the chroniclers. Slaves were in great demand in the eighth and ninth centuries, especially in Moslem Europe and the east. With their superb longships and sea-craft, the Vikings had the unrivalled ability to abduct people and transport them quickly for sale to distant markets and customers. And many slave raids, savage though they were, will have gone unreported.

Irish sources are clear that feast days were chosen not so much for the gold plate (never unwelcome) but much more because of the ready availability of a large number of people gathered in one place, as potential slaves. Pilgrims came to churches from some distance on saints' days, always held at the same time each year and therefore easily predictable, and these helpful concentrations of people made obvious targets for the Viking slave masters.

Thrall was the Norse translation and it survives in the phrase to be 'in thrall to' someone. A large slave market was established at Dublin and the longships hove to at the mouth of the Liffey with a steady supply of captives from across the Irish Sea and Ireland itself.

Repeated raids on Lindisfarne forced the monks to move St Cuthbert's shrine out of reach. There followed years of wandering. The saint first lay at Norham on the Tweed before being carried deeper into Bernicia, even further from the dangerous shore, possibly as far inland as Jedburgh. From the ruins of the medieval abbey, archaeologists have uncovered fragments of an elaborate and beautiful shrine which may have held the holy man's remains for a time. Cuthbert was moved to Ripon and then to Chester-le-Street before finding his final resting-place at Durham and becoming the inspiration for the raising of the great cathedral church. This long peregrination may have had one important cultural side effect. Having protected him from pagans and many having seen his shrine in all its stopping places, Bernicians began to see themselves as living in a blessed land, St Cuthbert's Land, and they called themselves the Haliwerfolc, 'the Holy Man's People'.

This was an identity recognised by outsiders and one which cuts across modern distinctions. The hagiographer of St Wilfrid, Eddius Stephanus, wrote of two peoples, the Northumbrians and the Southumbrians, as did Bede, and they are also recorded in *The Anglo-Saxon Chronicle*. By the ninth century, Asser, biographer of Alfred the Great of Wessex, was encouraging the notion of a north–south divide for obvious political purposes – 'a great dispute, fomented by the devil, has arisen amongst the Northumbrians, as always happens to a people which has incurred the wrath of God'. This sense of difference stuck and medieval writers reinforced it. Probably correctly, William of Malmesbury claimed that, by the twelfth century, Northumbrians spoke a different language from their Saxon cousins in the south.

Just as the Humber and the marshland which extended to the west of the estuary (a considerable barrier) was seen as a physical, cultural and political boundary for centuries, so the notional line drawn in the midstream of the Tweed and along the Cheviot watershed between Scotland and England has influenced attitudes to our history very greatly. Because the modern border cuts through the centre of the lost kingdom of Bernicia and the name of Northumbria has come to be attached to an English county to the south of the line, we have failed to see clearly the central importance of either to Scotland's early history. It is easily forgotten that the descendants of Ida and Aethelfrith had an absolutely determinant influence on the evolution of the Scottish nation, arguably one far greater than the Gaelic and Pictish kingdoms to the north. That is because Bernicia bequeathed the English language to Scotland or at any rate a recognisable and intelligible northern dialect of English. The ancient Celtic language of Old Welsh has been entirely effaced and, at the outset of the twenty-first century, Gaelic stands on the precipice of extinction.

The process of the adoption of English in Lowland Scotland can be glimpsed occasionally in changing place-names and progressively through the medieval period as written records accumulated. But the pace, scale and distribution of adoption must have been halting and patchy. More remote communities in the high valleys and less accessible inland districts will have clung on longer to the mouth-filling fluidity of Old Welsh and, for those forced to speak it, early English must have seemed like stones in their mouths. But the rippling subtleties of *yr iaith hen*, 'the old language', were still heard in southern Scotland for many generations after it had withered in the Bernician east. The kingdom known as Ystrad Clud, Strathclyde, survived the longest of any of the Old Welsh-speaking polities, only retreating into the shadows in 1018 when one of its last kings, Owain, died fighting the Bernicians on the banks of the Tweed.

8

Strathclyde

FOR MANY, THE ROAD to the Highlands begins when it reaches Loch Lomond and winds picturesquely around its bonny braes and bonny, bonny banks. The motorist quickly realises that he has left the Lowlands, the industrial valley of the Clyde and the bustle and busyness of Glasgow behind. As the steep sides of Ben Lomond plunge into the waters of the largest loch in Britain, travellers on the sometimes narrow and twisting road have the powerful sense of entering another culture, another country. But their instincts are premature. When the north road leaves the lochside and climbs up Glen Falloch to the watershed, a striking geological phenomenon rises up on the left of the A82. Set on a rocky knoll on a ridge, a huge jagged boulder sits, commanding the wild moorland. At more than two metres in height and its eminence much enhanced by its rocky platform, the stone is unmissable – and it was meant to be.

This is the Clach nam Breatann, the 'Stone of the Britons', and it marked an ancient frontier between three lost kingdoms. The lands of the Gaelic-speaking Scots of Dalriada lay to the west, the Pictish kingdom to the north and east and the Britons of Strathclyde to the south. Beneath the clichés and the sentimental music brought to mind by the bonnie banks rumbles the hidden history of a violent border between different languages and different politics. Lomond derives from the Old Welsh *llumon*, 'a beacon', and Ben Lomond was the beacon mountain where fires were lit if hostile ships were seen in the loch below. The Lomond Hills in the centre of Fife can also be seen from a great distance and they got their name in the same way.

Through the brilliant and tenacious research conducted over many years by Elizabeth Rennie and her colleagues in the Cowal Archaeological and Historical Society, a complete land border between the realm of the Strathclyde kings and the men of Dalriada has been traced. It runs south-west from the Clach nam Breatann and follows the line of the burn known as Allt na Criche to a low but conspicuous hill called Cnap na Criche. In Gaelic, *cnap* is 'a hill' and the word *criche* or *crioch* means 'a frontier'. *Na criochan* is the Gaelic term for 'the borders'.

South of the Cnap and at the head of Loch Goil in a very prominent position stands another unambiguous marker. At 8 metres high and 10 metres broad, Clach a Breatunnach is truly massive. Its name is a slight variant on its more famous cousin's in Glen Falloch and it means 'the Stone of the British'. Below it lies another beacon site at Blairlomond, 'the Field of the Beacon', on the loch shore. It was probably visible from another lochside location now lost which could have conveyed an alarm down to the mouth of Loch Goil where it joins Loch Long. The stone and the beacon site guard the high pass called Hell's Glen, a difficult but short through-route from Dalriadan territory along Loch Fyne.

Identifiable by a string of *criche* names and other Gaelic boundary names, the ancient frontier extends all the way south to Toward Point where it looks across to the Isle of Bute. To understand why it was placed some way inland, it is necessary to cast aside modern perceptions of geography.

When it is borne firmly in mind that, until the coming of the railways in the nineteenth century and a road network in the twentieth, the sea was not seen as a barrier but as a highway, then this recently discovered frontier comes into focus and makes every sort of economic, social and military sense. The upper reaches of the Firth of Clyde were an integral part of the kingdom of Strathclyde – in a real sense, its beating heart – and the communities who lived, farmed, hunted and fished on the shores of the Holy Loch, Loch Long, Loch Goil and Gare Loch were all linked by busy seaborne traffic. Navigation was easy. The coast-lines are all inter-visible except in the very worst of the weather and the crossing distances are short. When the tiderip is power-ful, sailors will have used the age-old practice of 'aiming off' – picking a landmark some way to the left or right of where they actually wish to make landfall – and knowing that the tide will alter their course. These devices and their seasonal variations will have been well known.

Easy navigation was not the sole consequence of the geo-graphy of the upper Clyde. The network of sea lochs and their settlements were protected to the south, where the firth ulti-mately opens out to the Irish Sea and the ocean beyond. The bulk of the Isle of Bute and the islands of the Cumbraes guard these approaches. The name of the Cumbraes resembles those of the great marker stones to the north of them for it simply means 'the Isles of the Britons', reinforcing the sense of a frontier zone. These sentinels encourage the impression of a near-landlocked Strathclyde lake. Elizabeth Rennie has identified a ring of coastal fortresses on Bute, Cumbrae and the mainland which are inter-visible and could quickly be in communication through beacons or signals in the event of any emergency. In addition, she and her colleagues have shown, through meticulous archaeology, that there was a homogenous cultural community living on the shores of the upper firth and its sea lochs.

Inspired by these findings, David Dorren and Nina Hendry, members of the Cowal Archaeological and Historical Society, began to look in the other direction, investigating the landscape to the north-east of the Clach nam Breatann. They discovered another clearly marked frontier. And in the wilder country many of its markers had survived more or less in situ. A series of cairns, standing stones and pointer stones (known as *merkie stanes* in Scots) divided the kingdoms of Dalriada and southern Pictland over a long distance – for nearly forty miles. The frontier extended to Glen Lochy, near Tyndrum, and, there, Dorren and Hendry made another discovery. Across the glen there runs a striking-looking ridge which glitters with deposits of quartz. This, they believe, was the Druim Albainn, 'the Ridge of Britain', referred to by Adomnan and others. It had been assumed that Drumalban was simply the name of the range of high mountains running north from the heads of lochs Long and Lomond but it may be that, in the Dark Ages, it was understood as a man-enhanced physical and demarcated line. As it descends to Glen Lochy, the easiest pass through the high mountains from east to west below the Great Glen, the frontier becomes necessarily more defined and it ran along the quartz ridge. It cannot be insignificant that the nearest settlement is Tyndrum, Taigh an Droma, 'the Farm on the Ridge' – *droma* is an older Gaelic rendering of *druim*.

Strathclyde's boundaries in the tamer and more densely populated Lowlands can hardly have been unclear or undefined even if they may have shifted more often. To the south the watershed hills at the head of the Clyde Valley almost certainly separated the kingdom from Rheged and later, Bernician Gallo-way, although no detailed research exists. To the north-east, Flanders Moss will have supplied a natural divide while, to the east, a rare scrap of documentary evidence may be helpful.

The Annals of Ulster recorded that, in the year 642, the king of Strathclyde ambushed a Dalriadan army. At Strathcarron, Eugein defeated the Scots and killed their king, Domnall Brecc, the grandson of Aedan macGabrain. This may well have been a skirmish on the frontier and it suggests that it lay somewhere along the low watershed ridge between the headwaters of the River Carron which flows into the Firth of Forth and the Kelvin which flows into the Clyde. The Bannock Burn is not far away and it is the descendant of the Dark Ages' name for this boggy border region, Bannawg.

Over its long history the name of Strathclyde changed. On his famous map of the second century AD, Ptolemy plotted the Damnonii on the Clyde Valley and their lands are briefly illuminated in the flicker of light that is St Patrick's letter to

Coroticus, probably a Damnonian king who commanded the great citadel called Alt Clut, the Rock of the Clyde. Like the stones in the north and the islands in the firth, the modern name of Dumbarton Rock remembers the Britons. It is from Dun Breatainn, 'the Fort of the Britons'.

Rising sheer and majestically out of the waters of the Clyde, Dumbarton Rock is a double summit – a split plug of volcanic basalt. More extensive fortifications were possible on the larger and flatter top of White Tower Crag but there was also a stockade on the more easterly summit known as The Beak. Boats could be beached below at the mouth of the little River Leven. It drains from Loch Lomond, less than five miles to the north and the likelihood that it was navigable gave Dumbarton Rock a strategic hinterland stretching all the way north to the Clach nam Breatann as well as an imposing command of the Clyde both up- and downriver. Admired by the chroniclers as *civitas Brettonum munitissima*, it was indeed 'the best-fortified city of the Britons'. For centuries the fortress and the kingdom were synonymous – Alt Clut.

In the 1970s, archaeologists discovered the remains of an impressive rampart on the steep eastern slopes of The Beak. Made from rammed earth and rubble with thick oak beams to support it and supply a flat fighting platform, the wall probably had a breastwork to shelter defenders. The beams had been burned at some point in a turbulent history but they allowed carbon dating. It appears that this awkward structure went up some time in the 580s or 590s.

Other finds suggested an even longer history. There were fragments of tableware from the time of Britannia, perhaps as early as the first century AD. Opulence and the presence of a wealthy royal court on the rock were evident in shards of wine amphorae from the Mediterranean and the jugs and glasses needed to drink it in the proper style. And, as on Dunadd, there were craftsmen jewellers at work on Alt Clut making objects from precious metals and gemstones – the sort of things kings could distribute to a royal war band.

The first ruler of the Rock of the Clyde to emerge is glimpsed only in a supporting role but his name adds to the sense of a king 'giving gold and horses' to his leading warriors. Rhydderch Hael means 'Riderch the Generous' and he reigned some time between 570 and 600. Adomnan knew of Rhydderch in his *Life of St Columba* and he was a contemporary of great kings in the north, Aethelfrith, Urien and Aedan. It may be that warriors from Alt Clut were at the siege of Lindisfarne when Morcant Bwlc had Urien murdered in his tent.

When St Patrick wrote to Coroticus at the end of the fifth century, it seems that at least the royal family were Christians. And, where rulers led in matters religious, their subjects tended to follow. Rhydderch rode to war as one of Y Bedydd, and he may have been an early patron of a famous saint. Kentigern's shadowy beginnings may have been at Traprain Law in the

Bonedd Gwyr Y Gogledd

The Descent of the Men of the North is a set of two lineages for the kings of Rheged, Gododdin and Alt Clut, and it lists the names of twenty kings of the sixth century. First transcribed in the twelfth century, the genealogies contain several ahistorical elements and connect two dynasties which had no connection. Nevertheless, there are famous names, real kings and a passion for a link to the Roman past. The first list descends from Coel Hen, thought to be the last Dux Britanniarum, 'the Duke of the Britains' (meaning all the four provinces of Britain in the late fourth century) and the last commander appointed by an Emperor. Two lines issue from Coel. Urien appears in the Rheged king list but not Owain. On the Gododdin side are Gwrgi and Peredur, the kings of Ebrauc who defeated Gwenddolau at Arthuret and also Cadrawd Calchvynydd, the king who ruled from Kelso. The second group descends from Macsen Wledig and, although Aedan macGabrain makes an unlikely appearance, it lists the Alt Clut or Strathclyde kings ending with Rhydderch Hael. These genealogies are too easily dismissed as fanciful and they have a good deal to say about attitudes and aspirations in north Britain in the sixth century.

lands of the Gododdin but it is as the apostle of Strathclyde he is known.

To become properly culted, all early saints needed their hagiographers to record miracles and an exemplary life but Kentigern's seems to have appeared very late. Jocelyn of Furness' *Life* was composed in the late twelfth century but it may have drawn on much earlier sources. The author claimed to have used old legends and a biography in Gaelic. Kentigern is certainly a Gaelicised version of Old Welsh Cyndeyrn and both mean something like 'Chief Lord' – a title rather than a name. The saint was also known as Mungo and that is a smoother version of *mwyn-gwr* or 'dear lad'. The nickname was said to have been coined by Kentigern's first patron, St Serf, when he and his refugee mother, Princess Thenu, turned up at the *diseart* at Culross in a coracle after a fabled journey across the Forth.

The story becomes less blurred when Jocelyn relates that the saint built a church on the Clyde, where the Molendinar Burn joins it. Now the site of Glasgow Cathedral, the foundation echoes the Celtic love of sanctity when it is bounded by water and God's own hand. A more prosaic reason for the location might be in the name for Molendinar means 'Mill Burn'. Kentigern went on to live, pray and preach on its banks for thirteen years before some unreported incident, perhaps a dispute with the royal family at Alt Clut, drove him south.

It seems that Kentigern established himself at the monastery at Hoddom in Dumfriesshire and archaeologists have discovered the remains of a baptistery he himself might have used. It is difficult to establish whether or not Kentigern was a founder of Hoddom (not least because his own dates are uncertain) but his association will have added prestige. After a return to the Clyde, possibly with the generous sponsorship of Rhydderch Hael, the saint built up a substantial community of monks on the Molendinar Burn. *Familia* was a versatile Latin term which could apply to such a community and some toponymists believe that *clas-gu*, an Old Welsh translation meaning 'dear family', is the origin of the place-name of Glasgow.

Mungo's Miracles

Every saint needed a stock of miracles to prove his holiness and Mungo performed four. They have become famous as the result of a verse which describes Glasgow's coat of arms, although quite why any of them seemed at all miraculous is difficult to see:

> *Here is the bird that never flew*
> *Here is the tree that never grew*
> *Here is the bell that never rang*
> *Here is the fish that never swam.*

Mungo brought back to life the pet robin of his first patron St Serf – although the point surely is that the bird did fly. Perhaps the reference is to its state before Mungo laid on his saintly hands. The second miracle seems not to have been a miracle at all. Again, at St Serf's community at Culross, Mungo fell asleep and allowed the fire to go out. To rekindle it, he took some branches from a tree. Perhaps it was a fire burning with green wood that amazed everyone. The bell sounds as though it was a preaching bell brought back from Rome by Mungo but why it should never ring is a mystery. The final miracle is based on a fable. King Rhydderch of Strathclyde believed that his queen, Languoreth, had given a ring to her lover. In fact, the king had thrown it in the Clyde. When told that she faced execution if the ring could not be produced, Languoreth appealed to Mungo for help. He had a fish caught in the Clyde (perhaps that is the miraculous part) and the ring was found inside it. This story harks back to the gospels and St Peter and the Tribute Money. An identical miracle was performed by St Asaph in Wales at the court of Maelgwyn of Gwynedd.

Towards the end of his *Life of Kentigern,* Jocelyn inserts a detail that sounds authentic. Through age, the old man's jaw had become slack and, to avoid unseemly gaping and perhaps drooling, his monks tied a bandage under his chin. There then follows an account of his death in a bath which sounds like a garbled version of Kentigern collapsing during a service of baptism. Whatever the truth of that, the likelihood is that the saint lived to a great age, almost a living relic.

Throughout the seventh and eighth centuries, Alt Clut remained defiantly independent, resisting the tide of Bernician arms and defeating Dalriadan armies. The names of vigorous kings like Beli (died 722) and Teudebur (died 752) appear in the chronicles and, despite a lack of detail, the overall impression is one of stability, certainly survival.

In the spring of 870, everything changed. Lookouts on the ramparts of Alt Clut must have turned to each other in disbelief. Rowing up the Clyde straight towards them was a vast fleet of warships, perhaps as many as 200 keels. On the prows of the leading longships stood two Viking kings, Olaf and Ivar. They had sailed from Dublin, broken through into the upper Clyde and were bent on storming the impregnable rock. Here is the entry for 870 from the Irish annals:

> In this year the kings of the Scandinavians besieged Strathclyde, in Britain. They were four months besieging it; and at last, after reducing the people who were inside by hunger and thirst (after the well that they had in their midst had dried up miraculously) they broke in upon them afterwards. And firstly all the riches that were in it were taken; [and also] a great host [was taken] out of it in captivity.

The Annals of Ulster offer a little more detail on the aftermath of the fall of the Rock: 'Olaf and Ivar returned to Dublin from Scotland with 200 ships, bringing away with them in captivity to Ireland a great prey of Angles, and Britons and Picts.'

A four-month siege was unheard of in the Dark Ages and it speaks of tremendous determination and organisation. It seems that the vast war fleet had overwintered somewhere on the Clyde and, safe for the moment in his citadel, King Artgal of Alt Clut must have expected an attack to come. But the scale of it was astonishing. Slaves were the principal prize and, since the list in the Annals of Ulster does not include any mention of Dalriada Scots, it must be suspected that the Vikings' siege was undertaken with the help of Alt Clut's neighbours. A year later, apparently at the request of King Constantine of Alba – the name given by the Dalriadic dynasts to their expanding realm – King Artgal was killed in captivity in Dublin. It appeared to be a sorry end for the continued independence if not the identity of the last of the Old Welsh-speaking kingdoms of southern Scotland.

Viking longships had been seen in the Irish Sea for most of the ninth century and the sea lords left their mark on the geography of its coasts and islands, especially in the northern basin. Seamarks were important navigational aids in the age of pilotage and the most striking and lofty of the hills and mountains around the Solway acquired Norse names for that reason. The practice of aiming off needed clearly visible fixed points on the horizon. When a sea lord wanted to beach his craft at, say, the mouth of the Nith, he might aim his course at Criffel, the singular hill to the west. If the Solway tides were rising, then they would push the longship eastwards and, depending on the season and the time of day, Viking seamen knew that aiming off at Criffel would bring them to the outfall of the river. These prominent seamarks all changed their names in the ninth century – Criffel is from Kraka Fjall or 'Raven Hill', Snaefell on the Isle of Man means 'Snow Hill' and Scafell Pike in Cumbria is 'the Mountain Meadow'.

More place-names confirm Viking settlement at the head of the Solway Firth especially where the suffix *-by* or *-bie* is found. It means 'farm' or 'settlement' and close clusters of 'by' names can be seen on road signs around Wiggonby, Thornby, Thursby and Oughterby, five miles west of Carlisle. And much closer to the city, on the east, are Botcherby, Rickerby, Harraby, Scotby, Aglionby and Corby. It seems likely that these dense concentrations were the result of enclaves established before the end of the tenth century.

Perhaps one of the most spectacular legacies of Viking contact in north-west Britain is the collection of tombstones in Govan Old Parish Church in the heart of the old kingdom of Strathclyde. On the west bank of the Clyde, downriver from Kentigern's monastery by the Molendinar Burn, the nineteenth century church stands on an ancient site. The original foundation certainly dates to the late ninth century and likely long before.

The dedication was to St Constantine, probably a reference to the son of the famous King Kenneth MacAlpine, the instigator of the murder of Artgal of Strathclyde. This Constantine reigned between 862 and 878 but, if he had been culted, then any dedication would have taken place some time after his death.

In the church lies a massive, richly carved sarcophagus which may have held the royal and sainted relics of Constantine. It is too narrow to have accommodated a recently deceased body but a set of disarticulated bones would have fitted in. On the sides of the sarcophagus (carved from an enormous single slab of sandstone, presumably in situ), there are hunting scenes interspersed with beautifully worked panels of interlace. It may be that the single block of stone was a conscious imitation of Roman sarcophagi – the sort of thing fit for emperors and therefore suitable for a king who bore the hallowed imperial name of Constantine. In any event, the depiction of a mounted huntsman in pursuit of deer with a hound running beside him is almost always applied to a royal subject which is another imitation – this time of the Old Testament King David. It was a particularly attractive association often found in Pictish art, most notably on the St Andrews sarcophagus of the mid eighth century. King David was seen as a holy warrior, dignified and severe, but from humble beginnings as a shepherd boy, and a defender of his people against mighty attackers. Most of all David was pious, a constant servant of God. Europe's greatest monarch of the Dark Ages was the Emperor Charlemagne and his nickname was said to have been David.

At Govan Old Parish Church, there are fragments of two high crosses, probably dating to the tenth century. They may have marked the entrance to the sacred precinct. Much worn after ten centuries of use and abuse, one cross shaft carries more allusions to King David. The carving has lost most of its definition but a standing figure with an arm outstretched over a seated figure can be made out. This is thought to be Samuel anointing the young King David. The other cross has a mounted huntsman riding across one face.

Two cross-slabs have also survived and one has an unusual motif. It is a boss, like a shield boss, with four stylised snakes curling outwards from it. This is an early metaphor for redemption. Snakes cast their skins and slither out of them renewed.

These fascinating Christian monuments are at the very least testament to Govan's importance as a prestigious, probably royal religious centre. Where patronage of that calibre left Kentigern's foundation upriver can only be a matter of conjecture. Some time after the fall of Alt Clut in 870, the sarcophagus, the crosses and cross-slabs were joined by a set of Viking tombs. Known as 'hogbacks' because of their humpbacked shape, five of these massive monuments are to be found in Govan. Taking the form of longhouses complete with wooden roof tiles clearly picked out by the sculptor's chisel, this group dates to the tenth century. Like Norse place-names around the Irish Sea, the Solway and the Clyde, these houses of the dead plot Viking contact and were probably monuments made for wealthy traders rather than the rulers of colonial settlement. They must have nevertheless been powerful, with enough local control to see their tombs made in the likely burial place of Strathclyde kings.

Twenty years after the siege and destruction of Alt Clut, a Welsh text, known as the *Brut Y Tywysogion*, the *Chronicle of the Princes*, marked an important cultural transmission: 'The men of Strathclyde, those that refused to unite with the English, had to depart from their country and go into Gwynedd.'

This seems confused. Union with or subjugation by the expanding kingdom of the Scots of Dalriada was the issue. By 890, the Bernicians were not only in retreat but the chroniclers mention that there were English people amongst those enslaved after the fall of Alt Clut. Perhaps it was simply the sense of the word *sais* to denote foreigners that was intended and the Dalriadic Scots may have been seen in that way in Wales. Whatever the interpretation, the traditions and some of the history of Strathclyde did linger in Welsh sources long enough to be written down in the medieval period. And the Gwyr Y Gogledd, the 'Men of the North', held an honoured place.

Artgal was not the last king of Strathclyde and it appears that, for 200 years after the siege of Alt Clut in 870, the kingdom continued to be seen as separate from Alba, what was becoming Scotland. Outsiders certainly made a clear distinction. In 924, Athelstan succeeded as king of Wessex and Mercia and almost immediately began to extend his power. Here is an entry from *The Anglo-Saxon Chronicle*:

In this year fiery lights appeared in the northern quarter of the sky and Sihtric died and King Athelstan succeeded to the kingdom of the Northumbrians; and he brought under his rule all the kings who were in this island; first Hywel, king of the West Welsh, and Constantine king of the Scots and Owain king of the people of Gwent, and Ealdred, son of Eadwulf, from Bamburgh. And they established peace with pledges and oaths in the place which is called Eamont, on 12th July, and renounced all idolatry, and afterwards departed in peace.

Eamont Bridge has long been a liminal place and it must have seemed appropriate for this important meeting. Close by are three prehistoric stone circles at Mayburgh, King Arthur's Round Table and the Little Round Table and, in the haughland where the Rivers Eamont and Lowther run parallel before meeting, there was a tall standing stone until the early eighteenth century. And, until the later twentieth century, Eamont Bridge stood directly on the old county line between Cumberland and Westmoreland.

The Anglo-Saxon Chronicle is almost certainly incorrect when it lists Owain of Gwent as present at the parley with Athelstan. The medieval chronicler, William of Malmesbury, identified him as another Owain, king of the Cumbrians and it seems that the ancient prehistoric landscape at Eamont Bridge was the widely recognised southern boundary of his kingdom. The takeover of Bernician territory on the Solway and in Cumbria by the Strathclyde kings is nowhere clearly documented but it certainly took place sometime in the latter half of the ninth century and before 924. King Owain, son of Dyfnwal, ruled this very substantial part of Britain in the 930s and he was obviously thought sufficiently powerful to be summoned to his borders to a meeting with the mighty Athelstan.

When, in imperial mode, the king of Wessex and Mercia demanded the presence of the king of Cumbria, he meant the ruler of the expanded kingdom of Strathclyde. Although decapitated by the Vikings (with the probable collusion of the Scots), it still compassed the Clyde Valley, ancient Rheged, that is, Galloway, Dumfriesshire, the old Roman city of Carlisle and Cumbria down to Eamont Bridge. In the ninth and tenth centuries the names of Strathclyde and Cumbria appear to have been interchangeable but the latter was probably more familiar to Athelstan and the clerks of his fledgling civil service. As has been noted, Cumbria derives from the same root as Cymru, the Welsh word for Wales. Both are from *combrogi*, the Late Latin term meaning 'fellow countrymen' and, by extension, the native British, the Cymry, the Northern Welsh as well as the West Welsh ruled over by Hywel. There is a sense of common cause against the Sais in the name even though the political realities were quite different. As Gildas complained in his 'On the Ruin of Britain' in the sixth century, the British kingdoms fought each other as much as they confronted the Sais and, as historians have shown, they also fought alongside the invaders against native British kings. The Cumber have left their name in more places than Cumberland and Cymru but many are now obscure – Cumberbatch, Comberton, Cumberlow, Camberwell and scores of others. The impression is of small communities clinging on to Old Welsh, *Yr Iaith Hen*, long enough for their places to be included in the Domesday Book of the 1080s.

For the year 934, *The Anglo-Saxon Chronicle* recorded:

King Athelstan, going towards Scotia with a great army, came to the tomb of St Cuthbert, commended himself and his expedition, and conferred on him many and diverse gifts befitting a king, as well as estates, and consigned to the torments of eternal fire any who should take any of these from him. He then subdued his enemies, laid waste Scotia as far as Dunnotar and the mountains of Fortriu with a land force, and ravaged with a naval force as far as Caithness.

The expedition appears to have been punitive but it also had motives of conquest behind it. It seems that Constantine of Scotland and Athelstan had disagreed about the future of the old kingdom of Northumbria. Deira and York had fallen to the Vikings in the ninth century but, although much reduced in the west, Bernicia had continued with a measure of independence. When an unnamed Bernician king died in 934, Athelstan moved north a year later to establish his overlordship there and to beat Constantine into submission.

The expedition far to the north was a complete success. In September 935, Athelstan held court at Buckingham and, when he issued a land grant to one of his courtiers, it was witnessed by Constantine of Scotland. While the Wessex king styled himself *Rex et Rector Totius Britanniae*, 'King and Governor of all Britain', Constantine was relegated to the status of *subregulus* and 'under-king' or, worse, 'underkinglet'. Submission clearly involved a great deal of wearisome travel up and down the length of Britain and, a year later, at the old Roman city of Cirencester, Constantine was again in attendance. Five kings acknowledged Athelstan's overlordship in what was almost certainly a public ceremony. In the tenth century, the Roman amphitheatre was still standing in Cirencester and it would have enhanced the imperial swagger of the king and governor of all Britain to imagine the province recreated under his governorship in such atmospheric setting. As it did with the Bernicians, the long echo of the Empire lent grandeur.

For the fragmentary story of Strathclyde, the Cirencester submissions are important. First in the order of precedence for the five underkings was Constantine but second was Owain of Strathclyde, coming before Hywel Dda, the greatest Welsh king of all. It seems that not only was Strathclyde seen as independent of Constantine and his Gaelic-speaking kingdom but the men of the Old Welsh-speaking north were seen as the leading native British nation, more powerful than their cousins in the west.

At Christmas 935, another court was held at Dorchester, also a

Roman city whose civic buildings were not all ruinous and whose amphitheatre was probably still usable, but, this time, Constantine was absent. Orders of precedence were not mere ceremonial frippery in the tenth century. They mattered and reflected political reality in a public context. Owain of Strathclyde was placed first and that meant Athelstan believed him to be the third most important monarch in Britain. And the choice of Roman cities for these state occasions can have been no accident. A clear point was being made.

A year later, all of this pomp and circumstance was forgotten and the diplomacy of the amphitheatres lay in ruins. Olaf, king of the Dublin Vikings, had been campaigning and making conquests in Ireland. It may be that he had a claim on Northumbria and resented Athelstan's takeover. At all events, an alliance was brokered with Constantine of Scotland and the king of Strathclyde. Doubtless both had tired of dancing attendance amongst the Roman ruins.

Vast armies were mustered. It was said that Olaf sailed with a huge fleet of 615 longships and they clashed in 937 at a place called Brunanburh. The name is lost but two locations have been advanced and each seems equally plausible. The Dublin fleet may have sailed due east and made landfall to fight at the Wirral, on the northern borders of Athelstan's kingdom of Mercia. Or they may have struck north-east to the head of the Solway and met the southern army at Burnswark, the old prehistoric hill fort and the site of Roman siege camps. Toponymic evidence leans towards a great battle at Burnswark but, wherever it took place, Brunanburh was an emphatic victory for Athelstan and the English. Its importance lay not in its immediate effects but rather in the battle lines drawn. On one side stood the Celtic nations of the north and west with their Viking allies while on the other were the ranks of an Anglo-Saxon army. The Welsh bards saw Brunanburh as a disaster, the last realistic hope of driving the Sais back into the sea and the turning historical moment when Celtic Britain was divided. Perhaps it was.

The Battle of Brunanburh

By the tenth century, The Anglo-Saxon Chronicle *was becoming poetical, something of a welcome departure from its customary terseness. Here is the text of a beautifully written piece of alliterative verse about the great battle:*

> Here King Athelstan, leader of warriors,
> Ring-giver of men, and also his brother,
> The aetheling, Edmund, struck life-long glory
> In strife round Brunanburh, clove the shield-wall,
> Hacked the war-lime, with hammers' leavings,
> Edward's offspring, as was natural to them
> By ancestry, that in frequent conflict
> They defend land, treasures and homes
> Against every foe. The antagonists succumbed,
> The nation of Scots and sea-men
> Fell doomed. The field darkened
> With soldiers' blood, after the morning-time
> The sun, that glorious star,
> Bright candle of God, the Lord Eternal,
> Glided over the depths, until the noble creature
> Sank to rest. There lay many a soldier
> Of the Men of the North, shot over shield,
> Taken by spears; likewise Scottish also
> Sated, weary of war. All day long
> The West Saxons with elite cavalry
> Pressed in the tracks of the hateful nation,
> With mill-sharp blades severely hacked from behind
> Those who fled battle. The Mercians refused
> Hard hand-play to none of the heroes
> Who with Olaf, over the mingling of waves,
> Doomed in fight, sought out land
> In the bosom of a ship. Five young
> Kings lay on the battle-field,
> Put to sleep by swords; likewise also seven
> Of Olaf's jarls, countless of the raiding-army
> Of Seamen and Scots. There the ruler of
> Northmen, compelled by necessity,
> Was put to flight, to ship's prow,
> With a small troop. The boat

Was pushed afloat; the king withdrew,
Saved life, over the fallow flood.
There also likewise, the aged Constantine
Came north to his kith by flight.
The hoary man of war had no cause to exult
In the clash of blades, he was shorn of his kinsmen,
Deprived of friends, on the meeting-place of peoples,
Cut off in strife, and left his son
On the place of slaughter, mangled by wounds,
Young in battle. The grey-haired warrior,
Old crafty one, had no cause to boast
In that clash of blades – no more had Olaf
Cause to laugh, with the remnants of their raiding-army,
That they were better in works of war
On the battle-field, in the conflict of standards,
The meeting of spears, the mixing of weapons,
The encounter of men, when they played
Against Edward's sons on the field of slaughter.
The Northmen, bloody survivors of darts,
Disgraced in spirit, departed on Ding's Mere,
In nailed boats over deep water,
To seek out Dublin and their own land again.
Likewise the brothers both together,
King and aetheling, exultant in war,
Sought kith, the land of Wessex.
They left behind to divide the corpses,
To enjoy the carrion, the dusky-coated,
Horny-beaked black raven,
And the grey-coated eagle, white-rumped,
Greedy war-hawk, and the wolf,
Grey beast in the forest. Never yet in this island
Was there a greater slaughter
Of people felled by the sword's edges,
Before this, as books tell us,
Old authorities, since Angles and Saxons
Came here from the east,
Sought out Britain over the broad ocean,
Warriors eager for fame, proud war-smiths,
Overcame the Welsh, seized the country.

In any case, there was no seismic change in the political landscape after 937. Athelstan died two years later and was succeeded by capable kings. Olaf briefly became king of Northumbria and raided into East Lothian where he died in 941. Some said it was in vengeance for his desecration of the shrine of St Baldred. Northumbria was reduced to the status of an earldom by King Eadred of Wessex in 954 although its boundaries were still extensive in the east, stretching to the Lammermuirs and probably beyond.

Strathclyde continued to act independently and to control Cumbria. There is a persistent tradition that Dunmail, 'the last king of Cumbria' (commemorated in a retail park near Workington), fought a battle at Dunmail Raise in 945. A large cairn marks the site on the pass between Thirlmere and Grasmere and it was also a meeting place on the old county boundary between Cumberland and Westmoreland. Dunmail was probably Dyfnwal III of Strathclyde and his opponents are reputed to have been on different sides at Brunanburh. The likelihood is that the earls of Northumbria were pushing westwards with the encouragement of their overlords in the south.

Whatever the reality behind the mists on Dunmail Raise, Strathclyde was aggressive elsewhere in the tenth century. King Amdarch attacked and killed Constantine's successor, Culen, and his brother Eochaid somewhere near Abington at the headwaters of the Clyde. *The Chronicle of the Kings of Scotland* states that Amdarch acted 'for the sake of his daughter'. Perhaps she had been raped.

By 973, Kenneth II, King of Scots, had persuaded Edgar of England to cede part of northern Bernicia to him and the territory to the north of the Lammermuirs became part of an expanding Scotland – but not until another elaborate ceremony of submission had taken place. This time it was marine as well as Roman. Here is an extract from the Melrose Chronicle:

In the year 973, Edgar the peaceful king of the English was at last consecrated king of the whole island, with the greatest honour and glory, in the city of Bath . . .

Some time afterwards, after sailing around northern Britain with a huge fleet, he landed at the city of Chester; and eight underkings met him, as he commended them, and swore that they would stand by him as his vassals, both on land and on sea: namely Kenneth, king of Scots; Malcolm, king of the Cumbrians; Maccus, king of very many islands; and another five: – Dufnal, Sigfrith, Higuel, Jacob, Iuchil.

With these one day he entered a boat, and, placing them at the oars, he himself took the rudder's helm, and skilfully steered along the course of the River Dee, and sailed from the palace to the monastery of St John the Baptist, the whole crowd of earls and nobles accompanying him in similar craft. And after praying there, he returned to the palace with the same pomp: and as he entered it he is related to have said to the nobles that then only could any of his successors boast that he was king of England, when he obtained the display of such honours, with so many kings submitting to him.

At Caddonlea, a few hundred yards south of the modern village of Clovenfords,which lies to the west of Galashiels, there is a wide and level area of haughland divided by the Caddon Water. A thousand years ago, a great army mustered on its banks. From the north, down Gala Water, rode the war bands of Malcolm II, the successor of Kenneth who had rowed Edgar, and down the Tweed from the west came the host of King Owain of Strathclyde. The humiliations of Chester would soon be banished to history.

In their tents on Caddonlea the kings and their captains planned a campaign – a war in the east against Bernicia, now a province of the English kings. As plans were laid, news of the arrival of the great host crackled like wildfire down the Tweed, undoubtedly reaching the ears of the Bernician Earl Uhtred. Probably without waiting for a full muster, the Bernicians hurried north from Bamburgh, anxious to keep the Scots and the Strathclyde Welsh out of their rich farming hinterland.

As reports ricocheted east and west, Malcolm and Owain put

on their war gear, struck camp at Caddonlea and moved down-river. They probably crossed the banks and ditches of the Catrail near the Rink fortress and marched into Bernicia when they forded the Tweed below Abbotsford.

Carham is a sleepy hamlet that lies only a few hundred yards beyond another frontier – the modern border between England and Scotland. There, on the banks of the Tweed, the armies clashed. The Bernician spearmen were cut to pieces but it seems that King Owain of Strathclyde was amongst the dead. In the wake of victory, Malcolm II gained all the territory north of the river. Carham did not establish the line of the modern frontier – there were still lands between the Tweed and the Cheviots in Bernician hands – but it did hasten the end of the old kingdom won by Aethelfrith four hundred years before.

Owain was not the last king of Strathclyde. His line lingered for another two generations. By the 1070s, however, the kings of the Scots were at last in control. Here is the entry from the *History of the Kings of England*: 'For at that time Cumberland was under the dominion of King Malcolm, not through just possession, but through violent subjugation.'

By 1070, Scotland was not yet a complete kingdom. The Norse earls of Orkney were powerful, there were aristocrats in Galloway with royal pretensions and Moray had recently made a king in the figure of Macbeth. But, after Malcolm Canmore's violent subjugation of Strathclyde, the old frontiers began to fade and the kingdoms they defined retreated into the shadows to be almost forgotten.

Bibliography

✷

I have made the conventional distinction between primary and secondary sources even though no bibliography could contain the most important archive, that of the feet and the eyes. In the primary sources listed below all of the introductions are very worthwhile.

Primary sources

The Anglo-Saxon Chronicle, ed. M. Swanton, J.M. Dent, 1996

Bede, *The Ecclesiastical History of the English People*, ed. B. Colgrave and R.A.B. Mynors, Penguin, 1969

Bede, *The Age of Bede*, ed. D.H. Farmer, Penguin, 1965

Calendar of Border Papers, ed. J. Bain, 1894

Liber de S. Marie de Calchou, The Bannatyne Club, 1846

Polybius, *The Rise of the Roman Empire*, Penguin, 1979

Tacitus, *Agricola and Germany*, trans. A.R. Birley, Oxford Paperbacks, 1999

Tacitus, *Annals of Imperial Rome*, trans. M. Grant, Penguin Classics, 1956

Vegetius, *Epitoma Rei Militaris*, ed. A.L. Jenkins, 1892

White, Rev. G., *The Natural History of Selbourne*, Wordsworth, 1996

Secondary Sources

Aitchison, N., *The Picts and Scots at War*, Tempus, 2003

Bates, C., *A History of Northumberland*, 1895

Birley, A.R., *Garrison Life at Vindolanda*, History Press, 200

Brooke, D., *Wild Men and Holy Places*, Canongate, 1994

Campbell J. ed., *The Anglo Saxons*, Penguin, 1982

Cowie, T. (ed.), *An Introduction to the Archaeology of the The Manor Valley*, Peebles-shire Archaeological Society, 2000

Cunliffe, B., *The Extraordinary Voyage of Pytheas the Greek*, Penguin, 2001

Cunliffe, B., *Europe Between the Oceans*, Yale UP, 2008

Darton, M., *The Dictionary of Place-names in Scotland*, 1992

Davies, J. *A History of Wales*, Penguin, 1990

Davies, J., *The Making of Wales*, Sutton 1999

Davies, N., *Europe: A History, Pimlico*, 1996

Fraser, A.F., *The Native Horses of Scotland*, John Donald, 1987

Fraser, J.E., *From Caledonia to Pictland*, EUP, 2009

Frere, S.S., *Britannia,* Pimlico, 1967

Gardiner, Robert (ed.), *The Earliest Ships*, Conway, 1996

Higham, N.J., *The Kingdom of Northumbria*, 1993

Hill, D. and Worthington, M., *Offa's Dyke*, The History Press, 2003

Hunter, J., *The Last of the Free: A Millennial History of the Highlands and Islands of Scotland*, Mainstream, 1999

Johnstone, P., *The Sea-craft of Prehistory*, Routledge, 1980

Koch, J.T., *The Gododdin on Aneirin*, University of Wales Press, 1997

Lowe, C., *Angels, Fools and Tyrants*, Canongate, 1999

Lynch, M., *Scotland: A New History*, Pimlico, 1991

Marner, D., *St Cuthbert*, The British Library, 2000

Miles, David, *The Tribes of Britain*, Weidenfield and Nicolson, 2005

Moffat, A., *The Borders: A History from Earliest Times*, Birlinn, 2002

Moffat, A., *The Wall*, Birlinn, 2008

Morris, J., *The Age of Arthur*, Weidenfeld & Nicolson, 1973

Nicolaisesn, W.F.H., *Scottish Place-names*, Birlinn, 2001

Ostler, N., *Empires of the Word*, HarperCollins, 2005

Ottoway, P, *Roman York*, Tempus, 1993

Reed, M., *The Landscape of Britain*, Routledge, 1990

Rennie, E B., *The Cowal Shore*, Argyll, 2006

Ridpath, G., *The Border History of England and Scotland*, 1778

Rivet, A.L.F. and C. Smith, *The Place-Names of Roman Britain*, Batsford 1981

Smyth, A.P. *Warlords and Holy Men*, EUP, 1984

The Source of Manor, Lyne and Manor Youth Group, 1999

Stenton, F.M., Anglo-Saxon England, *Oxford University Press*, 1989

Thomas, A.C. *Celtic Britain*, Thames & Hudson, 1986

Ward, B., *Bede*, Continuum, 1990

Watson, W.J., *The Celtic Place-Names of Scotland*, Birlinn, 1993

Whitrow, G.J., *Time in History*, OUP, 1988

Woolf, A., *From Pictland to Alba*, EUP, 2007

Yeoman, P., *Pilgrimage in Medieval Scotland*, Batsford, 1999

Index

Note: *Entries in small capitals refers to feature boxes*

Index

Bute, Isle of 241

Caddonlea 258–9
Cademuir hill forts 154
Cadwallon, King of Gwynedd 106, 176, 177, 197
CAEDMON 232
Caereni 78
Caerleon 55, 91
Cair Lion 111
Cairncross 184
Cairnryan 132
Caithness 252
Calchvynydd 73
Caledonia (and Caledonians) 9, 29, 52, 62, 63, 64, 65, 70, 81–2, 84, 87
Calgacus 64
Caligula 26
Callanish 21, 23
Callendar Park 75
Calpurnius 95
Camberwell 106
Camboglanna 116
Camlann 115, 116
Canna 108, 109, 178, 179
Caracalla 85
Cardoness 202
Carham, battle of 9, 259
Carlisle 22, 23, 24, 30–1, 35, 49, 93, 94, 95, 107, 124, 130, 132, 145, 208, 209
CARLISLE, KING ARTHUR IN 131
Carn na Marbh 225
Carpow 84
Carron River 242
Carsluith 202
Carthage 46, 117
Cartimandua 41, 84
Carvetii 30, 66, 93, 132, 145
Carwinley (Caer Gwenddolau) 126
Cassius, Dio 82, 84
Castlesteads (Camboglanna) 116, 127
Cat Bregion 111
Cat Coit Celidon 111, 112
Catraeth 145–7, 150, 157
CATRAETH, LORDS OF 144
The Catrail 2, 3, 4, 5, 6, 7, 44, 259
Catrawt of Calchvynydd 168, 172
Catterick 124, 138, 168, 185
Causewayhead 51
Celidon Wood 111
Celtic armies 64, 65
Celtic festivals 34
Celtic kingdoms of southern Scotland 116
Celyddon 130
Cenel Conaill 183
Ceolfrith, Abbot of Monkwearmouth 212, 218

Ceredigion 101
Ceretic 135
Cerialis, Petilius 22, 23, 24, 28, 29, 30, 38, 41, 49, 53
Charlemagne 166, 210, 211 (box), 249
Chester (Deva) 69, 91, 100, 258
    battle of 171–2
Chesterholm (Vindolanda) 23
Cheviot Hills 4, 30, 41, 43, 49, 68, 69, 73, 113, 114, 123, 169, 174, 226, 237, 259
Chlorus, Constantius 87
Christianity 92, 93, 96, 105, 107, 109, 110, 146, 154
    early Christian churches and crosses 227–8
    links between sacred and temporal power 165–6
    religion of the Word 185
Chronicle of the Kings of Scotland 257
Chronicle of the Princes 250
Cicero 219
Ciminian Forest 29
Cirencester 93, 253
Clach an Truiseal 21
Clach na Manau 9, 52
Clach nam Breatann ("Stone of the Britons") 239–40, 241, 243
Clackmannanshire 9, 52
Clan Chattan 9
Clan McEachern 60
Classis Britannica 63
Claudius 24, 26, 27, 40
Clemens, Quintilius 89, 96
Clovis, King 161
Clyde (Clota)
    Clyde Valley 72, 74, 75, 107, 242–3, 248–9, 252
    Firth of 51, 240–43
    River Clyde 89, 96
Cnap na Criche 240
Cocidius 126, 127
Coel Hen 201, 244 (box)
Coenwulf, King of Mercia 222
Colchester 26, 27, 40, 49
Coldingham, priory at 184, 202, 235
Colman, Bishop of Lindisfarne 203–4, 205
Commodus 80, 81
Coninia Stone 151, 152
Connaught, Queen Medb of 58
Constans 87
Constantine, King of Alba 247–8, 251, 253–4
Constantine III 90, 92, 93, 104
Constantinople 118, 119
Continental Celtic (P-Celtic) 43, 44, 45, 47, 56, 59, 75
Cooley, Brown Bull of 58
Corbridge 23, 30–1, 35, 49, 68, 80
Corionototae 66
Cornovii 101
Coroticus 96, 243, 244
Covenanters 151

Index